Focus

Focus

A College English Handbook

Kim Flachmann
California State College, Bakersfield

Houghton Mifflin Company   Boston
Dallas   Geneva, Illinois   Hopewell, New Jersey
Palo Alto   London

For Michael

Library of Congress Catalog Card Number: 80-82699
ISBN: 0-395-29728-1

Contents

Unit I: The Writing Basics

Contents

Contents

Unit III: Spelling

Unit V: Effective Sentences

Unit VI: The Writing Process

Preface: To the Student

Reading and writing are two skills basic to your success in college. To learn any subject, you must be able to read and understand your textbooks; to show what you have learned, you must be able to write correctly and effectively. Your achievement in any course can be severely limited by a weakness in either ability. Because your capability in one skill is dependent upon your capability in the other, you need to understand how these skills are related to each other. This book demonstrates just such a relationship by using reading to teach writing and writing to teach reading.

The text is divided into six units that are arranged progressively from basic to more advanced skills. Each unit teaches a series of writing skills and then asks you to show how these skills work in a reading selection that might be used in a typical college course. The identical selection is then used to give you special instruction in a few vital reading skills that can help you in your studies. Every unit also contains a second reading selection, comprehension questions, reading exercises, and writing or discussion assignments that are related to the reading selections. Within each unit, every chapter includes a review of the writing skills in that chapter and review exercises.

Finally, this book has two special features designed to help you and your instructor monitor your reading and writing progress: (1) a correction symbol chart for the writing skills covered in the text and (2) a reading chart to enable you and your instructor to measure your progress in speed and comprehension. A glossary of basic reading and writing terms is also included.

Understanding what you read and writing what you mean are two very rewarding activities. This book is designed to help you develop these skills and enjoy the rewards they bring.

Acknowledgments

I would like to express my appreciation to several colleagues who have commented on the manuscript and offered helpful suggestions as it developed: Professors John T. Becker, John Carroll University; Duncan Carter, Boston University; Diana Culberson, Kent State University; Katherine M. Fuller, Gainesville Junior College; Donald C. Green, California State College; Bruce Holland, The University of Akron; Josephine K. Moore, the University of Southwestern Louisiana; C. Stephen Rhoades, Illinois Valley Community College; John Scanlan, Quinsigamond Community College; David E. E. Sloane, the University of New Haven; and M. Beverly Swan, the University of Rhode Island. A number of other people have played a significant role in making this project a reality, and I am glad to have the opportunity to thank them individually as well: Linda Beyer and Marylee Rufert for their legwork, Joanne Silva for her prose studies, Stacey Haley for being dependable, Janine Strange for getting me through the final draft, and Victor Lasseter for proofreading. In addition, I thank my students for their continuing advice and encouragement from beginning to end.

K. F.

Unit I

The Writing Basics

This unit will furnish you with definitions and explanations of some basic facts about the English language. The unit begins with a definition of each part of speech and a demonstration of how the parts of speech work together. The first three chapters of this unit serve as an introduction to this entire section, because they include definitions of writing terms you will need to know throughout this handbook. All of these terms are also defined in a glossary at the end of the handbook.

Before you begin this unit, read the following passage about language. Look closely at the way the words and sentences work to get the author's message across. Various exercises in this unit will ask you to return to this passage to find examples of certain rules you will be studying.

(1)   Language is human speech, either spoken or written. It makes it possible for people to talk to each other and to write their thoughts and ideas. Language is the most common system of communication. The word *language* may be loosely used to mean any system of communication, such as traffic lights or Indian smoke signals. But the

Adapted from *The World Book Encyclopedia.* © 1980 World Book-Childcraft International, Inc. (Chicago: World Book-Childcraft International, 1980.) Vol. XII, p. 62. Reprinted by permission of the publisher.

origin of the word shows its basic use. It comes from the Latin word *lingua,* meaning *tongue.* And a language still is often called a *tongue.* About 90 per cent of all human communication takes place through spoken language.

(2) Thousands of years ago, prehistoric people began to develop speech. They probably discovered that speech had two great advantages over other systems of communication, such as gestures. First, speech could be used when two persons could not see each other, as in the dark. Second, it left the hands of both speaker and hearer free to do other things.

(3) Wherever there are people, there is language. Even the most primitive jungle tribe speaks a language. Most forms of human activity depend on the cooperation of two or more persons. The lack of a common language makes any close cooperation impossible. Language has accompanied human beings in their slow and difficult climb to higher civilization.

1   Parts of Speech

Most English words can be categorized as one of eight **parts of speech:** verbs, nouns, pronouns, adjectives, adverbs, prepositions, conjunctions, and interjections. Parts of speech are the working parts of a sentence. Like the parts of a machine, they must be joined properly to work properly. In order to combine parts of speech effectively, you should know how each part functions.

The name of a part of speech identifies each word by its use in a sentence. Some words can serve as several parts of speech, but most function only as one. Since no single definition is completely accurate, each part of speech is defined in a variety of ways.

1A Verbs

Verbs are considered the heart of a sentence because they describe an action (what someone or something does) or a state of being (how someone or something is).

Action: Last night the bakery *burned* down.
 This rain *will melt* the snow quickly.
Being: I *have been* sick for two weeks.
 You *seem* unhappy.

All verbs have five basic forms: (1) an **infinitive** (the "to" form: *to want, to buy, to break*); (2) a **third person singular, present tense form** (almost always formed by adding *-s* or *-es* to the infinitive); (3) a **present participle** (or *-ing* form); (4) a **past tense form** (stem of the infinitive plus *-d* or *-ed* in regular verbs); and (5) a **past participle** (identical with the past tense in regular verbs). Verbs like *break* or *buy* are called "irregular" because their past tense form and their past participle do not end in *-d* or *-ed*. See also 7A and 7B.

Infinitive	Third person singular, present tense	Present participle	Past tense	Past participle
to want	wants	wanting	wanted	wanted
to buy	buys	buying	bought	bought
to break	breaks	breaking	broke	broken

3

Practice 1–1 List the missing forms for the verbs in the following chart.

Infinitive	Third person singular, present tense	Present participle	Past tense	Past participle
to need				
	sells			
		requiring		
			built	
				stolen

The **tense** of a verb tells when the situation in a sentence took place or will occur—in the present, the past, or the future. Verbs show tense, or tell time, by changing their forms. Every verb has six tenses. See 7B for more information on tenses.

Present: I *walk* in the morning. He *walks* at night. When do you *walk?*
Past: They *walked* in the park.
Future: She *will walk* to class today.
Present perfect: I *have walked* to the movie theater many times.
Past perfect: You *had walked* to the store and back before breakfast.
Future perfect: They *will have walked* ten miles by Saturday afternoon.

The italicized verbs in these sentences are the **main,** or **finite, verbs.** Notice that these verbs follow their subjects; this is usually—though not always—the case.

Practice 1–2 List the main verbs in the following sentences. (Only one main verb appears in each sentence here, though some of the verbs are made up of more than one word.)

1. I have planned our band's trip to Los Angeles.
2. Tomorrow, George and I will work in the yard.
3. I still lack control of some of my tennis strokes.
4. I hope so.
5. She jogs every morning before work.
6. The job on Saturdays was ideal.
7. She tried to decide whether or not to go home next weekend.
8. Chemistry caused him more problems than any of his other courses.
9. I am nervous about getting my hair cut.
10. When will you pick me up?

Practice 1–3 List the main verbs in the reading selection at the beginning of this unit.

Main verbs can also be identified as transitive, intransitive, or linking. Each type of verb calls for slightly different elements to make a complete sentence.

1A(1) Transitive Verbs

When indicating action taken on someone or something, a main verb is **transitive.** The receiver of the action is the direct object. The actor is the subject. With a transitive verb, the direct object must usually be expressed to complete a sentence's meaning.

Transitive: He *filled* our cups.

In this example, *cups* is the direct object of the action verb. It receives the action of the verb in its sentence. The verb, then, connects the subject and the object.

5

1A(2) Intransitive Verbs

A main verb is **intransitive** when it indicates action not taken on someone or something. In other words, an intransitive verb is an action verb that does not need a direct object to complete its meaning.

> Intransitive: He *fell*.

In this sentence, the verb follows the subject, but no direct object receives the action of the verb.

You can remember the difference between transitive and intransitive verbs by keeping in mind that *trans-* means "across" or "over" (as in *transport*, "to carry across") and that *in-* means "not." Therefore, a *trans*itive verb carries its action across from subject to object, and an intransitive verb does not.

A verb's function in a sentence (whether it indicates action taken on something or not) determines whether it is transitive or intransitive. Just as a shoe can serve as an article of clothing, a weapon, or a doorstop, some verbs can be either transitive or intransitive—depending on their use in a given sentence.

> Transitive:　　He *rang* the bell.
> Intransitive:　The bell *rang*.

1A(3) Linking Verbs

Verbs that describe a state of being are **linking verbs.** Such verbs include *to act, to appear, to become, to feel, to grow, to look, to remain, to seem, to smell, to sound, to taste,* and *to turn.** The most common linking verb is *to be.*

---

*Some verbs can be linking or transitive. Linking: "The garbage *smelled* peculiar"; "the soup *tastes* good." Transitive: "The jogger *is smelling* the roses"; "they *tasted* the soup."

Present Tense	Past Tense
I am	I was
you are	you were
he/she/it is	he/she/it was
we are	we were
you are	you were
they are	they were

A linking verb connects the subject with a word describing its state of being.

$$\text{Subject} \qquad \text{Description}$$
$$\downarrow \qquad\qquad \downarrow$$

Linking verb: Jo *appeared* cheerful.

$$\text{Subject} \qquad \text{Description}$$
$$\downarrow \qquad\qquad \downarrow$$

Linking verb: Francisco *is* a businessperson.

Practice 1–4 Supply the following sentences with main verbs.

1. You _____ happy with the results.
2. When Mom comes to visit, we _____ and _____ as soon as we can.
3. As a result, his roommate _____.
4. My friend and I _____ a trip to the West Coast.
5. It is the wine that _____ the fun.

Practice 1–5 Label the main verbs you identified in the reading selection at the beginning of this unit as "transitive," "intransitive," or "linking." (See your answer to Practice 1–3.)

Practice 1–6 Write one sentence for each of the following verbs.

1. become
2. understand
3. act
4. buy
5. discover

7

1B Nouns

Nouns name persons, places, things, animals, actions, qualities, and ideas. Examples of nouns are such words as *jobs, humor, education, hero, dugout, Martha, pendulum, sincerity, Oregon, beach, scissors,* and *Rufus.* They function in sentences in a variety of ways. See 4A and 9A for additional information on how nouns function in sentences.

You can recognize nouns most easily by their forms. Most nouns change form to indicate singular or plural: *car/cars, child/children, fantasy/fantasies.* They also change form to indicate possession: *day's* excitement, *book's* pictures. One of the most reliable tests for identifying a noun is to put *a, an,* or *the* before it and decide whether or not the phrase makes sense (a *car,* the *children,* the *book*). However, this test does not always work with proper nouns (the names of people or specific places). We do not say, for example, *the Martha* or *an Oregon.*

In addition, nouns can frequently be identified by characteristic endings, such as *-age, -ance, -ence, -er, -ice, -ism, -ist, -ity, -ment, -ness, -ship, -sion, -tion,* and *-ure.* Some examples are *postage, annoyance, persistence, adviser, practice, materialism, socialist, celebrity, resentment, kindness, hardship, tension, convention,* and *failure.*

Practice 1–7 List all the nouns in the reading selection at the beginning of this unit.

Practice 1–8 Rewrite the following sentences, adding a word that is the part of speech named in parentheses.

1. Hobbies are like __(noun)__ to some people.
2. I __(verb)__ anyone who is over thirty years old.
3. __(noun)__ is a great idea for a class project.
4. When I draw pictures of people, I __(verb)__ funny habits.
5. Why are __(noun)__ necessary?
6. The __(noun)__ runs on batteries.

7. If you ___(verb)___, I'll ___(verb)___ the tree.
8. Energy is necessary for all of our ___(noun)___.
9. A shortage of jobs ___(verb)___ in the United States.
10. It is important for ___(noun)___ to understand the qualifications for the job.

Practice 1–9 Write one sentence for each of the following nouns.

1. language
2. speech
3. communication
4. English
5. knowledge

1C Pronouns

A **pronoun** takes the place of a noun in a sentence. The noun that a pronoun refers to is called the pronoun's **antecedent.** An antecedent usually comes before the pronoun it refers to. In the following sentence, the antecedent of the pronoun *they* is the noun *candidates.*

When the *candidates* finished speaking, *they* were applauded.

Without pronouns, sentences would be wordy and repetitious. The following paragraphs show the advantages of using pronouns. The first contains none, whereas many nouns have been replaced by pronouns in the second.

Without Pronouns
A reporter is interested in the opinions of people on the street. The people give the reporter valuable information. The information furnishes a reporter with signs of support for certain issues of public interest. In order to develop an accurate

9

article, a reporter needs to know people's opinions, people's reactions, people's concerns, and even people's accounts of people's personal experiences.

With Pronouns

A reporter is interested in the opinions of people on the street. *They* give the reporter valuable information, *which* furnishes *him* or *her* with signs of support for certain issues of public interest. In order to develop an accurate article, the reporter needs to know people's opinions, *their* reactions, *their* concerns, and even *their* accounts of *their* personal experiences.

There are several different kinds of pronouns in English: **personal, reflexive, intensive, demonstrative, relative, interrogative, indefinite,** and **reciprocal.**

Personal				Reflexive/ Intensive	Demonstrative
Subject	*Possessive Adjective*	*Possessive Pronoun*	*Object*		
I	my	mine	me	myself	this*
you	your	yours	you	yourself	that*
he	his	his	him	himself	these*
she	her	hers	her	herself	those*
it	its	its	it	itself	
we	our	ours	us	ourselves	
you	your	yours	you	yourselves	
they	their	theirs	them	themselves	

*When used with nouns, these pronouns become adjectives. Pronoun: *This* is the problem. Adjective: *This* car is the problem. Pronoun: *Some* are just arriving. Adjective: *Some people* haven't studied.

Relative[†]			Interrogative	Indefinite	Reciprocal
Subject	*Possessive*	*Object*			
who	whose	whom	who?	all*	each other
that		that	which?*	another*	one another
what		what	what?*	any*	
which		which	whom?	anybody	
whoever		whomever	whose?*	anyone	
whatever		whatever		anything	
whichever		whichever		each*	
				either*	
				everybody	
				everyone	
				everything	
				more*	
				most*	
				neither*	
				no one	
				nobody	
				none	
				nothing	
				one*	
				some*	
				somebody	
				someone	
				something	

[†]*Who* and *whom* refer only to persons. *Which* refers only to animals or things. *That* may refer to persons, animals, or things.

The following examples of pronouns might help you recognize this part of speech within a sentence.

Personal:	*I* have a red car.
	This red car belongs to *me*.
Reflexive:	Sam blames *himself*.
Intensive:	She did the calculations *themselves*.
Demonstrative:	I just carried *these** across campus.
Relative:	The person *whom* you hire needs to know *what* you want done.
Interrogative:	*What* are you doing?
Indefinite:	*Anybody* can see that *no one* knows the answer.
Reciprocal:	You should encourage *each other*.

Practice 1–10 List the pronouns in the following sentences.

1. I wonder why no one likes him.
2. Why are you making fun of me and my favorite hamster?
3. Whoever took it had better return it to them soon.
4. She had to replace the shocks on their car.
5. Without freedom or some form of free speech, we have nothing to encourage our different outlooks.

Practice 1–11 Rewrite the following paragraph, replacing the italicized nouns with pronouns. Use the pronoun chart to help you find pronouns that can replace these nouns logically.

> When students enter college, *students* often find that *students* are weak in various study skills. Among *the skills* are note taking, managing time, listening, outlining, remembering, and taking exams. Many problems with study skills begin with poor reading habits. If you can read efficiently the material you are studying, many other skills, *skills* are related to reading, will come naturally.

---

*When used with nouns, such words become **demonstrative adjectives** rather than pronouns. "I just carried *these* books across campus." Be careful when using these words as adjectives (as in *these books*) not to choose pronouns that cannot be used with nouns. Wrong: "I just carried *them* books across campus."

For example, if you can concentrate on *the material* you are reading, remembering will take care of *remembering.* If you can read *material* one time with a high degree of comprehension, your problems with time will begin to take care of *your problems with time. This lesson* applies to all disciplines *disciplines* are in most college curriculums. So if you have any reading problems *problems* you know of, take care of *the problems* as early in your college career as you can.

Practice 1–12 List the pronouns in the reading selection at the beginning of this unit. Do not count pronouns used with nouns (because they are adjectives, not pronouns).

Practice 1–13 Write one sentence for each of the following pronouns.

1. his
2. you
3. which

4. each
5. nothing

1D Adjectives

Adjectives describe, or modify, nouns and pronouns by giving information about their quality or quantity. Examples of adjectives include *an, a, the* (these three make up a special class of adjectives also known as **articles**), *free, clever, superstitious, thin, thinner, thinnest, clear, active, lovely, personal, two,* and *yellow.* Adjectives are usually placed immediately before or after the word or words they explain.

Adjective: She is *a frivolous* person.

To see if a word is an adjective, you can usually add either *-ly* or *-ness* to it and form another word.

13

Adjective	-ly	-ness
dark	darkly	darkness
active	actively	
lonely		loneliness

Also, an adjective will usually make sense when placed in the blank in a sentence of the following sort: "He/She/It seems _____."

An adjective can frequently be recognized by its ending: *-able, -ant, -ent, -ful, -ic, -ive, -less, -ory, -ous, -some,* and *-y.* Some examples are *portable, significant, prudent, forgetful, athletic, creative, speechless, sensory, continuous, bothersome,* and *happy.*

Basically, an adjective answers one of these questions about the word or words it modifies:

What quality?	gentle, heavier, suspicious, anxious, huge, strangest
What quantity?	sixteen, many, less, fewest

Adjectives are also used to make comparisons. They show degrees of quality and quantity by changing their forms. The three degrees are called **positive, comparative,** and **superlative.**

1D(1) Positive Degree

The positive degree of an adjective names a quality or quantity. No comparison with another person or thing is involved.

Positive Form
deep
nervous
bad
good

1D(2) Comparative Degree

The comparative form expresses a degree of difference between two persons or things. In general, short adjectives form the comparative by adding *-er* to the positive form; longer adjectives (including some adjectives with two syllables and most adjectives with more than two) form the comparative by placing *more* or *less* before the positive form. *More* or *less* or *-er* is all that is needed to express comparison. Using both (for example, *more deeper*) is incorrect because it is repetitious and awkward. Some adjectives form the comparative in an irregular way.

	Positive Form	**Comparative Form**
Regular:	deep	deeper
	nervous	more/less nervous
Irregular:	bad	worse
	good	better

1D(3) Superlative Degree

The superlative form expresses a degree of difference among three or more persons or things. In general, short adjectives form the superlative by adding *-est* to the positive form and long adjectives by placing *most* or *least* before the positive form. But *most* or *least* and the *-est* form are not used together to form the superlative (*most deepest* is incorrect). One or the other is enough; using both is repetitious. Some adjectives form the superlative in an irregular way.

Positive Form	**Comparative Form**	**Superlative Form**
deep	deeper	deepest
nervous	more/less nervous	most/least nervous
bad	worse	worst
good	better	best

Practice 1–14 List the adjectives (positive, comparative, and superlative) in the reading selection at the beginning of this unit. Include as adjectives all articles and all pronouns that act as adjectives (see note on page 10).

Practice 1–15 Write one sentence for each of the following adjectives.

1. active
2. fuller
3. most serious
4. more determined
5. pleasant

1E Adverbs

Adverbs modify verbs, adjectives, other adverbs, and occasionally entire sentences. Many adverbs can be identified by an *-ly* ending, but these should not be confused with adjectives ending in *-ly*, like *lonely* or *lovely*. Others lack this *-ly* feature but can be recognized by their function in a sentence. It is a good idea, however, to consult your dictionary when in doubt about whether a word may act as an adverb, since some words have two forms (adjective: *quick;* adverb: *quickly*) and others have only one (adjective: *fast;* adverb: *fast*). Examples of adverbs include *quickly, not, hopefully, soon, modestly, sadly, never, slightly, only, there, too often,* and *now*. Adverbs are usually placed close to the word or words they modify.

Adverb: The crime rate has increased *recently*.

Basically, an adverb answers one of these questions about the word or words it explains:

How?	quickly, well, severely, somehow
When?	tomorrow, daily, later, rarely
Where?	there, away, somewhere, outside
To what extent?	less, somewhat, more, very

When they tell how, when, where, and to what extent, these words are all adverbs. However, some of these words can describe nouns or pronouns; then they are adjectives.

Adverb   Adjective
↓   ↓
They swim *daily*. They read the *daily* newspaper.

Like adjectives, adverbs can make comparisons. They change their forms to show **positive, comparative,** and **superlative** degrees.

1E(1) Positive Degree

The positive degree of an adverb describes an action or clarifies an adjective by explaining how, when, where, or to what extent.

Positive Form
openly
sourly
far
well

1E(2) Comparative Degree

The comparative form expresses a degree of difference between two or more actions, persons, or things. In general, adverbs form the comparative just as adjectives do. Most adverbs, particularly those ending in *-ly,* form the comparative by adding *more* (or *less*) to the positive form of the word.

	Positive Form	**Comparative Form**
Regular:	openly	more/less openly
	sourly	more/less sourly
Irregular:	far	farther
	well	better

17

1E(3) Superlative Degree

The superlative form expresses a degree of difference among three or more actions, persons, or things. In general, adverbs form the superlative just as adjectives do. Most adverbs, particularly those ending in -*ly*, form the superlative by adding *most* (or *least*) to the positive form of the word.

Positive Form	Comparative Form	Superlative Form
openly	more/less openly	most/least openly
sourly	more/less sourly	most/least sourly
far	farther	farthest
well	better	best

Practice 1–16 List the adverbs in the reading selection at the beginning of this unit.

Practice 1–17 List the adjectives and adverbs in the following sentences.
1. Hockey is growing rapidly in popularity.
2. Mix dark molasses, fresh bananas, and active yeast to make my special bread.
3. Creative people are becoming increasingly successful in selling their crafts.
4. I often go to discount drugstores.
5. Basically, liberation from stereotypes brings a keener awareness of oneself and of others.

Practice 1–18 Write one sentence for each of the following adverbs.
1. carefully
2. more quickly
3. deepest
4. more quietly
5. best

Practice 1–19 Rewrite the following sentences, adding a word that is the part of speech named in parentheses.
1. Plants are very ___(adjective)___.
2. ___(adverb)___ ___(adjective)___ classes are my favorites.
3. You are a ___(adjective)___ athlete than I am.

18

4. You can usually trust someone with a <u>(adjective)</u>, <u>(adjective)</u> face.

5. If I had a preference, I would <u>(adverb)</u> choose a <u>(adjective)</u> car over a <u>(adjective)</u> one.

1F Prepositions

A **preposition** relates one word to another in a sentence. Some of the most common prepositions include *about, above, according to, across, after, against, ahead of, along, among, around, at, because of, before, behind, below, beneath, between, beyond, by, by means of, concerning, down, during, except, for, from, in, in addition to, in back of, in front of, in spite of, inside, instead of, into, like, near, of, off, on, out, outside, over, past, regardless of, through, throughout, to, together, toward, under, underneath, until, up, upon, with, within,* and *without.*

A preposition usually appears in a phrase with an object, which is usually a noun or pronoun. A prepositional phrase always begins with a preposition and ends with an object of the preposition. The following sentence contains two prepositional phrases:

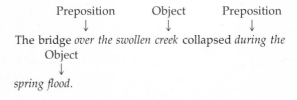

Preposition   Object   Preposition
↓   ↓   ↓
The bridge *over the swollen creek* collapsed *during the*
Object
↓
spring flood.

The first phrase explains the relationship between the bridge and the creek, telling where the bridge was. The second phrase tells when the bridge collapsed.

Practice 1–20 List the prepositions in the reading selection at the beginning of this unit.

Practice 1–21 List the prepositional phrases in the following sentences.

1. Politics requires open-minded citizens who can understand what the people of the world say to them.
2. Robert suggested that I go roller-skating with him and his friend after dinner.
3. A bed board offers good therapy for your back during sleep.
4. The parents of my roommate didn't understand what their youngest son was doing at school.
5. Fresh vegetables supply us with vitamins and minerals that we do not get otherwise—with or without vitamin supplements.

Practice 1–22 Write one sentence for each of the following prepositions.

1. across
2. because of
3. during
4. near
5. under

1G Conjunctions

Conjunctions are parts of speech that join words and groups of words. There are two main types of conjunctions: **coordinating** and **subordinating.**

1G(1) Coordinating Conjunctions

Coordinating conjunctions connect words, phrases, or clauses of equal weight. See Chapters 2 and 3 for definitions of phrases and clauses. The coordinating conjunctions are *and, but, or, nor, for, so,* and *yet.*

The following sentences show coordinating conjunctions linking elements of equal weight:

Verb   Verb
↓   ↓
Coordinating: He washed *and* combed his hair.

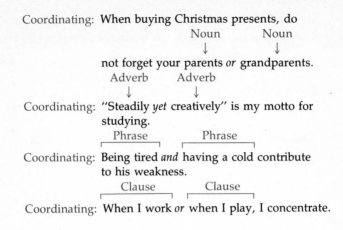

Coordinating: When buying Christmas presents, do

Noun → | Noun → |

not forget your parents *or* grandparents.

Adverb → | Adverb → |

Coordinating: "Steadily *yet* creatively" is my motto for studying.

Phrase | Phrase |

Coordinating: Being tired *and* having a cold contribute to his weakness.

Clause | Clause |

Coordinating: When I work *or* when I play, I concentrate.

Correlative conjunctions are coordinating conjunctions used in pairs. They include *either/or, neither/nor, not only/but also, not/but, whether/or,* and *both/and.*

Correlative: *Either* my work *or* my persistence is bound to pay off.

1G(2) Subordinating Conjunctions

Subordinating conjunctions connect clauses—units containing their own subjects and verbs—that are not equally stressed. See Chapter 3 for a detailed discussion of clauses. The dependent (less stressed) clause, often introduced by a subordinating conjunction, functions as a single part of speech (noun, adjective, adverb). Therefore it cannot stand alone as a sentence but *depends* for its meaning on the rest of the words in the sentence. The independent (stressed) clause can function as a sentence when standing alone; its meaning is *independent* of the rest of the words in the sentence.

Subordinating conjunctions include *after, although, as, as if, as long as, as though, because, before, how, if, in order that, since, so that, that, though, unless, until, when, whenever, where, wherever,* and *while.* Remembering how subordinating conjunctions work in a sentence will be more helpful to you than memorizing a list of them, because some of these

21

words can function either as subordinating conjunctions or as prepositions (*before, since*), pronouns or adjectives (*that*), or even nouns (*while*).

> Subordinating: *Because* you expressed genuine concern, we will be able to hire you.

Practice 1–23 List the conjunctions in the following sentences.

1. I often go to the movies, although I prefer live drama.
2. Antelope originally came from either Africa or Asia.
3. Good running shoes both increase speed and reduce the risk of injury.
4. Rain clears the air but makes waiting for a bus difficult.
5. Joan considered both sides of the proposition, and then she voted in favor of it.

Practice 1–24 List the conjunctions in the reading selection at the beginning of this unit.

Practice 1–25 Rewrite the following sentences, adding a word or phrase that is the part of speech named in the parentheses.

1. <u>(subordinating conjunction)</u> I was almost broke, I gave my father a wallet for Father's Day.

2. I enjoy <u>(correlative conjunction)</u> planting flowers <u>(correlative conjunction)</u> watching them grow, <u>(coordinating conjunction)</u> I am still learning how to water them properly.

3. I lost my key, <u>(coordinating conjunction)</u> I can't drive home.

4. <u>(subordinating conjunction)</u> circumstances at home are complex, the college life of a married person is different from that of an unmarried person.

5. <u>(subordinating conjunction)</u> Mother is sick in bed, I might wash the car, <u>(coordinating conjunction)</u> I might start dinner.

Practice 1–26 Write one sentence for each of the following conjunctions.

1. since
2. whether . . . or
3. after
4. so
5. and

1H   Interjections

Interjections are exclamations that express emotion: *ouch, hey, hallelujah, oh, aha, alas, well*. In sentences, mild interjections are followed by commas and strong interjections by exclamation points.

> Interjection: *Well,* that does sting a little.
> Interjection: *Hallelujah!* I passed that final.

Practice 1–27 List the interjections in the following sentences.

1. Oh, no! The dishwasher has broken down again!
2. My goodness, where on earth did you come from?
3. The camellias, alas, are late this year.

Practice 1–28 Write one sentence for each of the following interjections.

1. well
2. oh, dear
3. my goodness

Review

A. There are eight parts of speech in the English language:
  1. Verbs describe an action or a state of being.
  2. Nouns name persons, places, things, animals, actions, qualities, and ideas.
  3. Pronouns take the place of nouns.
  4. Adjectives modify (describe) nouns and pronouns by giving information about their quality or quantity.
  5. Adverbs modify verbs, adjectives, other adverbs, and occasionally entire sentences.

23

6. Prepositions relate a noun or pronoun to another word.
7. Conjunctions join words and groups of words.
8. Interjections are exclamations.

B. The names of the parts of speech identify words by their use, or function, in a sentence.

C. Each part of speech has its own specific role in a sentence.

D. The position and function of a word in a sentence indicate what part of speech the word is.

Review Practice 1–1 Label each word in the following sentences by its part of speech (verb, noun, pronoun, adjective, adverb, preposition, conjunction, or interjection).

1. Everything rests on my promotion, especially my ego.
2. Wow! What did you think of that final pass in the game?
3. All people have emotions.
4. When I have eaten breakfast, I will look at your car.
5. Students need some form of recreation.

Review Practice 1–2 Rewrite the following sentences, adding a word or phrase that is the part of speech named in parentheses.

1. Scuba diving is ___(adverb)___ one of the most ___(adjective)___ sports that I know of.

2. ___(preposition)___ the ___(noun)___ is a secret meeting room for ___(noun)___ only, explained the mayor ___(adverb)___.

3. ___(interjection)___, ___(subordinating conjunction)___ you will not see it my way, I will take my ___(noun)___ and go home.

4. She ___(pronoun)___ admitted that ___(pronoun)___ had been ___(adjective)___.

5. Jim ___(verb)___ and ___(verb)___ the car ___(subordinating conjunction)___ he bought it.

6. Track is really my favorite sport, ___(coordinating conjunction)___ I like to swim ___(subordinating conjunction)___ I can.

7. __(subordinating conjunction)__ I die, I want to visit __(noun)__.

8. I really think a (an) __(adjective)__, __(adjective)__ bag __(preposition)__ popcorn would __(adverb)__ taste __(adjective)__ about now.

9. If you have anything to say about it, you __(verb)__ before you do __(pronoun)__ again.

10. People __(verb)__ hobbies __(subordinating conjunction)__ their work is __(adjective)__.

2 Phrases

A **phrase** is a group of related words that does not contain a subject or a predicate. See 4A and 4B. Since a sentence must contain a subject and a verb, a phrase cannot stand alone as a sentence. Recognizing phrases helps you read effectively, because you can move through a reading assignment quickly with a high degree of comprehension when you have learned to see words in clusters. A phrase functions as a single part of speech in its sentence. Four common types of phrases are **noun phrases, prepositional phrases, verb phrases,** and **verbal phrases.**

2A Noun Phrases

A **noun phrase** is a group of words that usually begins with a noun or with words that modify nouns. It functions as a single noun in a sentence. In the following examples of noun phrases, the nouns are in italics.

Phrase

Noun phrases: Many valuable leather-bound *books* were

Phrase

destroyed in the great *fire.*

An **appositive** is a noun or noun phrase that explains or identifies another noun or noun phrase. The appositive is placed next to the word(s) it explains.

Phrase

Appositive: My stereo, my most valuable *possession,* keeps me company when I'm alone.

Practice 2–1 List the noun phrases in the reading selection at the beginning of this unit.

Practice 2–2 Write a sentence for each of the following noun phrases.

1. two nursery rhymes
2. a new language
3. an easy word
4. several kind looks
5. ink, pens, and books

2B   Prepositional Phrases

A **prepositional phrase** is a group of words that begins with a preposition and ends with an object of the preposition. Prepositional phrases function within sentences as adjectives, as adverbs, and occasionally as nouns. In the following examples of prepositional phrases, the prepositions are italicized.

Phrase

Prepositional phrase: He was standing alone *by* the pond

Phrase

when a child appeared *behind* him.

Practice 2–3 List the prepositional phrases in the reading selection at the beginning of this unit.

Practice 2–4 Write a sentence for each of the following prepositional phrases.

1. from my house
2. at track practice
3. under the desk
4. ahead of me
5. according to my instructor

2C Verb Phrases

A **verb phrase** consists of words that function together as the main verb of a sentence; see 1A. These phrases begin with **auxiliary,** or **helping, verbs.** Helping verbs are so named because they *help* the main verb express action or state of being. Common helping verbs include most forms of *to be, to do, to have, can, may, will* (or *shall*), and *must.* In the following examples of verb phrases, main verbs are italicized, and helping verbs are not.

Phrase Phrase

Verb phrase: I will be *needing* all the help I can *get.*

Practice 2–5 List the verb phrases in the reading selection at the beginning of this unit.

Practice 2–6 Write one sentence for each of the following verb phrases.

1. have seen
2. will be asking
3. is gone
4. am about to be
5. can't believe

2D Verbal Phrases

Verbal phrases, unlike verb phrases, cannot function in a sentence as main verbs. Verbal phrases—often called

27

verbals—are groups of words that begin with a participle (present or past) or an infinitive (*to* plus a verb); they have the general characteristics of a verb but function as other parts of speech in a sentence.

The **participial phrase**, one kind of verbal, begins with either a present participle (the verb form that ends in *-ing*) or a past participle (the verb form that often ends in *-d* or *-ed*). In each of the following examples of verbals, the participle is italicized. See 1A.

Adjective

Participial phrase: People *driving* a car at night should be extra cautious when they judge distances.

Present participial phrases used as nouns are called **gerunds.** The example here shows a gerund phrase as the object of the verb *liked*.

Noun

Gerund phrase: They liked *watching* the wrestlers.

An **infinitive phrase** begins with an infinitive (the *to* form of a verb). Infinitive phrases can be used in sentences as nouns, adjectives, or adverbs.

Noun

Infinitive phrase: *To swim* the English Channel requires remarkable physical endurance.

Adjective

Infinitive phrase: The time *to make* reservations is right now.

Adverb

Infinitive phrase: She got up *to answer* the phone.

Practice 2–7 List the verbal phrases in the reading selection at the beginning of this unit.

Practice 2–8 Write one sentence for each of the following verbals.

1. to see the cooperation
2. getting an important letter
3. having seen the movie
4. corrected by my friend
5. to be available

Practice 2–9 List all the phrases in the following sentences.

1. *Star Trek* has been shown on TV for a long time.
2. After going north on Weedpatch Highway and then right onto Brundage, you will be at my house in no time at all.
3. Combing his hair, he slowly walked toward the front door.
4. Citation was the first horse to win more than $1 million in racing.
5. Canonizing a person means recognizing that person as a saint.
6. "Scorpion" is a clever name for a sports car.
7. According to barrio folklore, tickling a baby will cause the child to have a speech defect.
8. Soccer is a very fast, stimulating sport.
9. "Bone of my bones and flesh of my flesh" is Adam's description of Eve.
10. Left outside in the rain, the dog howled in misery.

Practice 2–10 Write a paragraph on a topic of your choice. Then underline all the phrases in the paragraph.

Practice 2–11 Rewrite the following sentences, adding phrases that make sense.

1. _(phrase)_ are fun to ride _(phrase)_ .
2. It is time _(phrase)_ the race.
3. _(phrase)_ , Mary _(phrase)_ tomorrow.
4. _(phrase)_ took a great deal _(phrase)_ .
5. Every evening we eat dinner _(phrase)_ .

Review

A. A phrase is a group of related words that does not contain a subject or a predicate and cannot stand alone as a sentence.

B. Phrases function in sentences as individual parts of speech.

C. There are four types of phrases:

1. A noun phrase is a group of words usually beginning with a noun or with words that modify nouns and functioning as a single noun in a sentence. Appositives are special types of noun phrases.

2. A prepositional phrase is a group of words that begins with a preposition and ends with an object of the preposition.

3. A verb phrase consists of words that function together as a main verb of a sentence.

4. Verbal phrases, which cannot function as main verbs, are participial phrases, gerund phrases, and infinitive phrases.

Review Practice 2–1 List all the phrases in the following sentences.

1. Nowadays, some couples getting married are writing their own ceremonies.

2. In the United States, many people still suffer from economic and political discrimination.

3. He has always wanted to visit the cliff dwellings in Mesa Verde National Park in Colorado.

4. Being in love is a little bit like eating an artichoke.

5. To be young is to be inquisitive.

Review Practice 2–2 Rewrite the following sentences, adding phrases that make sense.

1. <u>(phrase)</u>, she wrote the assignment on the chalkboard.

2. <u>(phrase)</u> got very tired <u>(phrase)</u>.

3. Do you want __(phrase)__ with me?
4. The stars __(phrase)__ __(phrase)__.
5. They __(phrase)__ as a group __(phrase)__.

Review Practice 2–3 Write a complete sentence including each of the following phrases.
1. to study art history
2. taking her first patient's temperature
3. in the hands of fate
4. will be joining
5. unnecessary and costly trip

3   Clauses

A **clause** is a group of words that contains a subject and a predicate; see 4A and 4B. A predicate consists of the main verb in a sentence and the words that follow that main verb. There are two types of clauses: **independent** (or **main**) and **dependent** (or **subordinate**). The major difference between these two types is that an independent clause can stand alone as a sentence and a dependent clause cannot.

Independent: Some people like a crowd.
Dependent: Although some people like a crowd . . .

The dependent clause here leaves the reader wondering what point the writer wants to make about crowds and different people. A dependent clause is **dependent** on an independent clause for meaning.

Dependent Clause	Independent Clause
Although some people like a crowd,	others prefer solitude.

3A Independent Clauses

An **independent clause** can stand alone as a sentence, because it has a subject and a predicate and expresses a complete idea.

Subject

Independent: Jack and Margaret

Predicate

enjoy the strawberry season.

Practice 3–1 Write out the independent clauses in the reading selection at the beginning of this unit.

Practice 3–2 Write five independent clauses of your own.

3B Dependent Clauses

A **dependent clause** contains a subject and a predicate, like an independent clause, but it is introduced by words or expressions that make its meaning *depend* on the rest of the sentence.

> Dependent: Since Jack and Margaret enjoy the strawberry season . . .

Dependent clauses are introduced by relative pronouns or by subordinating conjunctions: see 1C and 1G(2).

> Relative pronoun: *that* overlooks the garden
> Subordinating conjunction: *unless* you had been there

Practice 3–3 List the dependent clauses in the following sentences.

1. Studying is important, but playing is also necessary.
2. Drugs are a strange business, because they cure as well as harm people.
3. Because his fiancée owns a men's clothing shop, his clothes always look sensational.
4. It's true that ivy can grow just about anywhere.
5. After the price of oil increased in September, our heating bill went sky high.

Practice 3–4 Write out the dependent clauses in the reading selection at the beginning of this unit.

Practice 3–5 Write five dependent clauses of your own.

Practice 3–6 List and label the independent and the dependent clauses in the following sentences.

1. The female image in commercials is slowly changing because the women's movement has pressured advertisers to avoid the old stereotypes.
2. When cranberries are dropped, they bounce.
3. All the theaters in our neighborhood show X-rated films, so none of our children can go to the movies by themselves.
4. If you want to go, you should ask Uncle John to take you.
5. Although girls seem to confide in other girls, boys usually confide in their mothers.
6. Wherever the bandits went, they saw their pictures on "wanted" posters.
7. The plumber whose shop is on the corner charges too much.
8. The highlight of her day was talking to her cat, who turned out to be a good listener.
9. Because even moderate drinkers are likely to have heart trouble, I am going to stop drinking.
10. "Black Power and the American Christ" is an essay that was written by Vincent Harding when he was at the height of his career.

3C Subordination

To *subordinate* anything is to assign it a lower rank or significance than something else. In writing, **subordination** allows you to play down less significant ideas by putting them in subordinate (or dependent) clauses and to emphasize main ideas by putting them in main (or independent) clauses. In addition to providing emphasis, subordination helps you indicate the logical relationships among ideas within a sentence.

Subordinate clauses are introduced by relative pronouns or subordinating conjunctions, which spell out the relationship between the main clause and the subordinate clause in a sentence: see 1C, 9B(2), and 1G(2). *Relative* pronouns *(who, whom, whose, which, that)* have a dual function in a sentence: first, they *relate* back to another word in the sentence; and second, they function as nouns and adjectives in their own clauses. In the following sentence, *who* refers to *man* in the main clause and serves as a subject of its own subordinate clause, *who won the match.*

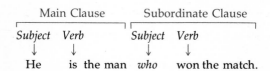

*Sub*ordinating conjunctions can best be remembered by recalling that *sub-* means "under" (as in *submarine* and *subway*). Like relative pronouns, subordinating conjunctions introduce clauses of less significance to the entire sentence than main clauses:

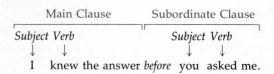

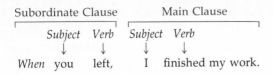

Subordinate Clause   Main Clause

Subject   *Verb*   *Subject*   *Verb*

When you left,   I   finished my work.

Without subordination, sentences are often choppy and uninteresting. The following paragraphs show the effect of subordination. The first contains no subordination. In the second, several clauses have been connected by relative pronouns and subordinating conjunctions.

Without Subordination

    The trees are bare and the streets are covered with ice and snow. I know about spring. Somewhere spring, with all its beauty, is ahead of us. I remember spring and its freshness. It helps me get through the winter. In spring there is an indescribable excitement in the air. Everyone feels it. The days are full of outdoor activity. Evening comes and is filled with smiling faces, people in spring clothes, and the sweet fragrances of lush greenery. In spring, everything blooms. It is good to be alive.

With Subordination

    Although the trees are bare and the streets are covered with ice and snow, I know *that* somewhere spring, with all its beauty, is ahead of us. *When* I remember spring and its freshness, it helps me get through the winter. In spring there is an indescribable excitement in the air *that* everyone feels. The days are full of outdoor activity *until* evening, *which* is filled with smiling faces, people in spring clothes, and the sweet fragrances of lush greenery. In spring, *while* everything blooms, it is good to be alive.

35

Practice 3–7 Rewrite these clauses, combining them by using relative pronouns or subordinating conjunctions as necessary. Add or subtract words to make your sentences clear.

1. The air is clear.
   The clouds are filled with rain.
2. I'm at school.
   You should clean the apartment.
3. He doesn't agree.
   He should present his side of the case.
4. You pay for the merchandise.
   I won't release it to you.
5. Photography is a growing art.
   This makes film appreciation a growing interest, too.
6. You're walking oddly.
   You have a thorn in your foot.
7. She wore a hole in her tennis shoe.
   She was playing very hard.
8. Cats enjoy the warmth of the sun.
   It makes them sleep.

Review

A. A clause is a group of words that contains a subject and a predicate.
B. There are two types of clauses:
   1. An independent, or main, clause can stand alone as a complete sentence.
   2. A dependent, or subordinate, clause is introduced by a relative pronoun or a subordinating conjunction and cannot stand alone as a complete sentence.
C. Subordination is the practice of combining independent and dependent clauses in order to emphasize

main ideas and show the relationship among the ideas in a sentence.

Review Practice 3–1 List the subject and the verb of each of the following clauses, and then label each clause "independent" or "dependent."
1. Bette Davis got the leading role
2. she went to the post office
3. that he decided on his career
4. they bought a car
5. if she wins the competition
6. which is on the floor
7. it won't be hers
8. because they wanted it a certain way
9. whose book he borrowed
10. the team fought for the title
11. after they left the dance
12. when the timer rings
13. although carbohydrates contain starch
14. we are happy to be here
15. which is my favorite song

Review Practice 3–2 In the following sentences, list each clause and label it "independent" or "dependent."
1. I entered the room slowly.
2. When I get my degree from college, I will be very proud of myself.
3. If you have ever played air hockey, you know it is easy to lose control of the puck.
4. Before she rode on the roller coaster, she ate two bags of popcorn and four hot dogs.
5. According to the religious beliefs that the couple holds, equality in marriage is not advisable.

Review Practice 3–3 Rewrite each set of clauses, combining them into a coherent sentence by using relative pronouns and subordinating conjunctions as necessary. Add or subtract words to make your sentences clear.

1. It is time to head for home.
   I have to be there by noon.
   I can go to work at one.
2. He likes strawberry milkshakes.
   He likes banana splits even more.
3. They could deny the accusation.
   It wouldn't get them anywhere.
   They wouldn't have any comeback.
4. She picks up her paycheck this afternoon.
   She can pay her debts.
   She will not be able to buy the new stereo.

4 Sentences

A **sentence** is a group of words containing at least one independent clause, which consists of at least one subject and one predicate. The words of a sentence are arranged so that they communicate a complete idea.

4A Subjects

The **subject** of a sentence tells who or what is doing an action or who or what is in a state of being; see 1A. Subjects are often phrases made up of nouns, pronouns, and their modifiers; see 1B for information on nouns and 1C for information on pronouns. To determine the subject, you can place *who* or *what* before the verb. The answer to the question you have formed is the subject of the sentence.

Simple subject: The *couple* rented the apartment.

Who rented? The couple.

Complete subjects include a simple subject and its

modifiers. If, however, the simple subject has no modifiers, it serves as the complete subject of a sentence. In the following examples of complete subjects, the simple subjects are italicized.

Complete subject: The *couple* from Kalamazoo rented the apartment.

Who rented? The couple from Kalamazoo.

Practice 4–1 List the simple subjects in the reading selection at the beginning of this unit.

Practice 4–2 List the complete subjects in the reading selection at the beginning of this unit.

Practice 4–3 Write sentences for each of the following subjects.

1. the friendly gestures
2. sign language
3. the team winning the spelling bee
4. a large portion of the population
5. the hermit living by himself on the top of the hill

4B Predicates

A **predicate** explains what is happening to the subject in a sentence. A predicate usually begins with a main verb. A simple predicate is a main verb and its auxiliary, or helping, words.

Simple predicate: We *have eaten*.
Simple predicate: The speaker at the conference *was* anxious.

A complete predicate contains a main verb and everything that follows or modifies the main verb. Depending on the type of sentence, this may include adverbs, indirect objects, direct objects, predicate nouns, and/or predicate adjectives: see 4C. In the following examples of complete predicates, simple predicates are italicized.

Complete predicate: She *bought* her books.

Complete predicate: My friend *told* me a secret.

Complete predicate: The farmer *was* a patriotic citizen.

Complete predicate: The clouds now *seem* heavy with rain.

Practice 4–4 You identified the simple predicates in the reading selection at the beginning of this unit when you listed the main verbs in Practice 1–3. How many main verbs are there in the passage?

Practice 4–5 List the complete predicates in the reading selection at the beginning of this unit.

Practice 4–6 Write sentences for the following predicates.

1. has finally won the debate and the trophy
2. soon will be here
3. wants to borrow some money but doesn't know when he can pay it back
4. is coming to talk to me next week
5. always wants things her way

4C Sentence Patterns

Most sentences are based on one of four sentence patterns: (1) **subject–verb**, (2) **subject–action verb–direct object**, (3) **subject–action verb–indirect object–direct object**, or (4) **subject–linking verb–complement**. These patterns differ mainly in the content of the predicate. All four patterns begin with subjects followed by verbs, but three of the patterns have objects or complements that follow the verb.

4C(1) Subject–Verb

Beyond a one-word sentence ("Stop!"), the simplest sentence consists of only two words.

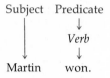

This statement makes sense and is complete even though it does not tell what Martin won. Verbs used in this pattern are usually intransitive; see 1A(2).

4C(2) Subject–Action Verb–Direct Object

Some verbs, however, need objects to complete their thought. These are transitive verbs; see 1A(1).

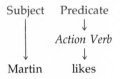

These two words are unable to stand alone as a sentence, because the meaning they are trying to express is not complete. We need to know what Martin likes. In other words, the subject *Martin* and the verb *likes* need a **direct object** for the sentence to make sense.

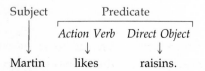

The addition of one word *(raisins)* makes this example a complete sentence. *Raisins* is the direct object that receives the action of the verb.

4C(3) Subject–Action Verb–Indirect Object–Direct Object

Here is another sentence that follows the second pattern.

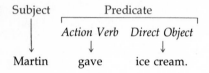

Although this group of words could stand as a complete sentence, we could add another element to make its meaning even clearer. That element, called the **indirect object,** explains to whom the ice cream was given. Indirect objects appear with such verbs as *ask, give, tell, award, leave, make, do, promise, send, assign,* and *throw.* They indicate to (or for) whom or what something is done. So, we can form a third pattern, in which the predicate includes a verb, an indirect object, and a direct object.

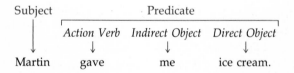

Notice that the indirect object comes before the direct object and can be converted into a prepositional phrase that begins with *to* or *for* and can follow the direct object: "Martin gave ice cream *to me.*"

4C(4) Subject–Linking Verb–Complement

A *linking* verb (which refers to a state of being) *links* its subject to the complement that follows it. The complement can be either a noun (also called a predicate noun) or an adjective (also called a predicate adjective). The best way to tell whether a sentence fits this pattern is to substitute an equals sign (=) for the verb. If the verb you replace is a linking verb, the meaning of the sentence will not change much.

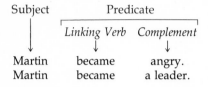

Subject	Predicate	
	Linking Verb	Complement
Martin	became	angry.
Martin	became	a leader.

Practice 4–7 Label each of the following sentences according to the pattern it follows: (1) subject–verb, (2) subject–action verb–direct object, (3) subject–action verb–indirect object–direct object, and (4) subject–linking verb–complement.

1. Nevertheless, I take sociology seriously.
2. Well, Joe baked me a pie for my birthday.
3. Forests burn.
4. Drinking can kill.
5. Sex education offers students knowledge.
6. Vocational training builds a community.
7. Traveling rests the soul, especially of the weary.
8. The stars might tell your future.
9. She felt strange after the ride on the ferris wheel.
10. They were the unhappy losers in the situation.

Practice 4–8 Compose five sentences following each of the four patterns.

4D Variations of the Patterns

Most sentences are constructed according to one of the four basic patterns. Sometimes, however, the pattern is hard to see, because the word order is changed or the sentence structure becomes complicated.

4D(1) Questions

In questions, the verb is divided into two or more parts—no matter how many parts it originally had. The helping word comes before the subject, and the rest of the verb follows the subject.

Statement: **Babies** *cry.*
Question: *Do* **babies** *cry?*

Statement: **Ruth** *is swimming.*
Question: *Is* **Ruth** *swimming?*

Statement: **Bert** *used to dance.*
Question: *Did* **Bert** *used to dance?*

Questions can also be introduced by interrogative words, such as *who, what, which, why, where, when,* and *how.*

Question: *Why* do babies cry?

4D(2) Negative Statements

To form negative statements, *not* is placed after the first helping word in a predicate. In most cases, the *not* splits the verb into two parts, even though the verb originally may have had only one part.

Statement: You *are going* home for vacation.
Negative: You *are* not *going* home for vacation.

Statement: They *made* soup for dinner.
Negative: They *did* not *make* soup for dinner.

Statement: We *had* to play soccer.
Negative: We *did* not *have* to play soccer.

4D(3) Expletives

The term *expletive* means "filler." Expletives *(it, there)* often combine with linking verbs (usually *is* or *are*) to get a sentence started. They direct attention to the words that follow them. A sentence that begins with an expletive is unusual in that its subject follows the verb.

Subject

Expletive: *It* is time to do your work.

Subject

Expletive: *There* are many solutions to this problem.

Practice 4–9 How many questions, negative statements, and expletives are there in the reading selection at the beginning of this unit?

4E Combining Clauses

One way of classifying a sentence is by the number and type of clauses it contains. Independent and dependent clauses can be **combined** to create four types of sentences: (1) **simple,** (2) **compound,** (3) **complex,** and (4) **compound-complex.** You should combine clauses that have logical relationships with each other, because combining usually clarifies and emphasizes these relationships. Combining clauses also gives your writing more variety of sentence structure, which usually makes it more interesting to read.

4E(1) Simple Sentences

A simple sentence expresses a single thought. It contains one independent clause that consists of one subject-predicate set.

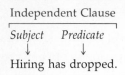

Independent Clause

Subject   *Predicate*
   ↓   ↓
Hiring has dropped.

Practice 4–10 Write out the simple sentences in the reading selection at the beginning of this unit.

Practice 4–11 Write five simple sentences on a topic of your choice.

4E(2) Compound Sentences

A compound sentence contains at least two independent clauses or two subject-predicate sets. Any independent clauses can be combined to form a compound sentence as long as they are logically related to one another. These clauses are of equal weight in a sentence and are usually connected by a coordinating conjunction; see 1G(1). Either clause can stand alone as a complete sentence, but a writer combines them to show their close relationship to each other.

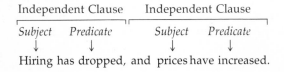

Independent Clause   Independent Clause

Subject   *Predicate*   *Subject*   *Predicate*
   ↓   ↓   ↓   ↓
Hiring has dropped, and prices have increased.

You should not confuse the structure of a compound sentence with the structure of a simple sentence that has two subjects or verbs.

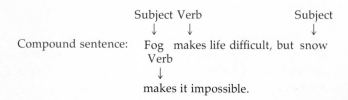

                    Subject Verb   Subject
                       ↓   ↓   ↓
Compound sentence: Fog makes life difficult, but snow
                     Verb
                       ↓
                     makes it impossible.

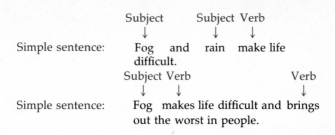

Simple sentence: Fog and rain make life difficult.

Simple sentence: Fog makes life difficult and brings out the worst in people.

Practice 4–12 Write two compound sentences on a topic of your choice.

4E(3) Complex Sentences

A complex sentence contains an independent clause and at least one dependent clause. Either type of clause can begin the sentence. Like compound sentences, complex sentences have at least two subject-predicate sets, but only the subject and predicate in the independent clause can stand alone as a complete sentence. In complex sentences, the dependent clause is joined to the independent clause by a subordinating conjunction or by a relative pronoun, which explains the relationship between the two clauses: see 1G(2) and 1C.

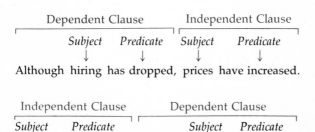

Practice 4–13 List the complex sentences in the reading selection at the beginning of this unit.

Practice 4–14 Write five complex sentences on a topic of your choice.

4E(4) Compound-Complex Sentences

Compound-complex sentences combine the features of compound sentences and complex sentences. A compound-complex sentence contains at least two independent clauses and one dependent clause. It uses subordinating and coordinating conjunctions or relative pronouns to connect the clauses. The clauses can be arranged in any order, as long as they are logically related to one another.

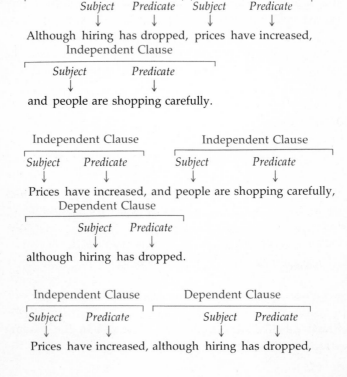

Independent Clause

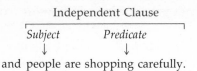

and people are shopping carefully.

Practice 4–15 Write two compound-complex sentences on a topic of your choice.

Practice 4–16 Answer the following questions.

1. What are the four clause combinations?
2. Give one example of each of these combinations.
3. Name four coordinating conjunctions. Write four compound sentences using these conjunctions.
4. Name four subordinating conjunctions. Write four complex sentences using these conjunctions.
5. Name four relative pronouns. Write four complex sentences using these pronouns.

Practice 4–17 Classify each of the following sentences as simple, compound, complex, or compound-complex. Refer to the models in the chapter whenever necessary.

1. Parents usually try to be consistent in setting down rules.
2. Electrons, which may be dispersed from solids or liquids, are basic to the study of electronics.
3. Feather paintings, which consist of feathers pasted on a background to make a picture, are a unique form of early Mexican art, and they originated with the Mayan and Aztec civilizations.
4. Marvin and Jack love to cook soufflés, and they seize upon any opportunity to show off their talents.
5. Liberation of any group in society usually brings a new awareness to the population.
6. Have you ever been to Lake Powell in Arizona?
7. Since Marge has been taking judo lessons, her friends have been treating her very nicely.
8. Shouldn't you put your book down and come to bed?
9. My brother tripped down the stairs, and he smashed the model airplane that I spent two months building.

10. Common sense will get you through a lot of college crises.

Practice 4–18 Classify as simple, compound, complex, or compound-complex the sentences in the paragraph "With Subordination" on page 35.

Practice 4–19 Rewrite the following sets of statements, connecting them with coordinating conjunctions, subordinating conjunctions, or relative pronouns so that each item reads smoothly as a compound, complex, or compound-complex sentence. Add or subtract words to make your sentences clear.

1. Concentration is a major part of reading.
   Reading is a major part of studying.
2. *Ladies' Home Journal* is a good authority on beauty.
   The magazine explains that sleep is the best possible beauty treatment.
3. People should be more tolerant of one another.
   Understanding is a partial solution to many of our social problems.
4. You sweep the garage.
   Then you can go to the movies.
5. Heart disease strikes those who work too hard.
   People shouldn't use up all their physical and emotional energy.
   They want to stay healthy.
6. I know this.
   People sometimes buy dogs that look like them.
   My roommate looks like a poodle.
   She bought one.
7. Keeping a secret from someone you love is difficult to do.
   It is especially difficult in some situations.
   The information you are keeping might be harmful to that person.
8. I think you should take a walk.
   It will do your temper good.
9. Teaching is both an art and a science.
   Some people just aren't good at it.

10. A piece of jewelry is a personal gift.
Giving a gift means you care.

4F   Sentences Classified by Use

Sentences can also be classified by the way they are used. According to **function,** a sentence may be (1) a **statement,** (2) a **question,** (3) an **exclamation,** or (4) a **command or request.**

4F(1) Statements

A statement declares a fact and ends with a period. See 12A and 7F(1).

> Statement: You are not taking Psychology 102 this term.

4F(2) Questions

A question makes an inquiry and ends with a question mark. See 12B and 4D(1).

> Question: Why aren't you taking Psychology 102 this term?

4F(3) Exclamations

An exclamation expresses sudden or strong feeling and ends with an exclamation point. See 12C.

> Exclamation: I wouldn't take Psychology 102 this term if my life depended on it!

4F(4) Commands

A command makes a request or gives an order and ends with a period. See 12A and 7F(2). The subject of a command *(you)* is not expressed.

51

Command: Take Psychology 102 this term or be prepared
to withdraw from school.
Command: Please let me take Psychology 102 this term.

Practice 4–20 Label each sentence in the reading selection
at the beginning of this unit as "statement," "question,"
"exclamation," or "command."

Practice 4–21 Rewrite the following sentences, adding correct
punctuation, and then identify each sentence as a
statement, question, exclamation, or command.

1. It will absolutely never work
2. Plagiarism is an advanced form of cheating and should
   always be avoided
3. Get out of here before I throw something at you
4. Will he ever learn not to argue with highway patrol
   officers
5. Go to work, and worry about dinner later

Practice 4–22 Write one example of each type of sentence:
statement, question, exclamation, and command. Use appropriate
punctuation.

Review

A. A sentence is a series of words that contains a subject
   and predicate and is arranged so that the words communicate
   a complete idea.
B. There are four common sentence patterns:
   1. subject–verb
   2. subject–action verb–direct object
   3. subject–action verb–indirect object–direct object
   4. subject–linking verb–complement
C. The word order of these four patterns varies in questions,
   negative statements, and sentences with expletives.
D. There are four clause combinations:
   1. simple sentence, one independent clause

2. compound sentence, two or more independent clauses
3. complex sentence, one independent clause and at least one dependent clause
4. compound-complex sentence, at least two independent clauses and one dependent clause

E. Sentences have one of four uses:
1. statements
2. questions
3. exclamations
4. commands or requests

Review Practice 4–1 List the complete subjects and verbs of each clause in the following sentences. Supply missing subjects, if necessary.

1. Animals and plants have different food needs.
2. Give him the dictionary and the historical atlas.
3. Confronting and evaluating problems of drug addiction and emotional depression in the United States are important to the welfare of our nation.
4. Economics does not deal with basic political demands in society, although its scope is broad and its topics are varied.
5. Why has religious interest decreased among young people in the last few years?
6. Renaissance art grew out of medieval culture, and it developed first in Italy.
7. In simple terms, one sperm cell from a male and one egg from a female join together to form one fetus.
8. As I have heard my mother say, only lazy people use sleep to procrastinate.
9. There are two major divisions in anthropology— physical and cultural.
10. Since the beginning of the women's movement, females have become more inclined to share the expense of a date.

Review Practice 4–2 How many clauses does each sentence in Review Practice 4–1 have?

Review Practice 4-3 How many clauses are in each sentence in the reading selection at the beginning of this unit?

Review Practice 4-4 Write one sentence for each of the following sets of characteristics.

1. a statement that contains a compound verb
2. a question that contains a direct object and indirect object
3. a statement that is a compound sentence
4. an exclamation that is a compound sentence
5. a question that contains a compound direct object
6. a statement that contains a phrase
7. a command that contains a phrase
8. a question that is a compound-complex sentence
9. an exclamation that is a simple sentence with an indirect object and a direct object
10. a command that contains a prepositional phrase

5   Sentence Fragments

A **fragment** is a part of a sentence that is capitalized and punctuated as if it were a complete sentence. A fragment leaves the reader hanging, because it is not a complete thought but is usually only a phrase or dependent clause.

Fragments are often heard in conversation and are also seen in written dialogue. Many exclamations, interjections, questions, and answers are acceptable fragments. Nevertheless, fragments in your writing should usually be developed into complete sentences so that your intention is clear and your thoughts are not misinterpreted.

5A   Identifying Fragments

Some fragments are phrases without subjects and predicates, and others consist of subjects and predicates introduced by subordinating conjunctions or relative pronouns. A sentence is complete (1) if it has at least one subject and predicate and (2) if no subordinating conjunction or relative pronoun appears before that subject and predicate.

Fragments that are phrases are missing a subject, a predicate, or both.

Fragment: Large, beautiful, white Canada geese . . .

This first example is missing a predicate; see 4B.

Fragment: And was elected to the office of class vice president . . .

This second fragment is missing a subject; see 4A.

Fragment: Always to be certain of the future . . .
Fragment: Canada geese flying in V-formation . . .

These last two examples consist of phrases only; each is missing a subject and a predicate.

Phrases occur most often as sentences when the writer mistakes a noun phrase for a sentence (as in the first example) or when the writer mistakes a verbal (especially an infinitive, as in *to be,* or a present participle, as in *flying*) for the main verb of a sentence. Fragments of this kind can be recognized and avoided by remembering three simple rules: (1) A noun phrase must be accompanied by a main verb to be a sentence. (2) An infinitive cannot act as the main verb of a sentence. (3) An *-ing* verb form cannot act as the main verb of a sentence unless it is accompanied by a helping verb; see 2C.

As you learned in 3B, dependent clauses cannot stand alone as sentences. As a result, a dependent clause that is punctuated as a complete sentence is a fragment.

Fragment: When he placed his bet . . .

55

This example contains a subject and a predicate, but it is a dependent clause that cannot stand alone as a complete sentence because of the subordinating word *(when)* that introduces it.

Phrase
┌─────────────────┐
Fragment: A small school
                    Dependent Clause
┌──────────────────────────────────────┐
where everyone knows everyone else.

This last example is a combination of a phrase and a dependent clause; it is missing a predicate.

Most fragments are written when someone has an afterthought. That is, the writer completes a sentence and then thinks of something to add to it. The addition often turns out to be a phrase or a dependent clause. These additions are often fragments because, rather than being complete thoughts by themselves, they describe or modify the ideas in the sentences before them. Both types of fragments can be avoided by making sure that each sentence you write has one subject and main verb and that a subordinating conjunction or a relative pronoun does not introduce this subject and verb.

Practice 5–1 List the fragments in the following practice.
1. By practicing every day. He knew he could win.
2. We will have to find a large apartment with a den and quiet neighbors. To produce an intellectual and emotional climate in which we can both flourish.
3. The book was overdue. Much to my surprise.
4. She takes long walks by herself. Enjoying her moments alone.
5. A friend to talk to when I am low. The pilot I met in Bermuda has been visiting me in the hospital.
6. To be successful in most of my endeavors. That is my goal.

7. I have tried. But never arrived on time.
8. Raising its head with a start. The dog seemed to hear someone outside.
9. A book that I absolutely could not put down. My instructor was proud of me.
10. A blank piece of paper staring at me waiting to be written on. That's how I spend Sunday night.

Practice 5–2 List the fragments in the following paragraph.

> The mother seal is an amazing creature. When the time arrives for her pup's birth. She raises herself up onto one of the many meeting places. Which are rocky pieces of land. Often an island of rock. In the ocean. Each female seal claims a territory. Where she will give birth. She then defends this territory. With her life. Male seals (bulls) are not allowed near the birthplace. Until several months after the pup is born. Because seals are mammals. The pup must nurse from its mother. To get its necessary nourishment. The pup stays with its mother. For one to two months. This is a time of growth and learning for the pup. Although the seal's life span is only about twenty years. It is not considered an adult until it is over five years old. When it takes full responsibility for itself.

5B   Correcting Fragments

If you can recognize fragments, you have taken the first step toward removing them from your writing, and you are ready to learn the two ways to correct them.

5B(1) Add to a Sentence

A fragment can be added to the sentence that comes before or after it.

Incorrect: It is quite a sight to watch birds migrate. *Canada geese flying in V-formation.*

Revised: It is quite a sight to watch birds migrate, especially Canada geese flying in V-formation.

5B(2) Rewrite as an Independent Clause

A fragment can be rewritten so that it is an independent clause.

Incorrect: It is quite a sight to watch birds migrate. *Canada geese flying in V-formation.*

Revised: It is quite a sight to watch birds migrate. Canada geese fly in V-formation.

Practice 5–3 Rewrite the sentences in Practice 5–1, eliminating all fragments. Use both methods of correcting fragments at least once.

Practice 5–4 Rewrite the paragraph in Practice 5–2 so that it consists of complete sentences. Use both methods of correcting fragments at least once.

Review

A. A fragment is a part of a sentence capitalized and punctuated as if it were a complete sentence.
B. A sentence is complete
   1. if it has at least one subject and predicate; and
   2. if no subordinating conjunction or relative pronoun appears before that subject and predicate.
C. Fragments are generally phrases, dependent clauses, or a combination of the two.
D. Most fragments are afterthoughts.
E. There are two ways to correct a fragment:
   1. It can be added to the sentence that comes before or after it.
   2. It can be rewritten so that it is an independent clause.

Review Practice 5–1 Rewrite the following sentences, eliminating the fragments by using both of the methods described in 5B.

1. The farmer's wife thought she had everything under control. When the goat began to eat the laundry.
2. Many spectators left before the game was over. Although some people still wanted to be part of the action.
3. As tired as you are. You should rest now.
4. Even if they had tried. They couldn't have been more helpful.
5. I decided to reveal everything. To be honest about the whole affair.
6. The fire fighters decided not to ask for additional bulldozers. They already had four.
7. The evil dwarfs approached the princess's realm. A land of hospitality and warmth.
8. Last night, after supper, we were working in the kitchen for six hours. Baking cookies for the annual bake-off.
9. Disney World in Florida is where we're going for vacation. A wonderland of fun and entertainment for the entire family.
10. Shaking like a fat lady on a weight-reducing machine. She was so furious that she trembled all over.

Review Practice 5–2 Rewrite the following paragraph, correcting the fragments.

The English language comes from a great tradition. Of variety and richness of words. In fact, there are almost one-half million words in English today. Most of the words, however, are latent. Which means they are words that are essentially unused. Even the most educated speaker in the language doesn't use nearly all of the words. That are in the language. We are still constantly borrowing words. And have received words from almost every other known language in existence. English speakers build words. From both ancient (especially Greek and Latin) and modern sources. A knowledge of classical languages often being necessary to understand the finer points of our language. We still do our best. In working with these symbols in our everyday world. In our language in particular for every speaker (and writer) to have a dictionary to use. This is important. Because our language is more varied and complex in origin and meanings than most.

6   Run-on Sentences

A **run-on or run-together sentence** contains two or more independent clauses linked by a comma **(comma splice)** or written together with no punctuation and no conjunctions between them at all **(fused sentence).** Both kinds of run-ons should be rewritten either as two separate sentences or as a compound or complex sentence.

6A   Identifying Run-ons

When two independent clauses are connected by a comma but no conjunction, the run-together that results is a comma splice.

> Comma splice: The weather is fair, we will be going on
> the picnic.

This first example is a comma splice because it includes two independent clauses separated by a comma but no conjunction. A comma is not the proper signal for warning the reader that a new independent clause is beginning.
When two independent clauses have no punctuation

between them, the run-together that results is a fused sentence.

> Fused: The wind blew hard she couldn't keep her skirt down.

This example is a fused sentence because it has no punctuation and no subordinating or coordinating conjunction between its two independent clauses. In other words, there is no indication that a second independent clause begins with *she*.

Practice 6–1 List the independent clauses that make up each of the following run-on sentences.
1. The Social Security Act protects the unemployed and the aged, furthermore it was passed by Congress in 1935.
2. Doric and Corinthian are styles of classical architecture they can be easily recognized.
3. He stayed after class he had not completed his exam.
4. Someone who majors in languages is usually called a "linguist," he or she is an expert in many languages.
5. Police science is becoming a popular area of concentration in community colleges it is drawing many students.

Practice 6–2 List the run-together clauses in the following paragraph.

> The art of writing is a difficult skill that is part natural and part learned it takes discipline and time to perfect, thoughts race through the writer's mind when the time comes to write these thoughts down they are gone and replaced by others. Writing can be frustrating when an assignment is due and the words won't come so why write this is a good question. Some people have to—like college students taking English courses others need to because certain thoughts running through their minds are demanding notice both types seem

trapped with the only escape being to surrender to words.

6B Correcting Run-ons

Comma splices and fused sentences can be rewritten in one of four ways.

6B(1) Separate by a Period

A period can separate the clauses.

Comma splice:	The weather is fair, we will be going on the picnic.
Revised:	The weather is fair. We will be going on the picnic.
Fused:	The wind blew hard she couldn't keep her skirt down.
Revised:	The wind blew hard. She couldn't keep her skirt down.

6B(2) Add a Semicolon

Closely related clauses can be connected with a semicolon.

Comma splice:	The weather is fair, we will be going on the picnic.
Revised:	The weather is fair; we will be going on the picnic.
Fused:	The wind blew hard she couldn't keep her skirt down.
Revised:	The wind blew hard; she couldn't keep her skirt down.

6B(3) Add a Coordinating Conjunction

A coordinating conjunction, preceded by a comma, can be used to connect the clauses.

Comma splice: The weather is fair, we will be going on the picnic.
Revised: The weather is fair, *so* we will be going on the picnic.

Fused: The wind blew hard she couldn't keep her skirt down.
Revised: The wind blew hard, *and* she couldn't keep her skirt down.

6B(4) Add a Subordinating Conjunction

A subordinating conjunction can be used to introduce one of the clauses.

Comma splice: The weather is fair, we will be going on the picnic.
Revised: *Since* the weather is fair, we will be going on the picnic.

Fused: The wind blew hard she couldn't keep her skirt down.
Revised: *When* the wind blew hard, she couldn't keep her skirt down.

Practice 6–3 Rewrite the sentences in Practice 6–1, correcting the run-on sentences. Use all four methods of correcting run-ons at least once.

Practice 6–4 Rewrite the paragraph in Practice 6–2, correcting the run-on sentences. Use all four methods of correcting run-ons at least once.

Review

A. A run-on sentence contains two or more independent clauses linked by a comma or written together with no punctuation or conjunctions between them. Run-on sentences do not give the reader adequate warning that one idea has ended and another is about to begin.

B. There are two kinds of run-on sentences:
  1. A comma splice is two independent clauses connected by a comma.
  2. A fused sentence is two independent clauses with no punctuation or conjunction between them.

C. There are four ways to correct run-on sentences:
  1. A period can separate the clauses.
  2. Closely related clauses can be connected with a semicolon.
  3. A coordinating conjunction, preceded by a comma, can be used to connect the clauses.
  4. A subordinating conjunction can be used to subordinate one of the clauses.

Review Practice 6–1 Rewrite the following items, eliminating run-on sentences. Not all items need correction.

1. Alcohol and heroin are addictive drugs, they are easily abused.
2. Music can regulate our moods by changing our feelings.
3. Instructors agree that logic is an important feature of a basic college education, it teaches students to think clearly.
4. Where there's snow, there's fun, that's just the way it is.
5. Eggs, lemon, and butter are in this recipe, it's delicious.
6. Natural foods are becoming a part of our diet, we are more interested in wholesome diets than we were ten years ago.
7. Driver training is now available in most high schools this seems to be a practical addition to the curriculum.
8. San Juan is the capital and the largest city of Puerto Rico.

9. A person's hair style is often considered an indication of his or her thinking on certain issues, especially on politics.
10. Where are you going, it's not time for the party to begin.
11. Soccer is becoming popular in the United States today it's an exciting sport.
12. The time is right, let's put it to the test.

Review Practice 6–2 Rewrite the following paragraph, correcting the run-on sentences.

> Slang is an important source of new words in our language, it appears in both speaking and writing. It is typical for slang to originate in very informal day-to-day conversation, then it works its way into our language or is discarded sometimes a slang or colloquial word will work its way up to the higher levels of the language it can gain status and become as socially acceptable in writing as the next word. Slang, however, is generally considered informal and is not usually used in written language, it indicates a statement of revolt against the restrictions of formal English language new words are usually developed by various groups of young people in each case the creation of slang seems to represent more than anything a desire for novelty.

7 Verb Forms

To work with verbs, you need to learn how their principal parts and their tenses are formed. This chapter explains how to form the principal parts of verbs and then how to develop the six tenses from those principal parts.

7A Principal Parts

Each verb in our language has three principal parts, from which all of that verb's tenses are formed. The first principal part is the **present stem,** which is the infinitive minus *to* (infinitive: *to talk;* present stem: *talk*); the second is the **past tense;** and the third is the **past participle.**

Present Stem	Past Tense	Past Participle
talk	talked	talked
write	wrote	written

Verbs whose past tense and past participle are formed by adding *-d* or *-ed* to the present stem are **regular** verbs; all others are **irregular.** The principal parts of some irregular verbs that cause students trouble are listed here.

Present Stem	Past Tense	Past Participle
be	was *or* were	been
begin	began	begun
bind	bound	bound
bite	bit	bitten
blow	blew	blown
break	broke	broken
bring	brought	brought (*not* brung)
build	built	built
burst	burst	burst
buy	bought	bought
catch	caught	caught
choose	chose	chosen
come	came	come
dive	dived *or* dove	dived
do	did	done
drag	dragged	dragged (*not* drug)
draw	drew	drawn
drink	drank	drunk
drive	drove	driven

Present Stem	Past Tense	Past Participle
eat	ate	eaten
fall	fell	fallen
fly	flew	flown
freeze	froze	frozen
get	got	got *or* gotten
give	gave	given
go	went	gone
grow	grew	grown
hang (execute)	hanged	hanged
hang (suspend)	hung	hung
know	knew	known
lay (place)	laid	laid
lead	led	led
lie (recline)*	lay	lain
lose (misplace)†	lost	lost
pay	paid	paid
prove	proved	proved *or* proven
put	put	put
raise	raised	raised
read	read	read
ride	rode	ridden
ring	rang *or* rung	rung
rise	rose	risen
run	ran	run
see	saw	seen
shake	shook	shaken
shrink	shrank *or* shrunk	shrunk *or* shrunken
sing	sang *or* sung	sung
sink	sank *or* sunk	sunk *or* sunken
sleep	slept	slept
speak	spoke	spoken
spread	spread	spread

*Different from *lie* meaning "to tell something untrue," which is a regular verb: *lie, lied, lied.*

†Often confused with *loose,* "to set free": "The crowd *loosed* the balloons." *Loose* is a regular verb.

Present Stem	Past Tense	Past Participle
spring	sprang *or* sprung	sprung
steal	stole	stolen
stink	stank *or* stunk	stunk
swear	swore	sworn
swim	swam	swum
swing	swung	swung
take	took	taken
teach	taught	taught
tear	tore	torn
thrive	thrived *or* throve	thrived *or* thriven
throw	threw	thrown
wake	woke	waked
wear	wore	worn
weave	wove	woven
write	wrote	written

Practice 7–1 Complete the following chart with the appropriate principal parts.

Present Stem	Past Tense	Past Participle
like		
buy		
	ate	
	handled	
form		
go		
		rented

Present Stem	Past Tense	Past Participle
		taught
	disappeared	
	spoke	

7B   The Six Tenses

Present, past, and **future** are the three main time divisions, and English has six **tenses** to express these times:

Present time: present tense
Past time: past tense, present perfect tense, and past perfect tense
Future time: future tense and future perfect tense

As you can see from the chart on page 70, all these tenses are formed from the principal parts we studied in 7A.

Here are some formulas that can help you form the different tenses of any verb, if you know its principal parts:

Present tense: present stem (add -s when subject is third person singular—*he, she,* or *it*)
Past tense: past tense
Future tense: *will* + present stem
Present perfect tense: *have* or *has* + past participle
Past perfect tense: *had* + past participle
Future perfect tense: *will* + *have* + past participle

A few tricks make these forms even easier to remember: (1) both tenses dealing with the future use *will;* (2) all perfect tenses use a form of the verb *to have* plus the past partici-

69

Verb Tense Formation

Principal parts (regular verb)
Infinitive: to hope

Present stem: hope

Past tense: hoped

Present tense

I hope	we hope
you hope	you hope
he hopes	they hope
she hopes	
it hopes	

Past tense

I hoped	we hoped
you hoped	you hoped
he hoped	they hoped
she hoped	
it hoped	

Future tense

I will hope	we will hope
you will hope	you will hope
he will hope	they will hope
she will hope	
it will hope	

Past Participle: hoped

Present perfect tense

I have hoped	we have hoped
you have hoped	you have hoped
he has hoped	they have hoped
she has hoped	
it has hoped	

Past perfect tense

I had hoped	we had hoped
you had hoped	you had hoped
he had hoped	they had hoped
she had hoped	
it had hoped	

Future perfect tense

I will have hoped	we will have hoped
you will have hoped	you will have hoped
he will have hoped	they will have hoped
she will have hoped	
it will have hoped	

ple; and (3) irregular verbs follow these same formulas but do not have identical forms for the past tense and the past participle, as regular verbs do.

Practice 7–2 Following these verb tense formulas, make a verb chart (like the one on page 70), for an irregular verb from the list on pages 66–68.

7B(1) Present Time

Present time is indicated by the present tense, which comes from the present stem. It expresses a current action or statement, a habitual action, a universal truth, a literary reference, a historical reference, and sometimes future time. The sentences here give examples of each of these uses of the present tense.

> Present: I *see* the difference.
> Present: My roommate *goes* to choir practice every Thursday.
> Present: Death *is* inevitable.
> Present: Hamlet *jumps* into the grave with Ophelia.
> Present: Then Patton *attacks* with everything he can.
> Present: The movers *come* tomorrow.

Emphasis can be achieved in the present tense by using a form of the verb *to do* with the present stem.

> Emphatic: They *do like* us after all.

Practice 7–3 List the present tense verbs in the reading selection at the beginning of this unit.

7B(2) Past Time

Three tenses in our language express past action or past states of being:

Past: The dog *chased* the fox.
Present perfect: The dog *has chased* the fox.
Past perfect: The dog *had chased* the fox.

Each of these tenses specifies a slightly different time in the past.

The past tense of a verb is one of its principal parts. It describes an action or state of being that took place at a definite time in the past.

Past: She *operated* on the patient this morning.

Emphasis can be achieved in the past tense by using *did* with the present stem of the verb:

Emphatic: I *did finish* one project before I started another.

Note that a form of *to do* adds emphasis only in the present and the past tenses.

Several verb phrases also indicate past time:

Past: My friend *was going to speak* for me.
Past: My friend *used to speak* for me.
Past: My friend *was to speak* for me.

You can tell that each of these verb phrases indicates an action that occurred in the past because the first word in each is a past tense verb itself. But notice how each communicates a slightly different shade of meaning from the simple past tense, *spoke*. The first indicates an action in the past that has not occurred yet (*was going to* [but hasn't yet]); the second, a regular action in the past that no longer occurs (*used to* [but no longer does]); and the third, a past commitment that has not come to pass yet (*was to* [but hasn't yet]).

The present perfect tense is written by combining *has* or *have* with the past participle of a verb. It describes an action or state of being begun in the past and completed (or *perfect*ed) prior to the present or continuing in the present:

> Present Perfect: They *have* already *bought* a new car.
> Present Perfect: I *have felt* sick for three weeks now.

The past perfect tense is written by combining *had* with the past participle. It describes a past action or state of being that was completed (or *perfect*ed) before a given time in the past.

> Past perfect: I *had seen* the movie in Chicago, so I didn't
> want to see it again.

Practice 7–4 List the verbs showing past time in the reading selection at the beginning of this unit.

7B(3) Future Time

The two tenses in our language that express future time are future and future perfect.

> Future: This afternoon we *will decide* whether or not
>   to go.
> Future perfect: By tomorrow we *will have decided* whether
>   or not to go.

Each of these tenses specifies a slightly different time in the future.

The future tense is written by combining *will* with the present stem of a verb. It describes an action or state of being that will take place.

> Future: They *will see* the results of the experiment.
> Future: I *will* always *be* there when you need me.

Several present-tense verb phrases also indicate future time.

73

Future: My brother *is about to leave* for the beach.
Future: My brother *is going to leave* for the beach.
Future: My brother *is to leave* for the beach tomorrow.

Just as the verb phrases indicating past time communicate slightly different shades of meaning from the past tense, so do these verb phrases differ slightly from the future tense, *will leave.* The first suggests that the action will occur very soon *(is about to);* the second is tentative *(is going to,* not *will);* the third suggests obligation or firm commitment *(is to).*

The future perfect tense is written by combining *will have* with the past participle of a verb. It describes an action or state of being that will be completed (or *perfect*ed) before a specific future time.

Future perfect: Mr. Warren *will have read* my term paper by next Friday.

Notice the difference between the future tense and the future perfect tense. Referring to the example here, you could say, "Mr. Warren *will read* [future tense] the term paper on Thursday." But "by Friday, Mr. Warren *will have read* the paper." By a specific time in the future, the action will have been completed (or perfected), so we use the future perfect tense.

Practice 7–5 Make four of the present-tense verbs in the reading selection at the beginning of this unit show future time by rewriting some of the sentences in the future or future perfect tense.

7C Use of Participle Forms

Two common faults in forming tenses concern the present and past participles of verbs. The present participle is written by adding *-ing* to the present stem of a verb *(want + ing)*; the past participle is the third principal part of a verb, ending with *-d* or *-ed* in regular verbs *(want + ed)*.

7C(1) Helping Words

Neither a present nor a past participle can stand alone (without a helping verb) in a sentence as a main verb; see 1A and 2C.

Wrong: Marge *buying* a new belt.
Right: Marge *is buying* a new belt.

Wrong: Fred *taken* his guitar to the beach.
Right: Fred *has taken* his guitar to the beach.

7C(2) Past Participles

In all three perfect tenses (present, past, and future), the past participle of a verb—not the past tense—follows the helping word.

Wrong: She *had wore* the same thing for three days.
Right: She *had worn* the same thing for three days.

Practice 7–6 List the incorrect verb forms in the following sentences.
1. She had already gave at the office.
2. May I be excuse, please?
3. There being a tremendous gap between what is fair and what exists in urban ghettos today.
4. The lake has froze over for the skaters.
5. The study of anatomy being a basic requirement for students who wanted to become pre-med majors.

Practice 7–7 Correct each mistake you identified in Practice 7–6 by rewriting each incorrect sentence.

7D Progressive Forms

In order to show an action or state of being that is continuing or is *in progress,* the English language has what are called *progress*ive verb forms for each tense. A comparison can help show the special use of the progressive form and its difference from other forms:

Past tense: Joe *smiled* when I saw him.
Past tense, progressive: Joe *was smiling* when I saw him.

The first sentence suggests that Joe smiled once at a specific time in the past. The second, in the progressive form, is also set in the past but differs from the first by implying that Joe's smile was already in progress when the writer of the sentence saw him. The progressive form, then, refers to action in progress, whereas most other forms refer to actions set at some specific time.

The progressive consists of a form of the verb *to be* and a present participle (-*ing* verb form). The form of the verb *to be* indicates when the action is taking place.

Present tense: I *am enjoying* the play very much.
Past tense: You *were enjoying* the play until the last scene.
Future tense: We *will be enjoying* the play together.
Present perfect tense: We *have been enjoying* the play very much, thank you.
Past perfect tense: You *had been enjoying* the play until the whispering started.
Future perfect tense: They *will have been* enjoying the play for an hour by the time I get there.

Practice 7–8 Rewrite four of the sentences in the reading selection at the beginning of this unit, changing the verbs to progressive forms.

Practice 7–9 Write one sentence using the progressive form of each of the following verbs.

1. *to stress,* present tense
2. *to carry,* past tense
3. *to open,* future tense
4. *to motivate,* present perfect tense
5. *to plant,* past perfect tense
6. *to love,* future perfect tense

Practice 7–10 Write a short paragraph narrating some sporting event, like a boxing match or a football game, as if you were there reporting the events as they occur. Use at least five progressive verb forms in your paragraph. Underline the progressive forms.

7E   Voice

The **voice** of a verb indicates whether the subject performs or receives the action of the verb. If the subject performs the action, the verb is in the **active voice.** If the subject receives the action rather than performs it, the verb is in the **passive voice.** A good way to remember this distinction is to remember the difference between an active person and a passive one. An active person initiates ideas, entertainment, activities, and so on, but a passive person sits around until someone else pressures him or her into action. Similarly, the subject of an active verb acts, but the subject of a passive verb is acted on.

Active: A student *started* an argument.
Passive: An argument *was started* by a student.

Notice that in a passive-voice sentence the performer of the action can be named in a *by* phrase; the verb consists of a form of the verb *to be* and a past participle.

Practice 7–11 Identify the voice (active or passive) of each of the verbs in the reading selection at the beginning of this unit. See Practice 1–3.

Practice 7–12 Write two sentences for each of the following verbs, the first using the active voice and the second using the passive.

1. to see
2. to want
3. to read
4. to spend
5. to write

Practice 7–13 Write a short paragraph about a very lazy person who simply wants to mind his or her own business but who has a series of strange events happen to him or her. Use at least five passive verbs in your paragraph. Underline the passive verbs.

7F Mood

A verb's **mood** is the manner in which a statement is made. Mood indicates a speaker's or writer's attitude or feeling toward the statement. The three moods in English are **indicative, imperative,** and **subjunctive.**

7F(1) The Indicative Mood

The indicative mood is used for factual statements and questions. It states (or inquires about) fact in all six tense forms discussed in 7B.

> Indicative mood: The porpoise *will perform* soon.
> Indicative mood: *Has* the porpoise *performed?*

7F(2) The Imperative Mood

The imperative mood is used for giving commands or making requests.

> Imperative mood: *Perform* the trick now.

The subject of this sentence is *you*, which is omitted in the imperative because it is naturally understood by both the writer or speaker and the reader.

7F(3) The Subjunctive Mood

The subjunctive mood expresses doubt, condition, wishes, and other states that are not based on fact. It describes actions that might take place and conditions that might be actual if some other detail were true. But since some specific detail is not true, actions do not take place and conditions are not actual when a writer uses the subjunctive mood.

> Subjunctive mood: If the porpoise *were performing* now, I *would be* happy.

In this example, the writer claims that he would be happy if the porpoise were performing. Because the writer chose the subjunctive mood, we know that the porpoise is not performing, so we can assume that the writer is not happy right now.

For all verbs except *be*, the subjunctive requires a special form for the third person singular of the present tense only; with *he, she,* or *it,* the *-s* or *-es* is dropped from the verb.

> Indicative: He *likes* me.
> Subjunctive: I ask only that he *like* me.

Four simple rules will help you form the subjunctive of the verb *to be:*

1. Where you would use *am, is,* or *are* in the indicative, use *be* in the subjunctive.

> Indicative: I *am* on time; he *is* on time; we *are* on time.

Subjunctive: They insist that I *be* on time; they insist that he *be* on time; they insist that we *be* on time.

2. Where you would use *was* in the indicative, use *were* in the subjunctive.

Indicative: I *was* on vacation.
Subjunctive: If I *were* on vacation [but I'm not], I would sleep for three straight days.

3. Where you would use *were* in the indicative, use *had been* in the subjunctive.

Indicative: They *were* at home.
Subjunctive: If they *had been* at home [but they weren't], we would have called.

4. Where you would use *have been* in the indicative, use *had been* in the subjunctive.

Indicative: I *have been* home for three days.
Subjunctive: If I *had been* home for three days [but I haven't], I would have called you.

The subjunctive mood most often appears in *if* clauses expressing impossible or unlikely conditions

If the ballet *had begun,* I *would be* content.
She *would like* the concert if she *were* to come.

and in *that* clauses stating commands or recommendations

I ask only that he *like* me.
I insist that he *be* on time.

The subjunctive mood of uncertainty or obligation is

usually expressed by the helping verbs *should, would, could,* and *might.*

> Subjunctive: He *should* be on time more often.
> Subjunctive: She *would* like the concert if she were to come.
> Subjunctive: She *could* have joined us, but she decided to stay home.
> Subjunctive: I *might* lend you the money.

Be careful not to use *of* for *have* in such constructions as *should have, would have, could have,* and *might have.* See 15A(2). This common error—like the substitution of *use to* for the proper form *used to*—probably occurs when our ears trick us. Read the following sentences aloud. One is grammatically correct and the other is not, but they sound similar:

> Wrong: I *would of* been on time if my car had not broken down.
> Right: I *would have* been on time if my car had not broken down.

Practice 7–14 Label the mood of each verb in the reading selection at the beginning of this unit. (See Practice 1–3.)
Practice 7–15 Rewrite the following sentences, adding the proper form and mood of the verb named in parentheses.

1. The captain suggests that every passenger _(to move; subjunctive)_ toward the stern of the boat.
2. _(to wash; imperative)_ your car tonight.
3. She _(to lead; indicative, future tense)_ the meeting.
4. If he had a job, he _(helping word + to be; subjunctive)_ able to pay his debts.
5. As you can see, he usually _(to cut; indicative, present tense)_ his own hair.

7G To Lie/To Lay, To Sit/To Set

These pairs of irregular verbs are especially troublesome because of similarities in spelling and meaning. Following are the principal parts of these verbs.

Present Stem	Past Tense	Past Participle
lie (to recline)	lay	lain
lay (to place or put)	laid	laid
sit (to be seated)	sat	sat
set (to place or put)	set	set

The main difference between these verbs is that *lay* and *set* take direct objects (they are transitive), but *lie* and *sit* do not (they are intransitive).

Intransitive: She *lay* there trying to fight off sleep.

Intransitive: He *sits* in the same seat for every class.

Intransitive: Abandoned soon after the Civil War, the house *has lain* vacant for more than a century.

Transitive: They *laid* their papers down and went to the front of the room.

Transitive: We *have set* the desk in its place.

Transitive: He *laid* the trousers over the back of the chair.

Practice 7–16 Select the proper verb form and tense to fit in the following blanks.

1. ___(sit, set)___ and worrying all day will accomplish nothing.

2. Please ___(sit, set)___ the folders on the table and then ___(sit, set)___ down until your name is called.

3. After I ___(lie, lay)___ out my bank statements, I realized where I made my mistake.

4. ___(lie, lay)___ the money on the table and close the door.

5. Silverman's dog has Silverman well trained: after one bark, he ___(lie, lay)___ down; after two, he rolls over; and after three, he ___(sit, set)___ up again. Finally, the dog gives him a chocolate bar.

Review

A. The key to using verbs is knowing their three principal parts:
   1. present stem (infinitive minus *to*)
   2. past tense
   3. past participle
B. There are six tenses in English:
   1. present
   2. past
   3. future
   4. present perfect (*have* or *has* + past participle)
   5. past perfect (*had* + past participle)
   6. future perfect (*will* + *have* + past participle)
C. Participles alone cannot be used as main verbs and are combined with helping words to form the perfect tenses.
D. The progressive tenses are made up of a form of the verb *to be* and a present participle (*-ing* form).
E. The voice of a verb indicates whether the subject acts or is acted on.
F. A verb's mood indicates the speaker's attitude toward a statement.
G. *Lay* and *set* take objects; *lie* and *sit* do not take objects.

Review Practice 7–1 List the principal parts of the following verbs.

1. cope
2. feel
3. develop
4. notice
5. show

Review Practice 7–2 Rewrite the following sentences, adding the proper forms of the verbs named in parentheses. Then, label the tense, voice, and mood of each verb.

1. A car is (steal) somewhere in the United States every thirty-seven seconds.

2. Thomas Edison said that success (be) 1 percent inspiration and 99 percent perspiration.

3. Ann Landers has often (give) sound advice to her large flock of readers.

4. (Polish) your shoes when you put them on today.

5. If my father were to (come) home, we (be) in big trouble.

Review Practice 7–3 Label the voice (active or passive) of the verbs in the following sentences.

1. The fire fighters rescued the children from the third story.

2. They read the first three chapters in one night.

3. The wood was burned in order to conserve natural resources.

4. The speech was delivered with enthusiasm.

5. You shouldn't have spent all of your money that quickly.

Review Practice 7–4 Rewrite the following sentences, changing the verbs to the tense indicated in parentheses. Make any other changes and additions that become necessary as you go along so that your sentences read smoothly and logically.

1. I used to feel sick before exams. (present)

2. The information I have received suggests he has won the competition. (future)

3. They do not want to see the movie. (past perfect)

4. My friend will arrive late tonight. (future perfect)

5. The magician travels constantly until he becomes physically exhausted. (past)

6. I was unable to see the game, but I heard the final basket was made just under the wire. (present perfect)

Review Practice 7–5 Rewrite the following paragraph, filling in the blanks with a verb in the tense indicated in the following sentences.

The product I __(present perfect)__ will solve all your problems with one application. It __(present)__ in an aerosol can, and I __(present perfect)__ it "Lla-eruc" ("Cure-all" spelled backwards). I __(future)__ that my product __(future)__ headaches, stomachaches, fits of anger, feelings of boredom and depression, and pangs of loneliness. All you need to do is __(present)__ it into the air in your room and it __(future)__. As of this summer, it __(future perfect)__ three years to perfect. Once I __(past)__ my product when I was overcome by all of these ailments and it __(past)__. I __(past perfect)__ it would. Basically, it just takes your mind off your problems. __(present)__ it; you __(future)__ it.

8 Modifiers

Modifiers limit, qualify, or add meaning to another word or group of words. The most common modifiers are adjectives and adverbs. To review the difference between adjective and adverb forms, see 1D and 1E.

8A Adjective Forms

As you know from 1D, adjectives modify nouns and pronouns.

Noun

Adjective: She prefers *realistic* novels.

Adjectives can also modify the subjects of linking verbs, which are either nouns or pronouns; see 1A(3) for more information on linking verbs.

Pronoun

Adjective: The party's over. It was *successful.*

Noun

Adjective: The *new* employee seemed *nervous.*

Noun

Adjective: The bread is *delicious.*

In these last three examples, the adjectives *successful, nervous,* and *delicious* describe the subjects of the sentences.

Practice 8–1 Name the nouns and the pronouns modified by the adjectives in the reading selection at the beginning of this unit. (See your answer to Practice 1–11 for a list of these adjectives.)

8B Adverb Forms

As you know from 1E, adverbs modify verbs.

Verb

Adverb: They did their work *well.*

In this sentence, the transitive verb *did* is modified by an adverb *(well).*

Verb

Adverb: She runs *quickly.*

In this next example, *runs* is an intransitive verb that is modified by an adverb *(quickly)*.

It helps to be able to distinguish linking verbs from transitive and intransitive verbs, since linking verbs may be followed by adjectives modifying their subjects

Adjective

Linking verb: The bread *is* delicious.

but transitive and intransitive verbs may not

Adverb

Transitive verb: The cooking class *baked* bread slowly.

Adverb

Intransitive verb: The bread *rose* perfectly.

Adverbs are also used to modify adjectives and other adverbs.

Adjective

Adverb: You were *completely* honest with your parents.

Adverb

Adverb: He responded *very* impolitely.

Double negative constructions, which are sentences containing two negatives, are generally wordy and unclear. Although some double negatives are acceptable

Right: She is *not un*happy now.

most double negatives are confusing.

Wrong: Some people do *not* pay *hardly* any attention to their pets.

Since *hardly* is a negative, it should not appear in a sentence with another negative word. One of the negatives should be omitted.

> Right: Some people pay *hardly* any attention to their pets.

Sometimes, writing double negatives has the same effect in language that multiplying two negative numbers has in math: you end up with a positive. If you say someone "wasn't never on time," you are really saying that person was sometimes on time. If, on the other hand, you are trying to stress how often this person was late, you can simply drop one of the negatives or change one of the negatives to a non-negative word.

> Right: He was *never* on time.
> Right: He was*n't* ever on time.

Notice that both of these revisions are not only more accurate but also less wordy than the original.

Practice 8–2 Name the words modified by the adverbs in the reading selection at the beginning of this unit. (See your answer to Practice 1–16 for a list of these adverbs.)

Review

A. Adjectives modify nouns, pronouns, and the subjects of linking verbs.
B. Adverbs modify verbs, adjectives, and other adverbs.
C. Most double negative constructions are not acceptable.

Review Practice 8–1 List any faulty adjective and adverb forms in the following sentences.
1. The school newspaper has been printed continuous since our school was founded.

2. I feel miserably about your father.
3. After a week in the shop, his cycle is working good.
4. She hasn't had hardly any decent breaks in her life.
5. Many students do not consider the value of some courses very careful.
6. You explained your problem so clear that I feel as if I'm going through it with you.
7. It tastes very well.
8. When a car hit him at an intersection, he began to yell uncontrollable.
9. She tested the brakes cautious.
10. The forensics instructor became very angry when someone spoke too rapid.

Review Practice 8–2 Rewrite the sentences in Review Practice 8–1, correcting any errors you found.

Review Practice 8–3 Compose sentences with the following constructions.

1. the adjective *hearty* following a linking verb and modifying its subject
2. the adjective *real* following a linking verb and modifying its subject
3. an adverb modifying the verb *collect*
4. an adverb modifying an intransitive verb
5. an adverb modifying a linking verb

9 Case Forms

Case refers to the function of nouns and pronouns. The names of the cases indicate how nouns and pronouns are used in a sentence. English has three cases: (1) **subjective,** (2) **objective,** and (3) **possessive.** Words in the subjective case serve as subjects of sentences and as predicate nouns (after linking verbs); words in the objective case serve as direct and indirect objects of verbs and as objects of prepositions; and words in the possessive case show ownership. Both nouns and pronouns change form to indicate their functions.

9A   Nouns

Nouns have three cases. In the subjective and objective cases, nouns are spelled exactly the same, but the possessive form of a noun changes. Most nouns add -'s to show possession: see 15A for more information on apostrophes.

> Subjective: *Penicillin* was discovered by Sir Alexander Fleming.
> Objective: We have put *penicillin* to active use on humans since 1941.
> Possessive: *Penicillin's* power is mainly antibiotic.

Although the form of the noun is the same in the subjective and objective cases, the subject comes before the verb and the object follows the verb.

Practice 9–1 Rewrite the following sentences, adding an appropriate noun in the case named in parentheses.
1. Pool is a game that _____ (subjective) likes.
2. If you can hit the _____ (objective), you will score.
3. It is _____ (possessive) turn to pay for the coffee.
4. There is no _____ (subjective) or _____ (subjective) for his behavior.
5. To many _____ (objective), dark rooms are scary.

9B   Pronouns

Some pronouns have distinctive forms in all three cases, but others change form only in the possessive case. The personal pronouns *I, he, she, we,* and *they* and the relative or interrogative pronoun *who* change form in all three cases. The personal pronouns *you* and *it* change form only in the possessive.

Personal Pronouns

Subjective

Singular: I, you, he, she, it
Plural: we, you, they

Objective

Singular: me, you, him, her, it
Plural: us, you, them

Possessive*

Singular: my, mine; your, yours; his; her, hers; its
Plural: our, ours; your, yours; their, theirs

Relative or Interrogative Pronouns

Subjective (singular and plural): who, whoever
Objective (singular and plural): whom, whomever
Possessive (singular and plural): whose

Subjective   Objective
↓   ↓

Of course, *I* will stay with *you* for a while.

Possessive
↓

When will it be *her* turn?

Many pronouns do not change form when they change case. *This, that, these, those,* and *which* have only one form.

Like nouns, some pronouns add -*'s* to show the possessive case—for example, *anyone's, everybody's, everyone's, no one's, nobody's, one's, somebody's,* and *someone's.* Note that every pronoun in this list is a singular indefinite pronoun.

Notice that none of the personal pronouns add -'s* to show possession. See 15A(1) for more detailed information on the use of the apostrophe to show possession.

Possessive: It was *someone's* task to see that *no one's* feelings were hurt.

For a detailed discussion of pronouns, see 1C.

Practice 9–2 Rewrite the following sentences, adding an appropriate pronoun in the case named in parentheses.

1. Between $\underline{\text{(objective)}}$ and $\underline{\text{(objective)}}$, $\underline{\text{(subjective)}}$ think Jan got a very high grade.

2. $\underline{\text{(Subjective)}}$ doesn't know much about flying a plane.

3. $\underline{\text{(Possessive)}}$ shock absorbers are faulty.

4. Math is $\underline{\text{(subjective)}}$ of $\underline{\text{(possessive)}}$ best subjects.

5. $\underline{\text{(Objective)}}$ are you going to ask to the dance?

Practice 9–3 Label the case of each pronoun in the reading selection at the beginning of this unit. (See your answer to Practice 1–10 for a list of these pronouns and see pages 10–11 for reference.)

9B(1) Personal Pronouns: Special Rules

In some instances, special rules govern the case of personal pronouns in sentences.

First, pronouns that form a compound subject are written in the subjective case, and pronouns that form a compound object are written in the objective case.

Subject

Right: *She* and the coach can get the job done in half the time.

Object

Right: I bought a plastic swimming pool for Paul and *him.*

To test a pronoun case, use the pronoun in its sentence by itself, without the compound construction.

Test: *She* can get the job done in half the time.
Wrong: *Her* can get the job done in half the time.

Test: I bought a plastic swimming pool for *him*.
Wrong: I bought a plastic swimming pool for *he*.

Second, when a pronoun is used with a noun (or appositive), it should be in the same case as the noun.

                                             Object
Right: The tiger's milk is for ‾us, Marsha and *me*‾.
              Subject
Right: ‾*We* students‾ find the proposal unacceptable.

Again, to test a pronoun case, try the pronoun in its sentence by itself, without the noun or appositive.

Test: The tiger's milk is for *me*.
Wrong: The tiger's milk is for *I*.

Test: *We* found the proposal unacceptable.
Wrong: *Us* find the proposal unacceptable.

Third, after the words *than* and *as*, you can determine what word is called for by completing the thought after *than* or *as*.

                    Subject
                      ↓
Right: She is stronger than *I* [am].
                                        Object
                                          ↓
Right: I related to her better than to *him*.

Fourth, the subjective case is used after any form of the verb *to be*.

                Subject
                   ↓
Right: It is *he*.

93

In spoken English, *it is him* is often used. But in writing, the subjective case should follow any form of *to be*.

Fifth, a possessive pronoun is used before a participle that functions as a noun (known as a gerund; see 2D).

> Possessive
> ↓
> Right: *His* enlisting caused his friends much heartache.
> [Not *he* but *his enlisting* caused his friends much heartache.]

Practice 9–4 Rewrite the following sentences, completing them with personal pronouns.

1. _____ and _____ are grateful to be given another chance in school.
2. His mother was proud of _____ receiving the English award.
3. I thought it was _____ .
4. It is clear that Mark is stronger than _____ .
5. Most of our friends applied, but scholarships were awarded only to _____ three.

9B(2) Relative and Interrogative Pronouns: Special Rules

The relative and interrogative pronouns *who* and *whoever* change form to indicate case. To determine what case of these pronouns belongs in a particular sentence, you must look at the pronoun's function in its own clause: see 1C and 3C for more information on these pronouns.

As you know from 3C, relative pronouns have a dual function in a sentence: (1) they relate back to another word in the sentence, and (2) they serve as nouns and adjectives in their own clauses. That these words serve as nouns and adjectives in their own clauses means that they can be subjects (*who, whoever*), objects (*whom, whomever*), or possessive adjectives (*whose* + a noun) in their own clauses. The first function of these pronouns—relating—requires that they appear early in their clauses (even objects are usually seen before their verbs), as in the following examples:

When these pronouns are subjects in their own clauses, the subjective forms (*who* and *whoever*) are used.

> Subjective: Jan knows the man *who is coming to dinner.*
>
> Subjective: *Whoever gets there first* should open the windows.
>
> Subjective: *Who is on duty now?*

When these pronouns are the objects of their own clauses, the objective forms (*whom* and *whomever*) are used.

> Objective: Father will give the car *to whomever you suggest.*
>
> Objective: Jan knows the woman *whom you have hired.*
>
> Objective: *Whom did you see* running from the scene of the accident?

A short phrase or clause within a clause does not affect the case of the pronoun. Remember to match the subject with the verb in its own clause.

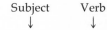

>   Subject   Verb
>
>   ↓   ↓
>
> Subjective: I went to visit my mother, *who* I think *feels* better.

In this sentence, *who* is the subject of *feels*.

> Objective: Jack has spent many years with his guidance
>
>   Object   Subject Verb
>
>   ↓   ↓   ↓
>
> counselor, *whom*, in my opinion, *he doesn't need.*

In this sentence, *he* is the subject of *doesn't need*, and *whom* is the direct object of *doesn't need*.

95

Whose is used in its own clause to show possession.

Possessive
↓

Possessive: I know the person *whose* house caught on
fire last night.

Notice that *whose* is different from *who's*. *Who's* is a contraction that stands for *who is* and follows the usage rules for
who; see 9B(2).

Subjective: *Who's* on duty now?

Practice 9–5 In the following sentences, label the *who*
clauses. Then, rewrite each sentence, completing each
clause with the correct form of *who*.
1. I believe that the man _____ committed suicide
   is the one _____ we needed to talk to about the
   murder.
2. _____ gave you the books was generous.
3. Jackie enjoys her literature instructor, _____
   class she has right after lunch.
4. I am sure that the personnel manager, _____ I
   believe you talked with, will hire _____ we
   recommend.
5. _____ do you think will win the election?

Review

A. The usage and position of nouns and pronouns in a
   sentence determine their cases.
B. There are three cases in the English language:
   1. subjective
   2. objective
   3. possessive
C. Nouns have only two forms, one to show subjective
   and objective functions and one to show possession.

D. Some pronouns have different forms for each of their cases.

E. Special rules govern the case of personal pronouns:

  1. Pronouns that form a compound subject are written in the subjective case, and pronouns that form a compound object are written in the objective case.

  2. When a pronoun is used with a noun (or appositive), it should be in the same case as the noun.

  3. After the words *than* and *as,* you can determine what word is called for by completing the thought after *than* or *as.*

  4. The subjective case is used after any form of the verb *to be.*

  5. The possessive pronoun is used before a participle that functions as a noun.

F. Some rules also govern the case of relative and interrogative pronouns:

  1. When these pronouns are subjects in their own clauses, subjective forms are used.

  2. When these pronouns are objects in their own clauses, objective forms are used.

  3. A short phrase or clause within a clause does not affect the form of a pronoun.

  4. *Whose* is used in its own clause to show possession.

Review Practice 9–1 List the incorrect pronoun forms in the following sentences.

1. The novelist who we took to lunch today laughed at our jokes.
2. It was her who was president of the Black Student Union.
3. She insists on them trying to snow ski.
4. Both Bruce and me should be happy with your final decision.
5. Why aren't you as miserable as me?
6. Along with he and I came five young children.
7. Tennis brings together people whom it seems have at least one interest in common.

8. It is us who want to learn to play bridge.
9. You are much more organized than me.
10. Linda and me, the two interested parties, fought over him yesterday.

Review Practice 9–2 Rewrite the sentences in Review Practice 9–1, correcting the incorrect forms you identified.

10 Subject-Verb Agreement

The verb of a sentence **agrees in number** with its subject. When you refer to only one item, the singular form for both the subject and the verb is correct. When you refer to two or more items, the plural form of both subject and verb is correct. Making subjects and verbs agree in number is especially difficult when the subject is not clearly singular or plural. See 1B for further information about number (singular and plural).

10A Phrases Separating Subject and Verb

Since singular verbs are used with singular subjects and plural verbs with plural subjects, you must first determine whether the subject is singular or plural. To do so, you should consider only the simple subject of a clause. The verb of a clause agrees in number with its simple subject, regardless of what words or phrases separate the simple subject from its verb.

Right: *Preferences* in lifestyle *differ* from person to person.

Since the subject of a sentence is never found within a prepositional phrase, one way to find the subject and verb of a sentence is to cross out all prepositional phrases and then choose the subject and verb from what is left. The first example would look like this:

Right: Preferences ~~in lifestyle~~ differ ~~from person to person~~.

The subject *(preferences)* and the verb *(differ)* of the sentence are left.

Notice how easy it is to locate the subject and the verb in the following examples when you cross out the prepositional phrases first.

Right: My *cousin,* ~~with his wife and sons,~~ has left ~~for London~~.

Practice 10–1 Choose the correct forms of the verbs in these sentences. Cross out the prepositional phrases first.

1. Different flowers in my garden _(was, were)_ growing.
2. Windows in a house _(serve, serves)_ many purposes.
3. I at least _(want, wants)_ a chance.
4. She, with all of her energy, _(has, have)_ swayed the judge.
5. Sam, with energy and enthusiasm, _(is, are)_ here to help.

10B   More Than One Subject

When two or more subjects are joined by certain conjunctions, they are considered **compound subjects.** See 1G for more information on conjunctions.

10B(1) Two or More Subjects

Two or more subjects joined by *and* take a plural verb.

Subject

Right: $\overline{\text{Sleep, food, and exercise}}$ *are* necessary to college life.

Subject

Right: A few friends and a variety of other interests *have kept* our minds healthy.

Certain words other than *and* suggest addition: *with, along with, including, as well as, like, together with.* But the phrases these words make are not part of the subject and, therefore, do not affect the number of the verb.

Right: Tom, together with Joe, *runs* daily.

Practice 10–2 Choose the correct forms of the verbs in these sentences. Cross out the prepositional phrases first.

1. Both laundry and homework (are going to be, is going to be) part of your responsibilities now.

2. A good mind and a healthy body (is, are) worth striving for.

3. He told his class that participation and mental discipline (was, were) both required.

4. Why (is, are) skiing and fishing so interesting to you?

5. Ethel, along with our luggage, (has, have) been traveling all day.

10B(2) Compound Subjects

The verb of a compound subject that is joined by *either/or, neither/nor, not only/but also,* and *whether/or* agrees in number with the part of the compound closest to it.

Subject

Right: Either the dog or the cats *are* bound to be gone tomorrow morning.

Subject

Right: Neither time nor energy *allows* me to go out with you tonight.

Subject

Right: Not only my term paper but also* my book reports *were* due last Monday.

Subject

Right: Whether fresh beans or a vegetable casserole *is* *served* with the roast is not important.

Practice 10–3 Choose the correct forms of the verbs in these sentences. Cross out the prepositional phrases first.

1. Either Joanne or Mabel _(has written, have written)_ good themes.

2. Neither you nor the party _(seems, seem)_ important enough to make me fail this exam tomorrow.

3. You should know that not only several magazines but also this book _(is, are)_ a good source of information.

4. Not only the apple pie but the oranges _(is, are)_ moldy.

5. The story, but not the pictures, _(remind, reminds)_ me of a past experience.

10C Indefinite Pronouns

Subject-verb agreement can be troublesome when certain indefinite pronouns are involved. For a list of indefinite pronouns, see 1C.

10C(1) Singular Pronouns

Singular verbs are used with the following words when they function as pronouns:† *another, anybody, anyone,*

Also is often implied in this construction rather than expressed: "Not only the guests *but* the food is stale."

†*Another, each,* and *one* are also adjectives; *anything, nobody, nothing, one,* and *somebody* are also nouns; and *either* and *neither* can serve as conjunctions ("*either* Sam or I"), adjectives ("I can't find *either* shoe"), or pronouns ("*Either* suits me"). *Either* can also be an adverb ("He is not happy, and I am not *either*").

anything, each, either, everybody, everyone, everything, neither, no one, nobody, nothing, one, somebody, someone, and *something.*

Singular verbs are used with these indefinite pronouns because these pronouns have singular meanings.

Right: *Each* of the men *uses* after-shave lotion.

Right: *No one* among all the students *knows* what I'm going through.

Right: *Neither* of them *wants* to assume responsibility for that.

10C(2) Singular or Plural Pronouns

Either singular or plural verbs are used with the following words: *all, any, more, most, none,* and *some.* A plural verb is appropriate when the meaning of the pronoun is plural; otherwise, a singular verb is correct.

Plural: *None were* as hard to please as your children.
Singular: *None* of us *owns* a green pen.

Plural: *Most were* willing to leave at 2 p.m.
Singular: *Most* of it *is* to take place tomorrow.

Practice 10–4 Choose the correct forms of the verbs in these sentences. Cross out the prepositional phrases first.

1. Neither of the spark plugs (has been, have been) useful.

2. Each of the six draftees (is taking, are taking) the army physical.

3. One authority says this is correct. Another (say, says) it is not.

4. More of them (use, uses) our brand than any other brand.

5. Everyone, even smokers, __(is, are)__ sensitive to the discomfort that smoke can cause others.

10D Relative Pronouns

Relative pronouns introduce their own clauses in sentences; see 3C and 9B(2). They include *that, what, whatever, which, whichever, who, whom, whose, whoever,* and *whomever.* See also 1C. A relative pronoun that is the subject of its own clause takes a verb that agrees in number with the word that the pronoun refers to.

> Right: Any person *who applies* for this job must have experience with children.
>
> Right: The vegetables *that were* gathered today will feed us for a week.

Practice 10–5 Choose the correct forms of the verbs in these sentences. Cross out the prepositional phrases first.
1. Are you the one who __(grade, grades)__ our papers?
2. My ability to observe and recall, which __(are, is)__ very well developed, will help me in my writing.
3. I want to buy the land that __(are covered, is covered)__ with vegetation.
4. Each of the contestants who __(have, has)__ entered the pie-throwing contest has a chance to win.
5. When the owners of the house take a trip, the dog that __(live, lives)__ there protects the place.

10E Linking Verbs

A linking verb is a state-of-being verb: see 1A(3). A subject usually precedes a linking verb, and a predicate noun or

103

adjective follows. A linking verb agrees with its subject—not with its predicate noun.

> Right: His constant *worry is* grades.
> Right: *Grades are* his constant worry.

Practice 10–6 Choose the correct forms of the verbs in these sentences. Cross out the prepositional phrases first.

1. Hummingbirds ___(has been, have been)___ the joy of his life.
2. Her job ___(involves, involve)___ constant contacts with people.
3. Horses ___(is, are)___ a part of their everyday life.
4. His major responsibility ___(has been, have been)___ the mechanics of the operation.
5. I ___(am, is)___ a robot when it comes to getting my work done.

10F Inverted Word Order

In English sentences, the subject usually, but not always, comes before the verb. When the subject follows its verb, the word order is said to be **inverted:** see 4D. But a verb still agrees with its subject, even when that subject follows the verb.

> Right: In my room *were pictures* of my favorite singing stars.
> Right: Beneath the trees *lies* a mossy *patch* of ground.

Achieving subject-verb agreement with *there is* and *there are* is sometimes difficult, because the word *there* is not a subject. In a construction that includes *there is* or *there are,* the verb agrees in number with the subject, which follows the verb.

Right: There *are* many *idiots* driving the highways on holidays.

Right: There *is* one major *problem* with your personality.

The expletive *it,* however, is always followed by a singular verb.

Right: *It is* miles to the next town.

Right: *It was* a mile to school.

Practice 10–7 Choose the correct forms of the verbs in these sentences. Cross out the prepositional phrases first.

1. Next to the fireplace <u>(is, are)</u> piles of wood.

2. There <u>(seem, seems)</u> to be trouble next door.

3. When did you realize it <u>(is, are)</u> grades that make the difference?

4. In the quadrangle at noon <u>(was, were)</u> a live band and three jugglers.

5. There <u>(is, are)</u> the actors and actresses I was telling you about.

10G Other Agreement Rules

Some additional rules about agreement can help you solve other subject-verb problems.

10G(1) Collective Nouns

Collective nouns are words that are singular in form but often plural in meaning. They are *collect*ive, because they refer to a *collect*ion of people: *orchestra, team, public, family, committee, band, class, navy, senate, majority, minority.*

Collective nouns that refer to a group as a whole take singular verbs.

105

Right: Our *team was* winning.

Collective nouns that refer to the separate members of a group take plural verbs.

Right: The *team were* wearing their letter sweaters.

Practice 10–8 Choose the correct forms of the verbs in the following sentences. Cross out the prepositional phrases first.

1. Humanity still ___(have, has)___ many difficult problems to solve.
2. A series of letters ___(is being sent, are being sent)___ to people who might want to buy the magazines.
3. Our committee ___(want, wants)___ people to believe in democracy.
4. A group of tourists ___(is, are)___ arriving at noon.
5. The team ___(were, was)___ on top this year.

10G(2) Plural Nouns with Singular Meanings

Words that are plural in form but singular in meaning (such as *news, measles, molasses, mumps*) take singular verbs.

Right: Campus *news travels* fast.
Right: *Molasses is* produced during the refining of sugar.

Words ending in *-ics* (such as *athletics, politics, ethics, statistics, mathematics, dynamics, physics, ceramics*) are singular when referring to a field of study

Right: *Statistics is* a difficult branch of mathematics.

and plural when they refer to the practical application of that field

Right: The *statistics were* so complex that I had to ask
a finance expert to explain them.

Practice 10–9 Choose the correct forms of the verbs in the following sentences. Cross out the prepositional phrases first.

1. News from home __(is, are)__ always welcome.
2. Mathematics __(causes, cause)__ some students trouble.
3. Measles usually __(occurs, occur)__ in children.
4. Physics __(concern, concerns)__ each of us.
5. In what way __(is, are)__ his politics affecting his life-style?

10G(3) Titles

The title of a book, article, play, movie, and so on takes a singular verb.

Right: *The Seasons is* a long poem written by James
Thomson.

Practice 10–10 Choose the correct forms of the verbs in the following sentences. Cross out the prepositional phrases first.

1. *The Three Musketeers* __(is, are)__ a novel by Alexandre Dumas.
2. *The Decline and Fall of the Roman Empire* __(challenge, challenges)__ our reading ability.
3. I recently read *A Farewell to Arms*, which __(capture, captures)__ some of Ernest Hemingway's war experiences.
4. *Love and Death* __(is, are)__ a movie by Woody Allen.
5. *Moll Flanders* __(depict, depicts)__ various episodes in the life of an eighteenth-century woman.

107

10G(4) Numbers, Letters, Words

Numbers, letters, and words that are referred to as such take singular verbs.

> Right: *Fifty-two is* my post office box number.
> Right: *Muscles is* a plural noun.

Practice 10–11 Choose the correct forms of the verbs in the following sentences. Cross out the prepositional phrases first.

1. There ____(are, is)____ at least one *i* in the word *Mississippi*.
2. *Consciences* ____(is, are)____ a commonly misspelled word.
3. *And* ____(are, is)____ a coordinating conjunction.
4. *S* ____(are, is)____ difficult for my little sister to pronounce.
5. Four ____(are, is)____ an even number.

Review

A. The subject and verb of a sentence agree in number.
B. The verb of a clause agrees in number with its simple subject, regardless of the words or phrases separating the simple subject from its verb.
C. Two or more subjects joined by *and* take a plural verb.
D. The verb of a compound subject that is joined by *either/or*, *neither/nor*, *not only/but also*, and *whether/or* agrees in number with the part of the compound closest to it.
E. Singular verbs are used with the following words when they function as pronouns: *another, anybody, anyone, anything, each, either, everybody, everyone, everything, neither, no one, nobody, nothing, one, somebody, someone,* and *something*.
F. Depending on the context, either singular or plural verbs are used with the following words: *all, any, more, most, none,* and *some*.

G. A relative pronoun that is the subject of its own clause takes a verb that agrees in number with the word that the pronoun refers to.

H. A linking verb agrees with its subject—not with its predicate noun.

I. A subject that follows its verb still determines whether the verb should be singular or plural.

J. Collective nouns, which name a collection of people, are singular when they refer to a group as a whole and plural when they refer to the separate members of a group.

K. Words that are plural in form but singular in meaning take singular verbs.

L. The title of a book, article, play, movie, and so on takes a singular verb.

M. Numbers, letters, and words that are referred to as such take singular verbs.

Review Practice 10–1 List and label as "singular" or "plural" the subjects and verbs of each clause in the following sentences. Cross out the prepositional phrases first.

1. My uncle and aunt live in Maine and raise horses.
2. Her mind at that point was clear because she had made her decision.
3. A series of books on that very issue is about to be published.
4. When everyone knows the answer, I pretend to know it too.
5. It is cockroaches that have the upper hand in their apartment.
6. My books are a source of comfort to me.
7. Not only the raisins but also the bran is good for you.
8. There are many methods that work for students trying to get high grades in college.
9. An *A* was embroidered on the heroine's gown in *The Scarlet Letter*, a novel by Nathaniel Hawthorne.
10. Athletics is basic to our health.

Review Practice 10–2 Label as "singular" or "plural" each of the subjects and verbs you have identified in the reading selection at the beginning of this unit.

Review Practice 10–3 Choose the correct forms of the verbs in the following sentences. Cross out the prepositional phrases first:

1. Trucks (are, is) a means of transport in our country.

2. I am told that neither skis nor boats (is, are) available at this resort.

3. A grade of 95 (is, are) hard to come by, even when you know the politics that (govern, governs) the grading system of a school.

4. It (was, were) our manners that (was, were) in question the other night.

5. We are happy to report that one of our members (is, are) going to have a baby.

6. Each of his friends (was, were) coming to his surprise party.

7. There (is, are) one hundred good reasons that you should stay here.

8. My cousin, but not my aunt and uncle, (use, uses) baking soda for toothpaste.

9. Either Richie Valens or José Féliciano (was, were) the first Chicano to have a hit record.

10. The children and I (am, are) the ones to blame for all the noise.

11. Neither television nor the movies (was, were) able to cheer them up.

12. Although the lectures as well as the entire textbook (is, are) hard to understand, my family always (help, helps) me through my assignments.

13. *The Sunshine Boys* <u>(were, was)</u> a classic in its own right.

14. *Acrobatics* <u>(is, are)</u> a word we might associate with the Olympics.

15. When there <u>(is, are)</u> funds available, I'll be able to hire the actors.

Review Practice 10–4 Write sentences that begin with the following thoughts, adding predicates that include verbs in the present tense.

1. The police
2. Athletics
3. Humanity
4. *Jaws*
5. There are times when
6. Anybody who cares
7. His interest in cars
8. Neither eating nor sleeping
9. Everyone
10. Math and science

---

11   Pronoun-Antecedent Agreement

Most pronouns in a sentence refer to a noun in that sentence or in a previous one. That noun is the pronoun's **antecedent.** The word *antecedent* comes from *ante-*, meaning "before" (one *antes* before each hand of poker), and *-cede,* meaning "go" (as in *precede* or *recede*); therefore, *antecedent* is our term for the noun that *goes before* a pronoun. A singular pronoun refers to a singular antecedent and a plural pronoun to a plural antecedent.

> Right: Most of my friends would be happy to share
> *their* notes with me.

The antecedent of *their* in this sentence is the word *most;* both the antecedent and the pronoun are plural.

111

Right: One of my sisters decided *she* wanted to spend *her* life in Oregon.

In this sentence, the antecedent of *she* and of *her* is *one*; both the antecedent and the pronouns are singular.

Besides these straightforward examples, however, your writing will include references to both males and females or to unknown persons. In these cases, the most generally accepted current practice is to use the appropriate forms of both *he* and *she* in the following way:

Right: A person can make good grades if *he or she* puts *his or her* mind to it.

Right: When someone asks you, do you give *him or her* any information?

If this reference becomes awkward, sentences can usually be rewritten with plural nouns and pronouns to avoid the *he or she* construction.

Right: People can make good grades if *they* put *their* minds to it.

Right: When people ask you, do you give *them* any information?

11A More Than One Antecedent

When two or more subjects are joined by certain conjunctions, they are considered compound subjects; see 1G for more information on conjunctions.

11A(1) Two or More Antecedents

A plural pronoun is used to refer to two or more words joined by *and*.

Right: Marsha and Shirley think *their* bicycles are fast.

11A(2) Compound Antecedents

A pronoun agrees with the closest noun of a compound antecedent joined by the conjunctions *either/or, neither/nor, not only/but also,* and *whether/or.*

Right: Either the dancer or the dance has to change *its* timing.

Right: Neither the coach nor the referees are in *their* positions for the game to begin.

Right: Not only the state but the farmers feel *their* responsibility to promote sound agricultural practices.

Right: Whether the chef or the owners will prepare *their* specialty is not certain.

Practice 11–1 Choose the correct pronouns to complete the following sentences.

1. Not only women but also other minorities are fighting for (her, their) rights.

2. Don and Al had (his, their) pool repaired.

3. Neither your understanding nor your attitudes will develop to (its, their) fullest if you don't apply yourself to your work.

4. Once the referee or the judge makes the final decision, (he or she, they) cannot change (his or her, their) position.

5. Either Maria or Kathy must take responsibility for (her, their) poor work.

11B Collective Noun Antecedents

Collective nouns are nouns that refer to a group—either as a unit or as a group of individuals.

113

11B(1) Singular Collective Nouns

A singular pronoun refers to a collective noun that is considered a unified whole.

Right: The committee was asked to present *its* report.

11B(2) Plural Collective Nouns

A plural pronoun refers to a collective noun when the individual members of a group are being considered separately—that is, when the activity described by the sentence is one that the group as a whole could not logically perform.

Right: The chair asked the committee to take *their* seats

Practice 11–2 Choose the correct pronouns to complete the following sentences.

1. I shot my arrows at the target, and (it, they) hit (its, their) mark.
2. The Women's Liberation Movement seeks freedom and personal growth for (its, their) followers.
3. The band put away (its, their) instruments after the half-time show.
4. The mountain full of gold deposits was (itself, themselves) valued at several million dollars.
5. The newspaper, although very biased, was asked to present (its, their) side of the bribery charges.

11C Indefinite Pronoun Antecedents

Singular pronouns refer to the following indefinite pronouns: *another, anybody, anyone, anything, each, either, everybody, everyone, everything, neither, no one, nobody, nothing, one, somebody, someone,* and *something.*

Right: One must have *his or her* pride in order to be successful.

Right: Each sneaked into *its* burrow.

Practice 11–3 Choose the correct pronouns to complete the following sentences.

1. You can have anything you want to eat here because <u>(it is, they are)</u> free.

2. Anyone working in the town hall knows <u>(his or her, their)</u> responsibilities.

3. In the folk dancing class, every one of the males got to <u>(his, her, their)</u> place on the right beat.

4. If someone in the crowd is a performer, <u>(he or she, they)</u> should come to the stage immediately.

5. Everybody is careless once in a while, but usually not when <u>(his or her, their)</u> life is at stake.

Review

A. A pronoun agrees with its antecedent in number.

B. A plural pronoun refers to two or more words joined by *and.*

C. A pronoun agrees with the closest part of a compound antecedent joined by *either/or, neither/nor, not only/but also,* and *whether/or.*

D. A singular pronoun refers to a collective noun that is considered a unit.

E. A plural pronoun refers to a collective noun when individual members are being considered separately.

F. Singular pronouns are used to refer to the following indefinite pronouns: *another, anybody, anyone, anything,*

115

each, either, everybody, everyone, everything, neither, no one, nobody, nothing, one, somebody, someone, and *something.*

Review Practice 11–1 Write out the antecedents of the pronouns you listed in Practice 1–12 at the beginning of this unit.

Review Practice 11–2 In the following sentences, list any pronouns that do not agree with their antecedents.

1. Each of our well-known proverbs has their own truth.
2. A football player gets a lot of attention if they make a touchdown during a game.
3. Even though a situation is complicated, a person may feel they have control of the daily transactions.
4. The professor requested that the class turn in its themes.
5. Everyone in their right mind can see that they should prepare for the future.
6. All of the stolen goods should be returned to its rightful owners.
7. A wild animal or plant will function best in their natural surroundings.
8. Where were the jack and lug wrench when I really needed it?
9. A family makes demands on each one of their members.
10. Every student who thinks for themselves will succeed in freshman composition.

Review Practice 11–3 Rewrite each sentence in Review Practice 11–2, correcting all of the pronoun errors that you found.

Reading Tasks

Comprehension

To check your comprehension, answer the following questions about the reading selection on language at the beginning of this unit. Refer to the selection when necessary.

1. Put the writer's definition of language (paragraph 1) in your own words.
2. What does the Latin word *lingua* mean?
3. What percentage of communication takes place through spoken language?
4. People discovered that speech had two advantages over other forms of communication. What were they?
5. According to paragraph 3 of this passage, how does language promote cooperation?

   For additional comprehension exercises, turn to the Unit I Appendix Selection.

Main Ideas

Main ideas are usually the most general statements in a reading selection. Every paragraph should include only one main idea, which is typically explained in one sentence, called the **topic sentence.** The rest of the sentences in a paragraph develop or illustrate the idea expressed in that topic sentence. A topic sentence is often the first or last **117**

sentence in a paragraph because these locations are most likely to capture the reader's attention.

In the passage on language, the topic sentence of the first paragraph is the first sentence, the most common place for a topic sentence. Read the sentence aloud; then read the first paragraph again. You will notice that the topic sentence is the most general statement in the paragraph.

In other cases, the topic sentence can be the last sentence of a paragraph, as in the second paragraph of the Unit I Appendix Selection. In a few instances, a topic sentence is implied; that is, no sentence stands out as the most general. Such a paragraph includes supporting material only.

6. Write out all the topic sentences in the reading selection at the beginning of this unit.
7. Write out all the topic sentences in the appendix selection.

Summary

A **summary** is a brief synopsis of the main ideas of a reading selection. A summary has the following features:

a. A summary explains in your own words the material that you read.
b. A summary usually identifies the writer and the passage being summarized in the first few sentences (except for a summary at the end of a textbook chapter).
c. A summary is about one-eighth as long as the original essay. (For a long essay, a summary should be even shorter.)
d. A summary of an essay is often one paragraph long.

e. A summary deals with main ideas only.

f. A summary usually does not include any detailed material or examples.

g. A summary uses the fewest words possible.

In writing a summary, you should first separate the main ideas from the details and then explain the main ideas in your own words. The success of a summary depends on your ability to recognize the relationships between these main ideas.

8. Referring to main ideas only, summarize the reading selection at the beginning of this unit.

9. Referring to main ideas only, summarize the appendix selection.

Discussion/Writing Assignments

The following questions are based on the reading selection at the beginning of this unit and on the Unit I Appendix Selection. Follow your instructor's directions for discussing and/or writing on the topics here. All discussion and written work should be in complete sentences.

10. According to the selection at the beginning of this unit, what makes language such an important part of human activity?

11. According to the same source, in what ways does speech make human beings different from all other animals? What does the ability to speak a language say about our thinking processes?

12. How have changes in our society affected our language? See the appendix selection. Give as many examples as possible.

Unit I Appendix Selection

(1)   Language, like the human beings who speak it, changes constantly. The rate of change depends on both human and historical causes. In a settled society, language change slows down. Several conditions help keep a language constant. These include a stable government, good communications, a centralized educational system, a set of beliefs and traditions, and a spirit of national unity. A breakdown in communications may create dialects in different areas. . . .

(2)   There are special vocabularies peculiar to religion, science, art, literature, and to military, political, and social life. These vocabularies add to the number of words in a language. It is possible, but not clearly proved, that geography and climate affect language.

(3)   A language remains alive and continues to develop as long as people speak it. A language that has lost all its speakers is called a *dead language.* Dead languages include Sumerian, ancient Egyptian, Akkadian, Hittite, Lydian, and Bithynian. Latin is not a dead language, mainly because the Roman Catholic Church still uses it.

Adapted from *The World Book Encyclopedia.* © 1980 (Chicago: World Book-Childcraft International, 1980). Vol. XII, p. 63. Reprinted by permission of the publisher.

To check your comprehension, answer the following questions:

1. What causes changes in language?
2. Describe the conditions that keep a language stable.
3. What kinds of special vocabularies exist in a society?
4. What is a "dead language"?
5. Name as many dead languages as you can.

Unit II

Punctuation and Mechanics

Proper use of punctuation and mechanics—that which conforms to widely accepted conventions—helps communicate your message to your reader. **Punctuation marks** are a form of nonverbal communication, indicating the end of a thought, a question, a strong emotion, the relation between thoughts, ownership, direct address, and so on. Punctuation marks are used in written language to replace the voice changes (stress, pause, pitch) of spoken language. The rules that govern punctuation were formed for the sake of both readers and writers. Notice how much clearer punctuation makes communication in the following example:

Without punctuation: I dont like the idea and I never have
it reminds me although much to my
surprise of my childhood.

With punctuation: I don't like the idea, and I never
have; it reminds me, although much
to my surprise, of my childhood.

The punctuated example would probably communicate the writer's thoughts immediately. The reader, however, would struggle with the first example, trying to figure out what the sentence means. Basically, punctuation is a shorthand aid to communication. It follows specific conventions and should not be used randomly.

This unit also gives you information on certain accepted mechanical aspects of writing. It answers some questions you might have about certain minor details in your papers.

Before you begin this unit, read the following selection about Charles Lindbergh. Look closely at the way punctuation, capital letters, italics, abbreviations, and numbers work to get the author's message across. Various exercises in this unit will ask you to return to this passage to find examples of certain rules you will be studying.

(1)   Thousands of people were massed around Le Bourget airfield just outside Paris, France, on the night of May 21, 1927. They waited anxiously, all eyes focused on the dark sky overhead. Somewhere in the vast black sea of space, a lone American flier was winging his way toward Paris in a fragile, single-engined monoplane.

(2)   The man at the controls was Charles A. Lindbergh, Jr., a boyish-faced, twenty-five-year-old former mail pilot and stunt flier. And the big question was whether he would make it. Would he successfully complete his transatlantic flight from New York to Paris?

(3)   The thousands gathered at Le Bourget believed that "Lucky Lindy," as the newspapers called him, could do it. Hours went by. The night grew cold. Still they waited.

(4)   Suddenly, the sound of an engine was heard. Giant searchlights lit the sky. There was a loud cheer as the crowd caught sight of a silver-gray plane. Moments later, at 10:24 p.m., Charles Lindbergh brought his plane, the *Spirit of St. Louis*, safely down to earth. The crowd went wild. A tidal wave of people broke through a cordon of police and soldiers and rushed madly toward the plane.

(5)   Cheering Frenchmen shouting *"Lindbergh! Vive Lindbergh!"* pulled the tall, slender American out of the cockpit and hoisted him onto their shoulders. Pale and weary, the youthful aviator

managed a smile as he said simply, "Well, I made it."

He had, indeed. On that memorable night in 1927, Charles Lindbergh became the first person to complete a solo nonstop flight across the Atlantic. Nicknamed the "Lone Eagle," he became an instant world hero and a legendary figure in his own lifetime. (6)

In 1977, the United States and France celebrated the 50th anniversary of Lindbergh's incredible feat of courage and flying skill. Special events were held. Commemorative stamps were issued, and on May 20, 1977, an exact copy of the *Spirit of St. Louis* took off from a Long Island, New York, airport in a re-enactment of the historic flight. (The original *Spirit of St. Louis* is on display at the Smithsonian Institution in Washington, D.C.) (7)

Fifty Years Earlier

The event these activities commemorate began on the morning of May 20, 1927, when Charles Lindbergh climbed into his silver airplane and prepared to take off from Roosevelt Field on Long Island. (8)

Lindbergh was one of many aviators who were competing for a $25,000 prize that was being offered to the flier, or fliers, who could make a nonstop trip across the Atlantic from New York to "the shores of France." (9)

From the moment he learned of the contest, Lindbergh decided to accept the challenge. At twenty-five, the lanky Midwesterner (called "Slim" by his friends) was already an experienced pilot. All he needed was a good plane. And thanks to a group of St. Louis businessmen, Lindbergh got the money he needed to have one built according to his own design. He named it the *Spirit of St. Louis* in honor of his backers. (10)

From THE NEW BOOK OF KNOWLEDGE ANNUAL, 1978, © Grolier Incorporated. (Danbury, Conn.: Grolier, 1978). Pp. 172–173. Reprinted by permission of the publisher.

12   Sentence End Punctuation

The **period**, the **question mark**, and the **exclamation point** all mark the end of a sentence, but each gives the sentence a different emphasis. As you talk, this emphasis is expressed by a change in your voice. Certain meanings that are communicated by your speaking voice can be recorded by punctuation in writing.

> Period: It's going to attack.
> Question mark: It's going to attack?
> Exclamation point: It's going to attack!

You should not, however, overuse these three punctuation marks to convey strong emotion.

> Unnecessary: I want some free time!!!!

To get the degree of emphasis you want, you should reorder the words in a sentence to say exactly what you mean and select only one punctuation mark:

> Clear: What I want is free time!
> Clear: Free time is what I want!

12A   Periods

The period is the most common form of end punctuation. It is used for this purpose in two distinct ways.

12A(1) Statements, Commands, Requests

A period marks the end of a statement, mild command, or request.

Statement: Motorcycles are becoming a popular means of transportation.

Command or request: Pick up some fresh fruit while you're out.

12A(2) Indirect Questions

A period ends a sentence that contains an indirect question.

Indirect question: He asked *how you are feeling* today.

Periods are also used for two other purposes besides end punctuation.

12A(3) Abbreviations

A period marks an abbreviation.

Abbreviation: I have a letter for Ms. Harris from Mr. Horn.

Abbreviation: She sent the package C.O.D.

We use many abbreviations in our writing, such as Dr., Sr., M.D., D.D.S., and Ph.D. Since most good dictionaries have a section on abbreviations, you can check your dictionary for the meaning and use of common abbreviations when you are in doubt.

12A(4) Ellipsis

Three spaced periods **(ellipsis marks)** indicate the omission **(ellipsis)** of one or more elements within a quoted passage.

A period is placed before the ellipsis marks when a complete sentence or an abbreviation comes before the omission. Ellipsis marks are not necessary at the beginning or the end of a quoted passage.

Reread paragraph 2 of the reading selection at the beginning of this unit, and compare it with the example that follows, which is the same paragraph with ellipsis marks in place of omitted material.

> The man at the controls was Charles A. Lindbergh, Jr. . . . And the big question was whether he would make it. Would he successfully complete his transatlantic flight from New York to Paris?

Three spaced periods are also sometimes used to indicate a pause or an unfinished statement, but they should not be overused in this way.

> Right: Will you join us . . . or not?
> Right: "I could tell her that I. . . ."

An entire line of spaced periods marks the omission of a full paragraph (or more) in prose or a full line (or more) in poetry. The format for omitting the second paragraph from the unit reading selection is as follows:

> Thousands of people were massed around Le Bourget airfield just outside Paris, France, on the night of May 21, 1927. They waited anxiously, all eyes focused on the dark sky overhead. Somewhere in that vast black sea of space, a lone American flier was winging his way toward Paris in a fragile, single-engined monoplane.
> . . . .
> The thousands gathered at Le Bourget believed that "Lucky Lindy," as the newspapers called him, could do it. Hours went by. The night grew cold. Still they waited.

Practice 12–1 Explain how all the periods are used in the reading selection at the beginning of this unit.

Practice 12–2 Write five sentences using periods.

12B Question Marks

The question mark is a form of end punctuation that distinguishes a question from a statement. When speaking, you probably make this distinction by raising your voice at the end of a question.

12B(1) Direct Questions

A question mark shows the end of a direct question.

Direct question: Did you have a good time?

12B(2) Direct Questions Within Statements

A question mark indicates a direct question within a statement.

Direct question: "Who started the argument?" he asked.

12B(3) Series of Questions

A question mark indicates the individual parts of a series of questions. See 16A(1) for an explanation of the use of the colon in the following example.

Direct questions: I have three questions: What time does the show start? Who is joining us? Where should I meet you?

12B(4) Uncertainties

A question mark indicates that the information preceding it is uncertain. Here the writer is not sure whether Edmund Spenser was born in 1552 or not.

Question: Edmund Spenser (1552?–1599) is a well-known Renaissance writer.

Practice 12–3 Rewrite as questions three statements from the reading selection at the beginning of this unit.

12C Exclamation Points

The exclamation point after words, phrases, or sentences usually designates surprise or some other strong emotion. In speaking, this emotion is conveyed by a combination of tone of voice, facial expressions, and gestures.

> Exclamation: No!
> Exclamation: Just get it over with!

Practice 12–4 Rewrite as exclamations three statements from the reading selection at the beginning of this unit.

Review

A. A period is used in the following ways:
  1. to mark the end of a statement, mild command, or request
  2. to mark the end of a sentence containing an indirect question
  3. to mark an abbreviation
  4. to mark an omission (ellipsis)
B. A question mark is used in the following ways:
  1. to mark the end of a direct question
  2. to indicate a direct question within a statement
  3. to mark the individual parts of a series of questions
  4. to mark a point of doubt in a sentence
C. An exclamation point is used after words, phrases, or sentences to mark strong emotion.

Review Practice 12–1 Rewrite the following sentences, adding end punctuation (periods, question marks, or exclamation points).

1. What was your time for the mile run
2. Ouch get off my foot
3. The Saint Bernard is a breed of dog that originated in Switzerland
4. Who sent you
5. Butterscotch is made by blending butter, brown sugar, and other flavorings
6. You'd better believe it
7. The saguaro cactus exists in the southwestern United States and in northern Mexico
8. What astrological sign were you born under
9. Absolutely not I refuse to come to that meeting
10. My camera never fails me

Review Practice 12–2 Rewrite the following paragraph, adding appropriate end punctuation (periods, question marks, and exclamation points).

> In Australia, an earthworm was found that was about thirteen feet (four hundred centimeters) long Even the tallest pro basketball player isn't that long
>
> At the other end of the scale is a worm that you would need a microscope to see You would need more than five hundred of these worms placed end to end to equal one inch (2.5 centimeters) How many would you need to equal that very long Australian worm Nearly eighty thousand

13   Commas

The comma marks brief pauses and connects words, phrases, and clauses to one another. As a result, the ability to recognize phrases and clauses in a sentence is an important part of knowing where to place a comma. A comma calls for a shorter pause than that indicated by a period. This chapter discusses the uses and misuses of the comma, focusing on the rule that governs each use. Following these rules can help you make statements clearly and precisely.

13A Uses of Commas

Eleven rules can help you use the comma to communicate effectively in your writing. Most of the rules governing single commas are probably familiar to you; these are the basic uses of this punctuation mark.

13A(1) Independent Clauses

A comma separates two independent clauses joined by the conjunctions *and, but, or, nor, for, so,* or *yet.* The comma is placed before the conjunction.

> Right: He raises ducks, and she runs a feed store.

For further information about these compound sentences, see 4E(2).

Practice 13–1 Write out the sentence containing the comma that separates two independent clauses in the reading selection at the beginning of this unit.
Practice 13–2 Write two compound sentences using commas to separate two independent clauses.

13A(2) Introductory Elements

A comma sets off introductory words, phrases, and clauses from the main clause of a sentence.

Right: First, let me introduce you to my cousin.
Right: In my opinion, the game shows on television are the best selections.
Right: When she won the swimming competition, Beverly felt proud.

As in the following example, a comma is often needed for clear communication:

Wrong: Do you want carrots for dinner? No beans.

The answer says that the person does not want any beans, even though the question was about carrots.

Right: Do you want carrots for dinner? No, beans.

This answer means that the person wants beans for dinner instead of carrots.

If the introductory phrase or clause is short and unlikely to be misunderstood, the comma is not required. However, because it is never wrong to use a comma after an introductory element, it is a good idea to develop the habit of inserting the comma after introductory phrases or clauses rather than having to stop each time to decide whether or not a comma is necessary. For clear communication, you should not use a comma when a word, phrase, or dependent clause follows an independent clause unless the element following the main clause presents a sharp break in thought.

Right: Let me introduce you to my cousin first.
Right: Beverly felt proud when she won the swimming competition. [The subordinating conjunction here is enough to alert the reader that a new idea (clause) is about to begin.]
Right: I prefer the bus to the trolley, all things considered. [Comma indicates a sharp break in thought.]

131

Practice 13–3 Write out the sentences containing commas that set off introductory words, phrases, and clauses in the reading selection at the beginning of this unit.

Practice 13–4 Write three sentences using commas to set off introductory elements: one sentence with an introductory word, one with an introductory phrase, and one with an introductory clause. Then, move the introductory elements to the end of each sentence, and adjust the punctuation.

13A(3) Direct Quotations

A comma separates a direct quotation from an explanation unless the quotation ends with another form of punctuation (as in the second example).

> Right: I heard her repeat, "Let him have it."
> Right: "That will be the day!" they exclaimed to each other.

In formal writing, a colon can be used in place of a comma to introduce a quotation. Therefore, a colon could be used in place of the comma only in the first example. See 16A(2) for more information on quotations introduced by colons.

13A(4) Interjections

A comma sets off mild interjections in a sentence.

> Right: Oh, I wish I were home now.

An exclamation point is used after strong interjections. See 12(C).

Practice 13–5 Write two sentences using commas that set off direct quotations from explanations and two sentences using commas that set off mild interjections.

Separating words in a series is also a common use of the comma. Two basic rules explain this function.

13A(5) Items in a Series

A comma separates three or more items in a series.

> Right: I recognized Herb, Kathy, and Sylvia.
> Right: I have to pick up the beer, clean the apartment, and call a babysitter.

Although the comma before the last item in a series is optional, it is a good idea to include it rather than to risk confusion.

> Unclear: For dinner, I had steak, salad, beans and rice.

The punctuation in this unclear statement implies that the speaker had steak, salad, and a combination of beans and rice.

> Clear: For dinner, I had steak, salad, beans, and rice.

Practice 13–6 Write four sentences using commas to separate items in a series.

13A(6) Adjectives

A comma separates adjectives modifying the same noun when they sound natural with the word *and* between them.

> Test: It was a cool and clear day.
> Right: It was a cool clear day.

The following examples do not sound natural when separated by *and*; therefore, they should not be separated by commas when *and* is removed.

> Test: He wore a washable and cotton shirt.
> Right: He wore a washable cotton shirt.

133

Another test is to reverse the order of the adjectives. If the adjectives can be reversed and the statement still makes sense, then commas are called for. If the adjectives cannot be reversed, no commas are needed.

Test: It was a clear, cool day.
Test: He wore a cotton, washable shirt.

The second sentence here does not make sense when the adjectives are reversed.

Practice 13–7 Write out the sentences containing commas that separate adjectives in the reading selection at the beginning of this unit.
Practice 13–8 Write four sentences using commas to separate a series of adjectives.

Finally, some commas are used in pairs. These commas enclose words, phrases, or clauses that can be moved elsewhere in a sentence or taken out of it altogether. Notice that one comma is omitted where the enclosed element comes at the beginning or end of a sentence.

13A(7) Parenthetical Elements

Commas set off parenthetical words, phrases, and clauses that interrupt the main train of thought in a sentence. **Parenthetical expressions** are expressions of clarification or emphasis that could be omitted from the sentence without altering the meaning of the main clause very much.

Right: The professor agreed, fortunately, to change my grade.
Right: The game shows are, in my opinion, the worst that television has to offer.

Practice 13–9 In the reading selection at the beginning of this unit, write out the sentences containing commas that set off words, phrases, and clauses that interrupt the sentence's main train of thought.

Practice 13–10 Write three sentences using commas to set off parenthetical elements: one sentence with a parenthetical word, one with a parenthetical phrase, and one with a parenthetical clause.

13A(8) Contrasted Elements

Commas enclose contrasted elements in a sentence.

> Right: It's Harry, not Sheila, whom the instructor wants to see.

The commas in this example signal a contrast between a word and the phrase that follows.

A comma is not used, however, when these items are reversed.

> Right: It's *not* Sheila *but* Harry whom the instructor wants to see.

This sentence stresses whom the instructor wants to see by its word order rather than by the use of commas.

Practice 13–11 Write four sentences using commas to set off contrasted elements.

13A(9) Nonrestrictive Clauses

A comma sets off phrases and clauses that are not needed to identify the word or words they modify.

> Nonrestrictive: She was suddenly confused by her roommate, *who is ordinarily a friendly person.*
> Nonrestrictive: The following sets of words, *known as idioms,* represent pecularities in our language.

Neither the clause nor the phrase in these examples is needed to identify the words it modifies. Each gives additional information, but if the information were taken out,

135

the sentence would still make sense. These are called **nonrestrictive** (or **nonessential**) modifiers, because they do not restrict the meaning of the preceding word, as the following examples do.

Restrictive: The man *who lives next door* rides a bicycle to work.

In this sentence, the clause is needed to identify the words before it. It tells which man is referred to and is called a **restrictive** (or **essential**) modifier.

Notice the difference in meaning caused by changing the punctuation in the following sentences:

Restrictive: The students who did most of the work at the carnival were glad that it was a success.

Nonrestrictive: The students, who did most of the work at the carnival, were glad that it was a success.

The first example says that the students who did the work (as opposed to the ones who did not work) were glad that the carnival was a success. The second example says that all the students did the work and were glad that the carnival was a success.

Practice 13–12 Identify one restrictive and one nonrestrictive clause in the reading selection at the beginning of this unit, and explain why they are restrictive and nonrestrictive.

Practice 13–13 Write five sentences containing at least one nonrestrictive clause each.

13A(10) Geographical Names, Dates, Addresses, Numbers

Commas are used in geographical names, dates, addresses, and certain numbers of four digits or more.

Right: He transferred to the University of California, Los
        Angeles, in September.
Right: He will be married by September 9, 1999.
Right: I live at 1234 East Pummel, Columbus, Ohio.
Right: The 16,492 people who live in my home town
        collected a total of $2,542,168 in their fund-raising
        campaign.

A comma is not used in years (1984), serial numbers
(#1436041), or page numbers (p. 1122).

Practice 13–14 In the reading selection at the beginning of
this unit, find three commas that are used in three different
ways explained in 13A(10).

13A(11) Direct Address

A comma sets off elements of direct address.

Right: Yes, sir, your package has arrived.

Practice 13–15 Write five sentences using the comma in
the five different ways explained in 13A(10) and 13A(11).
Practice 13–16 Rewrite the following sentences, adding
commas where needed. Not all the sentences need commas.

1. It's cold but I don't think it will snow.
2. Tonight I watched a special on TV.
3. No I don't want to go out with Sam who is supposed to
   have a bad temper.
4. I ate dinner and I still made it to the game on time.
5. I am positive that you will fall in love at first sight.
6. Alicia lives in Wichita Kansas.
7. Look at the awful industrial smog otherwise known as
   pollution.
8. I just read *The Catcher in the Rye* which is an exciting
   work of art.
9. November 3 1942 was a special day.

10. I assume his track record is good for he's always been a superior athlete.

13B Misuses of Commas

Writers sometimes misuse the comma because they are not sure of its exact functions. Following are examples of the six most common misuses of the comma.

13B(1) Between Subjects and Verbs

A comma is not used between a subject and its verb or between a verb and its object or complement.

Wrong: How can he, ask for a new suit?
Right:　How can he ask for a new suit?

Wrong: I have always wanted, a rose garden.
Right:　I have always wanted a rose garden.

13B(2) Between Compound Elements

A comma is not used between compound elements other than independent clauses. See 13A(1).

Wrong: I feel tired, and happy.
Right:　I feel tired and happy

Wrong: The photographer jogs every morning, and plays
　　　　tennis in the early evening.
Right:　The photographer jogs every morning and plays
　　　　tennis in the early evening.

Wrong: What she said, and what she felt were two
　　　　different matters.
Right:　What she said and what she felt were two
　　　　different matters.

13B(3) Between Adjectives

A comma is not used between adjectives that do not sound natural when *and* is put between them (or between adjectives that cannot logically be reversed).

Wrong: We live in the little, white house on the corner.
Right: We live in the little white house on the corner.

13B(4) With Restrictive Clauses

A comma is not used to set off a clause or phrase that is needed to identify the word it modifies.

Wrong: The person, who works the noon shift, should be here now.
Right: The person who works the noon shift should be here now.

Clauses beginning with *that* are never set off from the rest of a sentence by commas because they are always restrictive.

Wrong: The people, that I know best, leave town for the summer.
Right: The people that I know best leave town for the summer.

13B(5) With Items in a Series

A comma is not used before the first item or after the last item in a series.

Wrong: I have enjoyed my work in, botany, physics, and algebra.
Right: I have enjoyed my work in botany, physics, and algebra.

Wrong: His parents were always thrifty, tolerant, practical, people.

139

Right: His parents were always thrifty, tolerant, practical people.

13B(6) Before Quotations

A comma is not used before a quotation that is part of another phrase or clause.

Wrong: The sailor said the lake was as, "smooth as a baby's bottom."
Right: The sailor said the lake was as "smooth as a baby's bottom."

Here a comma after *as* would separate that preposition from its object.

Review

A. Commas are used in the following ways:
1. to separate two independent clauses joined by *and, but, or, nor, for, so,* or *yet*
2. to set off introductory words, phrases, and clauses
3. to separate a direct quotation from an explanation
4. to set off mild interjections
5. to separate three or more items in a series
6. to separate adjectives that sound natural when *and* is put between them or adjectives that can logically be reversed
7. to set off words, phrases, and clauses that interrupt the main train of thought in a sentence
8. to enclose contrasted elements
9. to set off clauses and phrases that are not needed to identify the word or words they modify
10. to set off geographical names, elements in dates, parts of addresses, and certain numbers of four digits or more

11. to set off elements of direct address
B. Commas are not used in the following ways:
    1. between a subject and its verb or between a verb and its object or complement
    2. between compound elements other than independent clauses
    3. between adjectives that do not sound natural when *and* is put between them or adjectives that cannot logically be reversed
    4. around a clause or phrase that is needed to identify the word it modifies
    5. before the first item or after the last item in a series

Review Practice 13–1 Rewrite the following sentences, adding commas where needed. Not all the sentences need commas.

1. I would like to order a hamburger a coke and fries to go.
2. If you help me I'll help you.
3. The couple got married on Tuesday and went to work on Wednesday June 18 1974.
4. The mechanic whom I met at school today lives down the street with that mean white dog.
5. In my opinion you should talk with people who encourage not discourage you.
6. Well since you asked I live at 2262 East 15th Street in a gray stucco house and I'm free for dinner tonight.
7. "The meeting is in Cincinnati Ohio" announced the director when everyone was finally silent.
8. I find that I enjoy assignments that are short coherent and practical but I still have trouble sitting through the long three-hour class session.
9. Your success which you deserve came early in your life.
10. "We demand Mr. President a meeting with you to discuss the proposed policy" insisted the program leader.

Review Practice 13–2 Rewrite the following paragraphs, adding commas where needed.

In 1969 more than 500000000 people witnessed the "impossible" coming true as the first men walked on the surface of the moon. For the next three years people watched as one of the great explorations in human history was displayed on their television screens.

Between 1969 and 1972 supported by thousands of scientists and engineers back on earth twelve astronauts explored the surface of the moon. In their space suits the astronauts were protected against the airlessness and the killing heat of the lunar environment. They stayed on the moon for days and some of them traveled for miles across its surface in Lunar Rovers. They made scientific observations and set up instruments to probe the interior of the moon. They collected hundreds of pounds of lunar rock and soil thus beginning the first attempt to discover the origin and geological history of another world from actual samples of its crust.

"What's New on the Moon?" From THE NEW BOOK OF KNOWLEDGE ANNUAL, 1978, © Grolier Incorporated. (Danbury, Conn.: Grolier, 1978). P. 96. Reprinted by permission of the publisher.

14 Semicolons

The **semicolon** separates ideas of equal weight. In reading, a semicolon represents a pause like that of a period. It is placed only between clauses that are closely related in thought, and it is followed by a word beginning with a small letter (except for the pronoun *I* and proper nouns).

14A Uses of Semicolons

The semicolon has three specific uses in written English.

14A(1) Two Independent Clauses

A semicolon separates two independent clauses that are not connected by *and, but, or, nor, for, so,* or *yet.*

> Right: She told me her reasons for quitting the job; I was amazed.

14A(2) Transitions

A semicolon separates two clauses when the second clause begins with certain transitional words or phrases.

> Right: Citizens have a moral obligation to their country; for example, they should vote as knowledgeably as possible.

14A(3) Long Phrases

A semicolon separates a series of long phrases or phrases that contain commas.

> Right: The law firms involved were Gonzales, Strauss, and Smith; Hazel, Logan, and Thomas; and Green, Brown, and Jones.
> Right: I know this section of the union handbook explains three things: the by-laws that we adopted; the ways of filing suit against employers, no matter what their stand; and the pros and cons of the situation at hand.

In these examples, semicolons separate the main elements of the series, whereas commas separate items within the main elements.

Practice 14–1 Write three sentences, each one showing a different use of the semicolon.

14B Misuse of Semicolons

Semicolons are most often misused when placed between items of unequal weight in a sentence—for example, between an independent and a dependent clause.

Dependent   Independent

Wrong: Because I was late; I skipped my morning coffee.

This sentence includes a dependent clause (beginning with *because*) and an independent clause. The clauses are not of equal weight and should be separated by a comma rather than a semicolon.

Right: Because I was late, I skipped my morning coffee.

Review

A. A semicolon is used in the following ways:
 1. to separate two independent clauses that are not connected by *and, but, or, nor, for, so,* or *yet*
 2. to separate two clauses when the second clause begins with certain transitional words or phrases
 3. to separate a series of long phrases, especially when some of them contain commas
B. A semicolon is not used between items of unequal weight.

Review Practice 14–1 Rewrite the following sentences, adding semicolons where needed.
 1. Love is passionate love is kind.
 2. Their children are polite—quick to apologize, whenever necessary hesitant, especially around strangers and soft-spoken.

3. I have attended your speech class therefore, I am qualified to enter the debate.
4. Minority programs are still expanding as a result, the demand for new levels of consciousness is rising.
5. Clothes are expensive however, they are more fun now than ever before.

Review Practice 14–2 Rewrite the following paragraphs, adding semicolons where needed.

Russia may seem like the Promised Land in one respect to schoolchildren of other countries homework is forbidden on weekends and holidays. However, children in Russia attend school six days a week—Sunday is the only free day.

Youngsters begin school at the age of seven, ten years education is compulsory in cities and many other areas, and seven years in rural sections where facilities are still inadequate. Many schools are on a two-shift basis plans call for nationwide ten-year schooling in the near future.

15   Apostrophes

The **apostrophe** has two major functions: (1) to show ownership (possession) and (2) to mark a contraction. In the possessive, the singular and plural possessives are formed according to specific rules. In a contraction, the apostrophe replaces the letter or letters that are missing in a word.

15A Uses of the Apostrophe

The apostrophe shows either possession or omission in a word. It is also used in letters, numbers, and abbreviations.

15A(1) Possession

An apostrophe marks ownership or possession in nouns and indefinite pronouns: see 1B and 1C.

> Right: The *boat's* rudder just hit bottom.
> Right: I have returned all the *students'* papers.
> Right: *Anybody's* guess is fair.

Possessive words are usually coupled with nouns and can also be written as *of* phrases. As phrases, the possessive words in these examples would read

> The rudder *of the boat* just hit bottom.
> I have returned all the papers *of the students*.
> The guess *of anybody* is fair.

The placement of the apostrophe is difficult with certain words and some final letters. Five rules can help you place the apostrophe correctly to show possession.

An -*'s* is added to words that do not end in an *s* or *z* sound.

> *popcorn's* kernels
> *people's* behavior

To singular words ending in an *s* or *z* sound, -*'s* is added to words of one syllable. Only an apostrophe is added to words of more than one syllable, unless you actually pronounce an additional *s* or *z* sound.

the *boss's* office
Ulysses' sacrifice
an *actress's* role

To plural words ending in an *s* or *z* sound, only an apostrophe is added.

the *drinks'* bubbles
the *candies'* wrappers

(A dictionary will usually furnish irregular plurals of words.)

An apostrophe is added to the last part of a compound word.

his *sister-in-law's* aunt
someone *else's* problem

For nouns showing joint possession, a possessive ending is added to the last word. For nouns showing individual possession, an apostrophe is added to each noun.

Claudia and Mike's house [one house: joint possession]
Both *Claudia's* and *Mike's* jobs [two jobs: individual possession]

15A(2) Contractions

An apostrophe marks a contraction by replacing the missing letter or letters in a word.

Right: Don't bother me now.
      (*Do not* bother me now.)
Right: It's ten o'clock
      (It *is* ten *of the* clock.)
Right: The class of '74 gave the school a bench.
      (The class of *1974* gave the school a bench.)

To form contractions, an apostrophe is placed exactly where the letter or letters are missing. Contractions are generally a sign of informality in written English. In more formal writing, you should avoid contractions.

15A(3) Letters, Numbers, Abbreviations

An apostrophe marks the plural of letters, numbers, and abbreviations.

> Right: Two *3's* equal 6.
> Right: The *P.O.W.'s*
> Right: three *B's* and two *C's*

Practice 15–1 In the reading selection at the beginning of this unit, label the one use of the apostrophe as either possession or contraction.

Practice 15–2 Write four sentences, two using apostrophes to mark possession and two using apostrophes in contractions.

15B   Misuses of the Apostrophe

Some common misuses of the apostrophe include its use with pronouns, plural words, and verbs. The following rules might help you avoid some of these errors.

15B(1) Possessive Pronouns

Apostrophes are not used with pronouns that are already possessive: *my, mine, your, yours, his, her, hers, its, our, ours, their, theirs, whose*. The troublesome words here are the words that end in *-s*; they are already possessive and need no extra mark to alert the reader.

> Wrong: *His's* sister is too young to play with us.
> Right: *His* sister is too young to play with us.

Wrong: This radio is *ours'*, not *theirs'*.
Right: This radio is *ours*, not *theirs*.

Also, the words *who's* and *it's* indicate not possession but contraction.

Right: *Who's* going to the show with us? *(Who is)*
Right: I know the person *who's* contributed the most money to our cause. *(Who has)*
Right: *It's* been a nice day, but *it's* getting late now. *(It has; it is)*

The possessive forms of these two words contain no apostrophes: *whose* (*whose* house) and *its* (*its* appeal).

15B(2) Plural Forms

Apostrophes are not used in plural words.

Wrong: Jacks *hamburgers'* are the best in town.
Right: Jack's *hamburgers* are the best in town.

15B(3) Verbs

Apostrophes are not used in verbs.

Wrong: The college graduate *want's* to start his own business.
Right: The college graduate *wants* to start his own business.

Review

A. An apostrophe is used in the following ways:
   1. to mark ownership or possession in nouns and indefinite pronouns
   2. to mark a contraction

    3. to mark the plural of letters, numbers, and abbrevia-
       tions

B. An apostrophe is not added to the following:
    1. a pronoun that is already possessive
    2. a plural word
    3. a verb

Review Practice 15–1 Rewrite the following sentences, adding any missing apostrophes. Label each apostrophe "possession" or "contraction."

1. Whos the winner today?
2. I couldnt do that without you.
3. Im sure I can understand its contents.
4. The childrens health is on my mind.
5. The popcorns ready; it is todays special.
6. Ive spent enough time listening to rock n roll.
7. I wish my schedule were someone elses problem.
8. John Joness trumpet was stolen from a house that wasnt his.
9. I got four Cs and two Bs on my finals this term.
10. I agree with the groups decisions, but the problem is hers.

Review Practice 15–2 Rewrite the following paragraphs, adding apostrophes where needed.

      Its Moms birthday, and the whole house is shaking with the excitement of the surprise party tonight. Mom is the only person who doesnt know about its plans and problems. Shes leaving for work now, so Ill be able to make the rest of the arrangements while shes gone for the day.

      At 6:00 sharp she will meet Dad for dinner downtown. Were not sure exactly whos going to join them, but we sent invitations to twelve of their friends. They should have responded to our invitations by now, but I hope they call while Im here today. Im supposed to bring the tables centerpiece and the champagne. Im looking forward to an enjoyable evening with my familys friends.

16   Colons

Basically, the **colon** is a mark of punctuation that introduces explanations. The statement before a colon is usually a complete statement, and what follows a colon generally expands upon that statement. A colon is a formal mark of punctuation and is seen in formal, rather than informal, writing; see 28A and 28B for an explanation of formal and informal writing.

16A   Uses of Colons

The colon functions in different ways. Each use has particular restrictions that you should follow.

16A(1) Introductory Statements

A colon is placed after an introductory statement when a list follows.

Right: When you go to the store, don't forget the main ingredients for lasagna: ground beef, noodles, cheese, and tomato sauce.

16A(2) Quotations

A colon is used before a quotation in formal writing.

Right: The student announced: "My classes are excellent, but the food leaves something to be desired."

In informal writing, a comma can be used in place of the colon in this example; see 13A(3).

16A(3) Explanations

A colon precedes an explanation.

Right: I have one main objective this year: self-control.
Right: Learning one another's names in class is important: you might need a friend sometime.

16A(4) Greetings

A colon follows the greeting of a business letter.

Right: Dear Ms. Gordon:

16A(5) Subtitles

A colon separates a title from a subtitle.

Right: *The Alchemy of Satire: A Study of Ben Jonson's Major Comedies*

16A(6) Time References

A colon separates the hours from the minutes in a time reference.

Right: 9:40

Notice that there is no space after a colon used in this way.

16A(7) Footnote and Bibliographical Entries

A colon separates the name of a city from the name of a publishing company in footnote and bibliographical entries.

Right: Boston: Houghton Mifflin Company, 1970

16A(8) Biblical References

A colon separates the chapter from the verse in a biblical reference.

Right: Relevation 20:4

16A(9) Parts of a Ratio

A colon separates the parts of a ratio.

Right: Mix the solution 3:2.

Notice there is no space after a colon used in biblical references or ratios.

Practice 16–1 Find the colons in the reading selection at the beginning of this unit, and explain how they are used. **Practice 16–2** Write four sentences using the colon in at least four different ways.

16B Misuses of Colons

Two common misuses of the colon confuse the process of communication.

16B(1) After Prepositions

A colon is not used after a preposition.

Wrong: I will never forget the feeling of: loneliness.
Right: I will never forget the feeling of loneliness.

16B(2) After Linking Verbs

A colon is not used after a linking verb.

Wrong:	Their reasons for choosing this dog are: temperament, size, length of hair, and general characteristics.
Right:	Their reasons for choosing this dog are temperament, size, length of hair, and general characteristics.
Right:	Their reasons for choosing this dog are the following: temperament, size, length of hair, and general characteristics.

Review

A. A colon is used in the following ways:
   1. to introduce a list
   2. to introduce a quotation
   3. to introduce an explanation
   4. to complete the greeting of a business letter
   5. to separate a title from a subtitle
   6. to separate the hours from the minutes in writing the time
   7. to separate the name of a city from the name of a publishing company in a footnote or bibliographical entry
   8. to separate the chapter from the verse in a biblical reference
   9. to separate the parts of a ratio
B. A colon is not used
   1. after a preposition
   2. after a linking verb

Review Practice 16–1 Rewrite the following sentences, adding colons where needed.
1. The steps are logical close the door, start the motor, release the emergency brake, and step on the gas.
2. It is 1130 and time to go to bed.

3. My father just finished reading a book entitled *Psychology A Study of Human Nature.*
4. The explanation is simple Clark killed his brother when their mother drove up.
5. I hope you can do these chores by 500 cut the grass, pick up the cleaning, and take the cats to the vet.

Review Practice 16–2 Rewrite the following paragraph, adding colons where needed.

> In 1951, a conference of weathermen decided to tag hurricanes with the letters of the alphabet. For radio messages, each letter was to be sent out as a word, using the army alphabet code Able, Baker, Charlie, Dog, Easy, and so on. But then they found that some foreign stations had just agreed to use other code words for the letters of the alphabet. So things were mixed up again. The next year the weathermen decided to solve the problem by giving each hurricane a name of its own, in alphabetical order. The first list read Alice, Barbara, Carol, Dolly, Edna, Florence, Gilda, Hazel, Irene, Jill, Katherine, Lucy, Mabel, Norma, Orpha, Patsy, Queen, Rachel, Susie, Tina, Una, Vicky, and Wallis.

"How Hurricanes Get Their Names," in *Hurricanes and Twisters* by Robert Irving. © 1955 by Alfred A. Knopf, Inc. Reprinted by permission of the publisher.

17   Quotation Marks

Quotation marks show that material is reproduced word-for-word. They are always used in pairs, showing the beginning (") and the end (") of a quotation.

17A   Uses of Quotation Marks

Quotation marks include both double (" . . . ") and single
(' . . . ') marks. This chapter explains the uses of quotation
marks and furnishes examples of each use; the following
rules apply to material that is taken from either written or
spoken sources.

17A(1) Written or Spoken Material

Double quotation marks enclose words taken directly from
written and spoken material. The material quoted can be a
word, a phrase, or full sentences.

> Right: She always said "yes" with a great deal of
> determination.
> Right: As my grandfather has said, I know I'm "going
> through only once," so I want to make the best of life.
> Right: According to Albert Einstein, *"The true value of a*
> *human being* is determined primarily by the measure
> and the sense in which he has attained liberation from
> the self."
>
> Taken from IDEAS AND OPINIONS by Albert Einstein.
> Copyright, 1954, by Crown Publishers, Inc. Used by permis-
> sion of CROWN PUBLISHERS, INC. P. 23.

17A(2) Titles of Short Works

Quotation marks enclose titles of short works: songs, short
poems, articles, short stories, and essays.

> Right: Have you read Randall Jarrell's poem entitled "Death
> of the Ball-Turret Gunner"?
> Right: I just finished "The Second Death," a short story by
> Graham Greene.

When you put a title on your own paper, however, do not
put that title in quotation marks, because you are naming
that paper for the first time rather than referring to it.

17A(3) Words or Phrases

Quotation marks show words or phrases used in a special sense.

Right: "Blitz" is a World War II term that has been taken into the professional football vocabulary.

Italics or underlining is also used in this way: see 20A(4).

17A(4) Single Quotation Marks

In quotations from both written and spoken sources, single quotation marks indicate a quotation within a quotation.

Right: "I told you that she actually said, 'I'll never get married,' even though the wedding date is set for next week," he sighed.

17B   Punctuation of Quotations

Quotations taken from either spoken or written sources are punctuated according to three rules.

17B(1) Periods and Commas

The period and the comma are placed inside the quotation marks.

17B(2) Colons and Semicolons

The colon and semicolon are placed outside the quotation marks.

17B(3) Dashes, Question Marks, Exclamation Points

The dash, the question mark, and the exclamation point are placed inside the quotation marks when they are part of the quoted material and outside the quotation marks when they apply to the whole sentence, including the quotation.

> Right: "I don't know what to—" she gasped.
> Right: "Victory with honor"—that's a slogan often heard.
> Right: "What's for dinner?"
> Right: Who wrote "The Homecoming"?
> Right: He shouted, "Get out!"
> Right: She had the nerve to call me "rude"!

Practice 17–1 Find the quotation marks in the reading selection at the beginning of this unit, and explain how they are used.

Practice 17–2 Write four sentences using quotation marks in at least four different ways. Add commas when necessary.

17C Misuse of Quotation Marks

Only one common error is connected with quotation marks: the overuse of quotation marks to achieve humor or to mark slang or colloquial expressions. Quotation marks are appropriate in these situations, but only when added very sparingly. Overuse of this device suggests that the writer is making fun of his or her own language. So in this situation you should drop the quotation marks or, if the word is unsuitable, as in most formal writing, replace it with another.

> Wrong: He is a real "slob" when it comes to living.
> Right: He is a real slob when it comes to living.

> Wrong: **His music is** "**out of sight.**"
> Right: **His music is terrific.**

Review

A. Double quotation marks are used in the following ways:
   1. to enclose direct quotations from both written and spoken sources
   2. to designate titles of short works
   3. to show words or phrases used in a special sense
B. Single quotation marks indicate a quotation within a quotation.
C. The following punctuation rules govern the use of quotation marks:
   1. The period and the comma are placed inside the quotation marks.
   2. The colon and semicolon are placed outside the quotation marks.
   3. The placement of the dash, the question mark, and the exclamation point depends on whether they are part of the quotation.
D. Quotation marks are used sparingly to achieve humor and to mark slang.

Review Practice 17–1 Rewrite the following sentences, adding quotation marks and other punctuation where needed. Not all sentences need punctuation.

1. We need jobs is the cry of the Vietnam veterans.
2. The word sensitivity is a key word in friendship.
3. I know myself better than anyone else knows me wrote the student.
4. I said to him that it's never too late to improve.
5. I said to her Why don't you take a shower and cool off.
6. Martha asked John to grow a moustache.
7. The instructor gave precise directions: Go home early and read Ode on a Grecian Urn again; it's a very short poem.
8. Henry Ford said an idealist is a person who helps other people to be prosperous.

159

9. Tell Tom hello shouted the woman.
10. Is it true that fame is the perfume of heroic deeds, as Socrates said? asked the philosophy major.

Review Practice 17–2 Rewrite the following paragraph, adding quotation marks and commas where needed.

> A serious-looking dictionary editor, tuned in to the Bergen show, leaned forward in his chair. Hubba hubba again he murmured. Next morning in his office, he went to an imposing file marked New Words. Thumbing rapidly through the cards, he reached H. There it was—Hubba hubba: a cry of enthusiasm; popular expression in Army camps.
>
> Adapted from "How Words Crash the Dictionary" by Paula Phillips, in *Coronet,* August 1948.

18 Dashes, Parentheses, and Brackets

All three of these punctuation marks signal breaks in a sentence. They are also all used in pairs except the dash, which can appear in pairs or as a single mark, depending on whether the break it signals occurs at the beginning, at the end, or in the middle of a sentence.

18A Dashes

A **dash** is a line (—) longer than a hyphen that separates two parts of a sentence for one of the following reasons.

18A(1) Sudden Breaks

A dash indicates a sudden break in thought or change in tone.

Right: Can I—will I ever become a fulfilled person?

18A(2) Explanations

A dash sets off an explanation or summary from the rest of a sentence.

Right: I have tried to cool her off—in more ways than one.
Right: You can cure your ringworm with walnuts—the insides of walnuts.

18A(3) Parenthetical Elements

A dash sets off parenthetical elements in a sentence.

Right: I can't understand why Margaret—a nice person—would hurt Martin's feelings.

On a typewriter, a dash is two unspaced hyphens. Do not leave a space between the dash and the words it separates unless the dash occurs at the end of a line. Dashes should be used sparingly because they are an informal kind of punctuation and signal only abrupt changes in thought or tone. Commas can often be chosen instead of dashes to mark less abrupt breaks in a sentence.

Practice 18–1 Rewrite the following sentences, adding dashes where needed.
1. Can I I mean will you let me go on the hike with you?
2. I would like to know her better or at least try to know her.
3. Sometimes he visits me that is when I'm lucky and takes me to a show.
4. W. C. Fields remember him was a great comic actor.
5. Could I should I ask him to the dance?

Practice 18–2 Write two sentences using dashes in at least two different ways.

18B Parentheses

Parentheses are written in pairs, like this: ( ). They enclose certain items in sentences.

18B(1) Supplementary Material

Parentheses set off supplementary or explanatory material in a sentence.

> Right: You will find the answer to your questions in the *OED (Oxford English Dictionary)*.
> Right: People are sometimes insulted by the personality types portrayed in television commercials. (Perhaps the commercials and not the people should be altered.)

Notice that the period goes inside the parentheses when a full sentence is enclosed in parentheses.

You should use parentheses only when you want certain information to be isolated from the rest of a sentence, as if it were an aside. Parentheses communicate a longer pause than a comma does and are meant to set off a word, phrase, or sentence from the rest of a sentence.

18B(2) Numbers and Letters

Parentheses enclose numbers or letters in a sentence.

> Right: The United States railroads serve a dual purpose: (1) to carry passengers and (2) to move freight.
> Right: The American Indians were (a) exploited, (b) dehumanized, and (c) exiled to reservations by the early settlers.

Practice 18–3 Rewrite the following sentences, adding parentheses where appropriate.

1. Her sign Capricorn indicates that she is compulsive.
2. Las Vegas offers weddings for $50.00 that is if you have no music, no flowers, and no rings.

3. Mother's Day May 10 is a perfect time to remember your mother in a special way.
4. Burt Bacharach and Hal David wrote my favorite song "I'll Never Fall in Love Again."
5. I gave him three commands: 1 Clean your room, 2 Do your chores, and 3 Get dressed.

Practice 18–4 Find the sets of parentheses in the reading selection at the beginning of this unit, and explain how they are used.

18C Brackets

Like parentheses, **brackets** are written in pairs and enclose certain items within a sentence. They look like this: [ ].

18C(1) Corrections

Brackets set off corrections or necessary information that a writer has added to quoted material.

Right: "It seemed to me [Anna] that the warm strength of my body's happiness was enough to drive away all the fear in the world."

Doris Lessing, *The Golden Notebook* (New York: Simon & Schuster, 1962), p. 612.

Right: A student in freshman composition wrote: "It is there [*sic*] problem."

[*Sic*] is Latin for "as it was" or "thus." It marks a mistake in something a writer wishes to quote. But someone who thinks there is a mistake in his or her own writing should not add [*sic*]. Rather, the writer should correct the mistake.

18C(2) Parentheses Within Parentheses

Brackets replace parentheses within parentheses.

Right: I know the importance of friendship. (Someone to talk to [like a roommate] is invaluable.)

The principle here is very much like that requiring single quotation marks for a quotation within a quotation. In both cases, if the inner marks were the same as the outer marks, confusion would result because the reader would not know which sets of parentheses went together. Look at the confusing use of parentheses in the following example: "I know the importance of friendship. (Someone to talk to (like a roommate) is invaluable.)"

Practice 18–5 Rewrite the following sentences, adding brackets where appropriate.
1. Poker is a good pastime (especially for lonely or should I say boring evenings).
2. Potato salad (made of potatoes, mayonnaise, eggs, pimento, salt, and peper *sic*) was on the menu for the picnic.
3. Henrietta (Ralph's girlfriend you know, the one who frowns all the time) looks as if she lost her best friend today.

Practice 18–6 Write two sentences using brackets in at least two different ways.

Review

A. A dash serves
   1. to indicate a sudden break in thought or change in tone
   2. to set off an explanation or summary
   3. to set off parenthetical elements
B. Parentheses are used
   1. to set off supplementary or explanatory material
   2. to enclose numbers or letters

C. Brackets are used
   1. to set off corrections or necessary information a writer has added to quoted material
   2. to replace parentheses within parentheses

Review Practice 18–1 Rewrite the following sentences, adding dashes, parentheses, or brackets where appropriate.
1. Father's Day June 20 is a celebration my father will enjoy.
2. You shouldn't have lied or exaggerated to your sister.
3. A pussy willow *Salix discolor* is a North American shrub.
4. This sentence shows Bruce's spelling problem: "I was hopping *sic* for your quick recovery."
5. "Cougar" is a great name for a car or is it?
6. Bean salad made of kidney beans, green beans, onion, oil, vinegar, and sometimes garbanzo beans is on the menu for our picnic.
7. I think I have a strep short for streptococcus throat.
8. She said, "I enjoyed the play, and I'd like to see more of his Edward Albee's dramas."

Review Practice 18–2 Rewrite the following paragraph, adding dashes, parentheses, and brackets where appropriate.

I've never believed in outer space life forms. I've always been I think I was born with it a synical *sic* person. So imagine my surprise when one day while flying my kite in the hills I saw what appeared to be a shiny round object descending in a vertical path heading in my direction. My first instinct was to run naturally; so I hurled myself with a great deal of force into the back door of my motor home, and, after regaining consciousness, I sat up in a daze. I still don't believe in outer space life forms, but now although I won't admit it to anyone else there will always be that question in my mind.

19 Capitalization

The use of capital letters in your writing should follow certain rules, which are listed in this chapter. In addition to these rules, a brief explanation of the use of small (or lower-case) letters is included at the end of this chapter.

19A Uses of Capitalization

Capitalization highlights a certain word or series of words in a sentence. The three main uses of capitalization are for proper nouns, for titles with proper nouns, and at the beginning of sentences.

19A(1) Proper Nouns

Proper nouns are names of persons, places, or things, including some geographical locations, buildings, organizations, institutions, celestial bodies, and most references to religion. Brand names are also proper nouns.

All proper nouns and parts of proper nouns are capitalized.

> Abraham Lincoln, Statue of Liberty, Thomas Hobbes, Ireland, Socrates, Methodism, the South, a Southerner, God, Asia, Congress, Revlon, New York, Peace Corps, Mars, Lake Isabella, Civic Center, Henderson Boulevard, Midwest College, Forest Park, Rogue River, the Humanities Building, Chesterfield Avenue

Directions of the compass are not capitalized: see 19B(1).
Many words that are formed from proper nouns are capitalized.

> American, Asian, Hobbesian, Irish, Martian, Methodist

166

Abbreviations of proper nouns are capitalized.

NATO, HEW, UFW, YMCA

Practice 19-1 List one example of each of these rules in the reading selection at the beginning of this unit.

19A(2) Titles with Proper Nouns

Titles showing office, rank, degree, position, or the like are written both with and without proper nouns. These titles are capitalized according to three rules.

A title that precedes a proper noun is capitalized:

Lieutenant Roberts, Professor Miller, Governor Jones, Sister Dorothea

A title is often capitalized when it substitutes for a name.

Right: Have you heard the President's decree on nuclear pollution?

A degree or title after a name is capitalized:

Thelma Moore, M.A.; Pat Burgess, Executive Director; Willard B. Christiansen, M.D.; Dean Johnson, Editor

19A(3) Beginnings of Sentences

As you may recall from Chapter 4, a sentence begins with a capital letter and ends with some form of end punctuation. Three rules apply to capital letters in sentences, quotations, and direct questions.

The first word of every sentence is capitalized.

Right: He must be on the next plane.

167

The first word of a quotation that is a complete sentence and any other words capitalized by the author of the quotation are capitalized.

Right: He read, "Night fell on the small town of Otter Rock."

The first word of a direct question within a sentence is capitalized.

Right: She asked, "Where will you spend your summer?"

Practice 19–2 List four examples of these rules from the reading selection at the beginning of this unit.

19A(4) Other Uses

Other usage rules for capitalization apply to titles of publications, works of art, and names of television programs; words referring to relatives; months, days of the week, and holidays; historical references; and courses.

The titles of publications (books, magazines, newspapers, stories, poems), works of art (plays, movies, musical compositions, sculptures, paintings), and names of television programs are capitalized.

The French Connection, The American Heritage Dictionary, Swan Lake, Who's Afraid of Virginia Woolf? Psychology Today, The Other, Star Trek, The New York Daily News

The only exceptions to this rule are articles, conjunctions, and prepositions, which are not capitalized unless they are the first or last word of a title or subtitle.

Words referring to a relative are capitalized when used as a substitute for names or with names, but not when used with possessive pronouns.

Right: When *Mother* called, she said she would be home right away.

Right: My *uncle* is joining us for dinner.

Right: My *uncle Jason* is joining us for dinner.

Right: Is *Uncle Jason* joining us for dinner?

Months, days of the week, and holidays are capitalized.

September, Saturday, Christmas, May, Tuesday, Hanukkah

Seasons or numbered days of the month are not capitalized: see 19B(3).

Names of movements, periods, and historical events are capitalized.

Romantic Movement, the Battle of the Bulge, the Bill of Rights, the Renaissance

The names of centuries are not capitalized: see 19B(4).

Names of specific courses and all languages are capitalized.

Right: I am taking *Botany* 101, *Math* 210, and *English* 100.

Right: Have you ever studied *Russian?*

The words *I* and *O* are capitalized.

She said, "On Sunday, *I* raised my voice in praise of thee, *O* God."

Practice 19–3 List four examples of how these rules are applied in the reading selection at the beginning of this unit.

19B **Misuses of Capitalization**

The most common errors in capitalization involve directions, occupations, seasons, centuries, courses of study,

169

and diseases. Some guidelines can help you avoid these faults.

19B(1) Directions

General compass directions are not capitalized: *north, south, east, west.*

These same words are capitalized, however, when they refer to sections of the country (the *South,* the *East*) or to people from a section of the country *(Southerner, Easterner):* see 19A(1) for further information.

19B(2) Occupations

An occupation used as a general description is not capitalized.

> Right: Victor Lasseter, the professor, will be in his office to answer your questions.

See 19A(2) for more information on occupations and titles.

19B(3) Seasons and Numbered Days

Seasons or numbered days of the month are not capitalized.

> Right: The rains come in the fall.
> Right: Let's have a party on the fifth of next month.

See 19A(4) for more information on months, days of the week, and holidays.

19B(4) Centuries

The names of centuries are not capitalized: *eighteenth century, sixteenth century, twentieth-century values.* See 19A(4) for more information on historical references.

19B(5) Study Courses

General courses of study are not capitalized (but languages are always capitalized).

Right: I am taking botany, math, and English.

See 19A(4) for more information on courses.

19B(6) Diseases

Names of diseases, except when they are formed from proper nouns, are not capitalized: *rheumatic fever, Hodgkin's disease, mononucleosis, influenza.*

Review

A. The following are capitalized:
    1. all proper nouns (and parts of proper nouns), which are names of specific persons, places, or things
    2. words that are formed from proper nouns
    3. abbreviations of proper nouns
    4. a title that precedes a proper noun
    5. a title of high rank when used as a substitute for a name
    6. a degree or title after a name
    7. the first word of every sentence
    8. the first word of a quotation that is a complete sentence and any other words capitalized by the author of the quotation
    9. the first word of a direct question within a sentence.
    10. the important words in titles of publications, works of art, and television programs

11. words referring to a relative when used as a substitute for a name or with a name
12. months, days of the week, and holidays
13. names of movements, periods, and historical events
14. names of specific courses and all languages
B. The following are not capitalized:
   1. directions
   2. an occupation used as a description
   3. seasons or numbered days of the month
   4. the names of centuries
   5. general courses of study
   6. names of diseases, except when they are formed from proper names

Review Practice 19–1 List all the capital letters in the reading selection at the beginning of this unit, and explain why they are used.

Review Practice 19–2 Rewrite the following sentences, capitalizing any words that should be capitalized.

1. in my philosophy course this quarter, we studied hegel, kierkegaard, hobbes, locke, and their theories on god and human development.
2. if we go to hendricks park for our picnic, i hope we don't run into jeff squires, our local representative in congress, who is sponsoring a fund-raising outing there.
3. aunt bertha is picking me up in ten minutes to take me shopping at the coburg mall.
4. my sister and brother will be arriving with dad on this coming wednesday for the thanksgiving holidays.
5. although it is very demanding, i like physics 280, but i do not like studying psychology.
6. have you ever studied latin or greek?
7. in the spring, the wonders of the world are obvious even to the skeptic who asks, "what's it all about?"
8. the baptist community sponsored a benefit for doris

welby, who is running for state representative to the senate.

9. a un meeting was held just before the united states presidential election.

10. mom and dad are going to the southwest for their vacation this year because they both suffer from sinus conditions.

Review Practice 19–3 Rewrite the following paragraph, capitalizing any words that should be capitalized.

photography is a medium that is very familiar to us today. chester newby, my cousin, took up photography as a hobby and developed into a great artist with his camera. he claims that a simple photography course (photography 102) in college stimulated his interest in this medium. cousin chester went east after college and studied under a man named eric bernhardt. when chester got his b.a. in fine arts in june 1978 (on a wednesday), he said, "a camera is all i need to translate life into art." his first book, *the art of photography*, was published in 1980 and was introduced to the market in time for christmas sales. last spring he moved to the country where he claims the best subject of art is—nature itself. i am proud of my cousin. as i watch his fame increase, i have begun to understand what he means when he says, "photography is the language of today."

20   Underlining or Italics

Underlining or **italics** are used to emphasize words or phrases in sentences. Italics are preferred when they are available (in printed works and on some typewriters). If your typewriter does not have italics (which is generally the case) or if you are writing out a paper in longhand, you may use underlining where you would otherwise use italics. Underlining and italics mean the same thing, but you should be consistent once you decide on one method or the other.

20A Uses of Underlining or Italics

Underlining or italics are used for titles of long publications, works of art, and names of television programs; specific vehicles; foreign words and phrases; and words, figures, and letters in certain constructions.

20A(1) Titles of Long Works

Titles of long publications (books, magazines, newspapers), works of art (plays, movies, major musical compositions, sculptures, paintings), and names of television programs are underlined or italicized.

> Right: Do you subscribe to *Newsweek* or *Time?*
> Right: Did you see *American Graffiti* when it was in town?

20A(2) Ships, Trains, Airplanes, Spacecraft

Names of specific ships, trains, airplanes, and spacecraft are underlined or italicized.

> Right: The people who observed the successful flight of the *Spirit of St. Louis* were thrilled by the experience.
> Right: The *U.S.S. Enterprise* is Captain Kirk's starship in the *Star Trek* series on TV.

20A(3) Foreign Expressions

Foreign words and phrases are underlined or italicized, but not words and phrases that have become part of our language, such as *cliché* (French), *tomahawk* (Algonquian), and *psyche* (Greek).

Right: *Barri* is an Arabic word meaning "of an open area."

Consult a dictionary if you are unsure whether or not a word or phrase has become a part of our language.

20A(4) Words, Figures, Letters

Words, figures, and letters are underlined or italicized when referred to as such.

Right: When I tried to find the word *eliminate* in the
        dictionary, I made the mistake of looking under *a*.
Right: You should dot your *i*'s clearly to distinguish them
        from your *e*'s.

Notice that the apostrophe and the -*s* that make single words, figures, and letters plural are not underlined or italicized.

Quotation marks are also used in this way: see 17A(3). Most authorities, however, prefer italics, because italicized words are less easily confused with quoted words.

20B Misuses of Underlining or Italics

The most common misuses of underlining or italics occur within sentences and in titles of student papers.

20B(1) Emphasis

Emphasis is not achieved by underlining or italics except in very rare cases.

Weak: I don't want your *money* but your *time*.

The use of underlining or italics for emphasis often reveals a weakness in the writer's style. The words in a sentence ought to be arranged to give the proper stress; therefore, rather than resort to underlining to catch your reader's attention, you should reword your sentences.

Stronger: Not your money but your time is what I want.

20B(2) Titles of Original Papers

The titles of your own papers are not underlined or italicized.

Titles of large works other than your own are underlined or italicized; titles of short works other than your own are enclosed in double quotation marks.

Review

A. The following are underlined or italicized:
1. titles of long publications, works of art, and television programs
2. names of specific ships, trains, airplanes, and spacecraft
3. foreign words and phrases
4. words, figures, and letters when referred to as such
B. Underlining or italics are not appropriate
1. to achieve emphasis in a sentence
2. to mark the titles of your own papers

Review Practice 20–1 Find the uses of italics in the reading selection at the beginning of this unit, and explain why they are used.

Review Practice 20–2 List the words and phrases that require italics in the following sentences.
1. The Electric Kool-Aid Acid Test is one of Tom Wolfe's best books.
2. Did you see the latest issue of Ebony?
3. Etc. is an abbreviation for the Latin phrase et cetera, meaning "and so on."
4. My brother once served on the U.S.S. Shelton.
5. The Joy of Cooking has been a best seller for years.

6. Arlo Guthrie once sang a popular ballad about the famous train named the City of New Orleans.
7. Bonita is a Spanish word meaning "beautiful."
8. Popcorn went well with the play Barefoot in the Park.

21   Abbreviations

The abbreviations explained in this chapter are acceptable in all kinds of writing. Other abbreviations are listed and defined in your dictionary.

21A   Uses of Abbreviations

Many words and phrases in our language can be abbreviated. Following are some general guidelines to help you use **abbreviations** in your writing.

21A(1) Titles Preceding Names

Titles before proper nouns are abbreviated.

Dr., Mrs., Ms., Mr., Rev., St. (for *Saint*), Messrs. (plural of *Mr.*), Mmes. (plural of *Mrs.*)

21A(2) Titles and Degrees Following Names

Titles and degrees after proper nouns are abbreviated.

Sr., Jr., A.B., B.A., M.A., M.D. (medical doctor), Ph.D. (doctor of philosophy), Ed.D. (doctor of education), D.D.S. (doctor of dental science), D.D. (doctor of divinity), J.D. (doctor of jurisprudence), D.M.V. (doctor of veterinary medicine), D.Lit. or D.Litt. (doctor of literature), LL.D. (doctor of laws)

177

21A(3) Dates and Figures

Words used with dates and figures are abbreviated.

> 8:00 a.m., 45 mph (also m.p.h.), no. 4, 10:00 p.m., 3,000 rpm (also r.p.m.), $44.00

21A(4) Government References

References to the District of Columbia and to government organizations are abbreviated.

> Washington, D.C.; UN; CIA; NATO; FBI; IRS

Notice that the abbreviations of the organizations are written without periods after each letter.

21A(5) Latin Expressions

Certain Latin expressions are abbreviated.

> i.e. (that is), e.g. (for example), etc. (and so on), c. (about)

21A(6) Footnote and Bibliographical Entries

Parts of footnote and bibliographical entries are abbreviated.

> p. (page), pp. (pages), ibid. (the same reference as that immediately before it)

21B Misuses of Abbreviations

Only a fine line separates abbreviations that are acceptable in writing and those that are not. Generally, abbreviations should be held to a minimum in formal writing. The following guidelines list the abbreviations that are not acceptable in either formal or informal writing; see 28A and 28B.

21B(1) Titles of Individuals

Titles of individuals are not abbreviated.

Wrong: Prof. Martin and Sen. Stein are discussing the main issues of the debate.

Right: Professor Martin and Senator Stein are discussing the main issues of the debate.

21B(2) States and Countries

States and countries are not abbreviated.

Wrong: Some friends and I drove through Ca. this summer.

Right: Some friends and I drove through California this summer.

21B(3) Months and Days

Months and days of the week are not abbreviated.

Wrong: Our papers are due Mon., Oct. 14.

Right: Our papers are due Monday, October 14.

21B(4) Measurements

Terms denoting measurements are not abbreviated.

Wrong: I learned how to convert ft. and yds. to the metric system.

Right: I learned how to convert feet and yards to the metric system.

21B(5) Parts of Proper Nouns

The words *street, avenue, road, park, mount, river, company, court,* and *boulevard* are not abbreviated when used with a proper noun.

Wrong: You can see Mt. Hood from Century Blvd.

Right: You can see Mount Hood from Century
         Boulevard.

21B(6) *Volume, Chapter, Page*

The terms *volume, chapter,* and *page* are not abbreviated
except in footnotes and bibliographical entries: see 21A(6).

Wrong: In class today, the instructor emphasized p. 30
         from chap. 12.
Right: In class today, the instructor emphasized page 30
         from chapter 12.

21B(7) First Names

First names are not abbreviated.

Wrong: The hero's name in the book is Robt. Cohn.
Right: The hero's name in the book is Robert Cohn.

21B(8) Common Words

Common words are not abbreviated.

Wrong: For many yrs. we haven't known what the gov't
         was going to do next.
Right: For many years we haven't known what the
         government was going to do next.

21C   Other Related Information

Etc., ampersands (&), and plus signs (+) are not used in
formal writing except in special situations.

21C(1) *Etc.*

The word *etc.* is avoided in formal writing. If you have
more details to support your point, you should include
them rather than write *etc.* Using this abbreviation

180

suggests a writer is too lazy to specify what those "other things" are.

21C(2) Ampersands and Plus Signs

Neither the ampersand (&) nor the plus sign (+) is correct in formal writing as an abbreviation for *and*. They appear in formal writing only when they are part of a corporate name or title: Harper & Row, *U.S. News & World Report*.

Review

A. The following are abbreviated in formal and informal writing:
  1. titles before proper nouns
  2. titles and degrees after proper nouns
  3. words used with dates and figures
  4. references to the District of Columbia and to government organizations
  5. certain Latin expressions
  6. parts of footnote and bibliographical entries
B. The following are not abbreviated in formal and informal writing:
  1. titles of individuals
  2. states and countries
  3. months and days of the week
  4. terms denoting measurement
  5. the words *street, avenue, road, park, mount, river, company, court,* and *boulevard* when used with a proper noun
  6. the terms *volume, chapter,* and *page,* except in footnote and bibliographical entries
  7. first names
  8. common words
C. The following information is related to the use of abbreviations:
  1. The word *etc.* is avoided in formal writing.

181

2. Neither an ampersand nor a plus sign is used in formal writing.

Review Practice 21–1 Find the abbreviations in the reading selection at the beginning of this unit, and explain why they are used.

Review Practice 21–2 Rewrite the following sentences, using abbreviations that are acceptable in all kinds of writing.

1. Jan Gabrielson, doctor of jurisprudence, got a job in a respectable firm in Los Angeles.
2. At 2:00 in the afternoon today, I hope to be on my way to the District of Columbia for a government meeting.
3. In my letter to Mister Adams, I found it difficult to explain why I did not contact him on February 8 when I was in Colorado.
4. If I buy two pounds of this cheese, will you split it with me?
5. If you go to Madison Avenue and take a right, you will be about 300 yards from Charles Cooper's house.

22 Numbers

The main concern in using **numbers** is whether to spell out numbers in your writing or to substitute figures for those numbers. The following guidelines can help you make that decision.

22A Numbers Written as Words

In written work, some numbers are spelled out in words rather than written as figures.

22A(1) One or Two Words

Numbers of one or two words are spelled out. All two-word numbers lower than one hundred are hyphenated.

Right: There are about *three thousand* students in our school.
Right: I had *five* mistakes on a spelling quiz of *twenty-five* questions.

22A(2) Beginning Sentences

Numbers at the beginning of sentences are spelled out.

Right: *One hundred ten* people marched for the cause.
Right: *Sixty-seven* years is the average life expectancy for a black female.

22B Numbers Written as Figures

Other numbers in your assignment ought to be written as figures.

22B(1) More Than Two Words

Numbers of more than two words are written as figures, unless they begin a sentence: see 22A(2).

Right: This year *204* students took driver's training at our local high school.

22B(2) Mathematical References

Numbers in a series, mathematical problems, and statistics are written as figures.

Right: My locker combination is *52, 8, 4.*
Right: If the head of produce in a grocery store bought *6* dozen oranges, gave *4* oranges to a special employee, sent *12* oranges back to the distributor because they

were damaged, and used *31* to make the store's fresh orange juice, how many were left?

22B(3) Decimals and Fractions

Decimals and fractions are written as figures.

Right: This meat weighs *3.74* pounds.
Right: One can no longer borrow money at *6¼* percent interest.

22B(4) Code Numbers

Code numbers are written as figures.

Right: You can call me in my office at any time at *833–2295*.
Right: Her social security number is *499–52–8489*.

22B(5) Measurements

Measurements of all kinds, page numbers, and amounts of money preceded by a dollar sign (\$) are written as figures.

Right: I need a piece of plywood that is *8"* by *4"* by *1"*.
Right: You can copy the chapter beginning on page *40* for about *\$2.20* at the library copy machine.

22B(6) Dates, Addresses, Time

Dates, addresses, and time written with a.m. or p.m. are written as figures.

Right: On March *15*, we will be moving into our new home at *2452* Conway Road.
Right: At *8:04* a.m., a gun was fired in apartment 2B.

Review

A. The following numbers are written as words:
   1. numbers of one or two words

2. numbers at the beginning of sentences

B. The following numbers are written as figures:
   1. numbers of more than two words
   2. numbers in a series, mathematical problems, and statistics
   3. numbers with decimals and fractions
   4. code numbers
   5. measurements, page numbers, and amounts of money preceded by a dollar sign
   6. dates, addresses, and time written with a.m. or p.m.

Review Practice 22–1 List all the numbers in the reading selection at the beginning of this unit, and explain why they are written as words or as figures.

Review Practice 22–2 Rewrite the following sentences, correcting any numbers that are not written according to the guidelines in this chapter.

1. Seventeen people showed up at a special party for our boss at three p.m. last Friday.
2. If we can borrow $ five thousand at eight percent, we can put a down payment on the house we liked at four-hundred twenty-nine Spruce Avenue.
3. My extension is two-three-five-nine, and you can reach me there every afternoon between two p.m. and six p.m.
4. Out of the one hundred seventy-eight items that were in the auction, I bid on two.
5. Although I have twenty good reasons for staying home tonight, I'm going to the party with you anyway.

Reading Tasks

Comprehension

To check your comprehension, answer the following questions about the reading selection on Lindbergh at the beginning of this unit. Refer to the selection when necessary.

1. How old was Charles Lindbergh when he made the flight from New York to Paris?
2. What nickname did the newspapers give Lindbergh?
3. What was the name of Lindbergh's plane?
4. What did Lindbergh say when he landed safely in Paris?
5. Where is Lindbergh's original plane now?

For additional comprehension exercises, turn to the Unit II Appendix Selection.

Details

Details explain main ideas. In other words, details support main ideas that are expressed in topic sentences. Several details are usually needed to explain one main idea. In most paragraphs, everything but the topic sentence is a detail.

In the first paragraph of the reading selection at the beginning of this unit, for example, the main idea is contained in the first sentence: "Thousands of people were massed around Le Bourget airfield just outside Paris, France, on the night of May 21, 1927." The other sentences in the first paragraph explain this main idea: the second

186

sentence explains how people were waiting at the airport, and the third sentence describes what they were waiting for.

6. List the main ideas and details of paragraphs 6 and 7 in the reading selection on Lindbergh.
7. List the main ideas and details of paragraphs 11 and 14 in the appendix selection.

Paraphrasing

Paraphrasing is stating what you have read in your own words, including main ideas and details. A paraphrase is usually about the same length as the reading selection itself, unlike a summary, which is usually much shorter than the original. A paraphrase of the first paragraph of the reading selection at the beginning of this unit might read something like the following:

> On the evening of May 21, 1927, Le Bourget airfield, which is near Paris, France, was packed with people. They were awaiting the arrival of a single person flying a one-engine plane.

8. Paraphrase the last paragraph of the reading selection at the beginning of this unit.
9. Paraphrase paragraphs 15–17 from the appendix selection.

Discussion/Writing Assignments

The following questions are based on the reading selection at the beginning of this unit and on the Unit II Appendix Selection. Follow your instructor's directions for discussing and/or writing on the topics here. All discussion and written work should be in complete sentences.

187

10. Do you agree that Lindbergh's flight in 1927 was an "incredible feat of courage and flying skill"?
11. From your own experience or from your knowledge of history, discuss some examples of one culture learning from another, as Peary and his team of men learned from the Eskimos. Give some details of what the cultures you mention learned from other cultures.

Unit II Appendix Selection

(1)   Robert E. Peary had found his life's work. He wanted to be an arctic explorer. Someday, he dreamed, he might be the first man to cross Greenland.

(2)   But in 1888, this dream was shattered. The great arctic explorer Fridtjof Nansen had crossed southern Greenland. He had covered a three-hundred-mile route much like the one Peary had hoped to take. For days Peary was angry. Then he stopped feeling sorry for himself. There was still much to do in Greenland, he thought. And he would do it.

(3)   Nansen's journey told nothing of northern Greenland. Suppose it went far to the north? Was it possible to reach the Pole that way? That would be a great scientific feat and a great event in history.

(4)   For nearly three years, Peary tried to set up an expedition. He spoke to scientists, wrote letters to important people, and outlined his plans. Gradually people began to notice his efforts. Top United States scientists got behind him. They agreed to provide money for an expedition to Greenland.

Peary immediately set to work rounding up a (5) team of men. On June 6, 1891, they sailed for Greenland on the *Kite.*

A month later the ship was moving deep into (6) the arctic off Greenland's west coast. Peary was on deck standing next to the wheel. Suddenly a huge cake of ice crashed into the rudder. The wheel swung loose and hit Peary. It snapped two bones above his right ankle.

The leg was set, but Peary was told that he (7) wouldn't be able to walk for months.

"We are not going back," he insisted. "People (8) are depending on me. I can't let them down. It will take more than a broken leg to stop me now."

Two weeks later, the *Kite* sailed into Whale (9) Sound, far up Greenland's western coast. The men started building a winter camp. They put up a wooden house at the foot of the cliffs. To keep busy, Peary directed their work from a chair. For five weeks, he could not take a step. But by mid-August, he got around with crutches. Every day his leg felt a little stronger. He was able to join the men on hunting trips.

In October, the days grew shorter. Cold (10) weather set in, and strong winds whipped down from the north. Ice began to form on the sea, and the first snow fell. By November, the sun had all but disappeared from the sky. In January, the temperature dropped to twenty below. A heavy snowfall half buried the wooden house. Inside, Peary and the men prepared for the trip.

They learned as much as they could from the (11) Eskimos who visited the camp. They built sledges and trained dog teams. Peary designed winter clothes and sleeping bags much like those used by the Eskimos. His men cut, stretched, and dried animal skins. Peary then called in Eskimo women to sew the skins. They made bearskin pants, deerskin mittens, and fur coats with fur hoods. They also spent much time preparing a special food called pemmican. It was a kind of arctic hamburger—chopped walrus, whale fat, spices, and sugar.

(12) Peary's plan was to start moving north as soon as daylight returned in February. The worst part of the winter would be over then. Yet it would still be cold enough to keep the ice firm under the sledges.

(13) From February to May, the men moved supplies by dog team from the base camp to an igloo base. Then, on May 4, 1892, they set out on the great journey.

(14) During the next few days, the temperature dropped sharply. One man's heel became frozen, and Peary had to send him back to camp. The rest of the expedition pushed north. Each day the going grew worse. Icy winds tore across the land. Three of the dogs died. Food supplies began to run low. At last Peary had to send two more men back to camp. He and Eivind Astrup went on alone. They began the great "white march" toward unknown northern Greenland.

(15) For weeks they pushed across the ice. Each day was like the one before—icy winds, flashing glare, long marches. At last they saw low coastal mountains in the distance. They were nearing Greenland's northern coast.

(16) On July 4, they climbed to the edge of a cliff. Spread out below was a bay opening into the Arctic Ocean. Huge icebergs stuck out from its frozen waters. From this high view, Peary could see that Greenland was not a continent, as people thought. It was an island! On the northern shore of that island, Peary planted the American flag.

(17) Peary returned to the United States in the fall of 1892. Newspaper stories of his white march across Greenland thrilled millions of Americans. Scientists of many lands praised him. His maps showed that he had crossed Greenland one thousand miles north of Nansen's route. On a later expedition, he succeeded in reaching the North

Pole. For his determination and courage, many honors were given him. One was especially fitting. The northernmost land region of the world, in northern Greenland, was named for him: Peary Land.

Excerpt from NORTH POLE by Tony Simon. (Garden City, N.Y.: Doubleday, 1961). Copyright © 1961 by Doubleday & Company, Inc. Reprinted by permission of the publisher.

To check your comprehension, answer the following questions:

1. What was Robert E. Peary's dream?
2. How was Peary's plan changed after Fridtjof Nansen crossed southern Greenland?
3. In what year did Peary sail for Greenland?
4. Explain the accident that happened to Peary a month after he set sail.
5. What was the great "white march"?
6. What did Peary find out about Greenland when he got to its northern coast?

Unit III

Spelling

An effective way to review or learn spelling skills is to make sure you understand the sound system of the English language. The word **phonics** refers to the relationship of letters and sounds in a language. Our sound system, which is fairly simple and straightforward, is the basis of our spelling rules.

A knowledge of phonics helps us make general observations about the spelling of certain words in English. These observations are then translated into spelling rules. For example, notice the spelling pattern in the following words in relation to how they are pronounced:

cap	cape	hop	hope
rod	rode	not	note
dim	dime	us	use
cut	cute	tub	tube

It seems that the vowel in a one-syllable word is pronounced as a short vowel when the word ends in a consonant. But when a silent *e* is added to these words, the first vowel is pronounced as a long vowel. From these observations, we might derive a rule: a silent *e* at the end of a one-syllable word makes the previous vowel long.

As you will see, spelling in our language is not as mysterious as you might think. It follows certain rules, explained in this unit, that will help you see some standard patterns in English words.

Before you begin this unit, read the following selection about remembering and forgetting. Look closely at the way specific words work to get the author's message across. Various exercises in this unit will ask you to return to this passage to find examples of certain spelling rules you will be studying.

Remembering is closely linked to learning. (1)
People need more than the ability to learn swiftly and well. They must be able to remember what they learn.

Psychologists have tried to explain how (2)
people remember and why they forget many of the things they learn. No one has yet found all the answers, but there are several theories to explain remembering and forgetting.

It is believed that, when a person learns (3)
something, a physical change of some kind takes place. A trace, or pattern, is left in the brain. According to one theory, memories or the traces memory may leave in the brain simply fade away in the course of time. Thus, things learned long ago are forgotten before things learned more recently. This is largely true, but there are enough exceptions to make scientists look for further explanations of forgetting. Old people, for example, often remember clearly events of their childhood, but they are unable to remember things they did only a few hours earlier.

According to another theory, memories of (4)
different things sometimes interfere with one another. When this happens, one displaces the other from memory. Something that you have just learned may cause you to forget something you already knew. Or something you have already learned may prevent you from learning and remembering something new.

The way you felt about a particular experience (5)
may also determine whether you remember it or forget it. In general, people are apt to forget things

193

that are unpleasant or upsetting and remember things that are pleasant.

(6)   With some effort on your part, it may be possible to improve your ability to remember. In trying to recall a simple thing like a name or a word, it often helps to stop trying to remember and to think of something else. The forgotten name or word may pop up in your memory. Or you may recall a name that is not the one you are trying to remember but resembles it in some way. It may start with the same sound as the correct word, or it may rhyme with it. Looking at different features of the incorrect word may help you recall the correct one.

(7)   In order to remember something you are studying, it helps to go over the material a number of times, even after you have mastered it. This is called overlearning. (You must be careful, though, to go over the material correctly each time. You do not want to repeat and learn a mistake.)

(8)   In studying to understand and remember, it is important for the learner to be active. This does not mean that he must move around the room. But he must be awake and alert, and he must pay close attention to the film or demonstration he is watching, the book he is reading, or the lecture to which he is listening.

(9)   Students have many methods for getting more out of study. They may outline a chapter in a textbook as they read it or underline key passages (if they own the book). When they listen to a lecture, they may take notes so that they learn and remember what they are hearing.

(10)   Sometimes students are even advised to go through special routines to help them retain what they study. One of these routines is called the **SQ3R method.** "S" stands for surveying, or skimming, the material to see what is covered and to look for important topics. "Q" stands for questions that the student is advised to make up for each heading or topic. "3R" stands for reading,

reciting, and reviewing. This means reading through the material to find answers for the questions that have been made up. Reciting means stopping every so often and, without looking at the book, trying to recall the material that has been covered. The third "R," reviewing, means going over the material once it has been learned. Rereading and reciting may both be part of reviewing.

Students sometimes use another method to improve their memory of subjects they are studying. They invent categories into which they place the material they must learn. In studying the French Revolution, a student might invent such categories as "causes," "major events," "important figures," and "results." (11)

People also help themselves remember facts by inventing special aids to memory, called **mnemonics** (from the Greek word for memory). If you wanted to memorize the names of the early presidents of the United States (Washington, Adams, Jefferson, Madison, Monroe, Adams, Jackson, and Van Buren), you might make up a saying like this: "When a just man makes a just vow." You would then remember the names, because the first letter of each word in the sentence stands for a president. (12)

Ernest Z. Rothkopf, "Learning: Remembering and Forgetting." From THE NEW BOOK OF KNOWLEDGE, vol. 11, 1979, © Grolier Incorporated. (Danbury, Conn.: Grolier, 1979.) Pp. 105–106. Reprinted by permission of the publisher.

23   Syllables

Being able to break words into **syllables** can help you in two ways: (1) it can help you sound out words when reading so that you can pronounce them and perhaps figure out their meanings, syllable by syllable; and (2) it can help you improve your spelling skills because you will be able to break words into small parts.

The basic terms you need to know in order to understand this chapter are the following:

Vowel: *a, e, i, o, u,* and *y* when it is pronounced like *i* (as in *dry*) or *e* (as in *happy*)

Vowel sound: a single vowel or a combination of vowels that makes only *one* sound (like *au, ou,* and *ie*)

Consonant: all the other letters in the alphabet, including *y* in such words as *yellow, yet, yesterday*

23A Number of Syllables in a Word

Basically, the number of syllables in a word depends on the number of vowel sounds (not just the number of vowels) in the word. Although the following words contain several consonant sounds, they consist of only one vowel sound and, therefore, have only one syllable. The vowel sounds are italicized here:

*a*te	sch*oo*l	c*ou*gh
m*ea*t	t*ou*ch	r*ea*ch
t*ie*	ch*ea*t	f*ee*t

Practice 23–1 List the vowel sounds in the following words.

1. crate
2. vein
3. cold
4. sin
5. yes
6. pain
7. scale
8. food
9. pose
10. guess
11. faint
12. best
13. town
14. find
15. yell
16. coat
17. front
18. seen
19. put
20. hand

Practice 23–2 By counting the vowel sounds in the following words, determine the number of syllables in each word.

1. parasite	4. today	7. fascinating
2. create	5. rebuild	8. balance
3. globe	6. transfer	9. castle

23B Dividing Words

In a dictionary, **syllable divisions** in a word are usually marked by dots within its alphabetical listing (dy •nam •ic). But some guidelines can help you learn how to divide words yourself.

When a single consonant follows the first vowel sound, the word is divided after the first vowel sound.

> Examples: fi •nish, ca •mel, e •lect, de •vice

When two consonants follow the first vowel sound in a word, the word is divided between the two consonants.

> Examples: for •mal, pas •sion, sup •port, con •duct

When the first vowel sound of a word is followed by two consonants that make a single sound, the word is divided after the vowel sound.

> Examples: fra •grance, se •cret, de •grade, a •gree

Review

A. The number of syllables in a word depends on the number of vowel sounds in the word.

B. Three general rules can help you divide words into syllables.

Review Practice 23–1 According to the guidelines in this chapter, divide the following words into syllables. Record the number of syllables in each word before you divide it.

1. federal
2. animation
3. candidate
4. famous
5. winner
6. courtesy
7. benefit
8. animalistic
9. carnival
10. hatred
11. mastery
12. carbonated
13. college
14. shepherd
15. quarterback

Review Practice 23–2 According to the guidelines in this chapter, divide into syllables the difficult words from the unit reading selection listed on page 217. Record the number of syllables in each word before you divide it.

24   Stress in Words

Every word in the English language has one main **accent** or main **stress.** Finding the main stress in a word can help you pronounce the word, and pronouncing the word correctly can help you spell the word properly.

A dictionary shows where the main stress comes in any word, but some general guidelines can help you figure it out on your own.

When two identical consonants follow the first vowel sound in a word, the main accent falls on the first syllable.

Examples: fal′ lacy, ac′ cent, pat′ tern, bat′ tle

If a word contains *ck* or ends in a consonant followed by *-le,* the main accent falls on the first syllable.

Examples: jack′ et, buck′ et, ca′ ble, scram′ ble

If a word contains a final *-e* or two vowels in the last syllable, the main accent falls on the last syllable.

Examples: pro ceed', re frain', ex pose', re solve'

In words ending with the suffixes *-ial, -ic, -ical, -ion, -ious, -ty,* the main accent falls on the preceding sylla-ble.

Examples: fan tas' tic, com bi na' tion, op por tu' ni ty,
glo' ri ous, com' i cal, in dus' tri al

Some words of more than one syllable have different pronunciations when they serve as different parts of speech.

Nouns: con' duct, pro' test, re' search
Verbs: con duct', pro test', re search'

Review

A. Every word in English has one main accent or main stress.
B. Five rules can help you determine where the main ac-cent of a word falls.

Review Practice 24–1 By following the guidelines in this chapter, determine where the main accent belongs in each of the following words.

1. persuasion	6. aggravate	11. impose
2. arrogance	7. racket	12. succeed
3. superficial	8. ticket	13. curious
4. accent	9. discrete	14. special
5. billion	10. humble	15. assume

Review Practice 24–2 By following the guidelines in this chapter, determine where the main accent belongs in each of the difficult words from the unit reading selection listed on page 217.

25 Hyphens

A **hyphen** is most frequently used to connect parts of compound words. A dictionary can usually help you determine whether or not a compound word requires a hyphen. The following examples show that some words need a hyphen and others do not.

Right: one-way, single-handed, sure-footed
Right: water system, spotlight, toothpaste

25A Uses of Hyphens

Three general principles regulate the use of the hyphen.
A hyphen is placed between two or more words when they serve as a single modifier before a noun.

Example: the well-liked track star

A hyphen is used in writing compound numbers from twenty-one through ninety-nine.

Examples: thirty-two, eighty-four, seventy-three

A hyphen signals the continuation of a word on the next line. It can divide a word only at the end of a syllable.

Examples: At the end of the day, the clerk was unmis-
takably sarcastic.

25B Misuses of Hyphens

Two errors in using the hyphen are common. The following rules are meant to help you avoid these faults.

A hyphen is not used when a compound modifier appears after a noun.

Example: The track star was *well liked.*

A hyphen is not used when the first word of a compound modifier ends in *-ly.*

Example: The *poorly written* exam did not count.

Note that the hyphen is perhaps the least stable feature of the English language. Typically, two words that are often paired gradually come to be hyphenated *(basket-ball, air-port);* then the hyphen disappears altogether *(basketball, airport).* So if you have any doubt about whether a compound word should be spelled as two words, one word, or a hyphenated word, consult a dictionary.

Review

A. Hyphens are used to connect parts of compound words.
B. A dictionary can usually help you determine whether or not a compound word contains a hyphen.
C. Five rules can help you use the hyphen properly.

Review Practice 25–1 Rewrite the following sentences, adding hyphens where necessary by following the guidelines in this chapter.
1. They are both single minded people.
2. At age twenty four, she ran for the board of directors of the local junior college.
3. His well spent hours paid off on the final exam.
4. Ninety four people signed up for the long awaited classes in photography.
5. Can I trust you to represent the group's thoughts at the gathering tomorrow night?

Review Practice 25–2 Find the hyphens in the reading selection at the beginning of this unit, and, applying the rules in this chapter, explain why they are used.

---

26   Spelling Rules

Spelling rules are derived from our English phonic system, the sound system of the language. In fact, pronunciation and spelling are directly related. Therefore, if you do not pronounce all the syllables in a word, you will be likely to misspell the word.

Some spelling rules are included here, with examples, so you can see each rule in operation. The basic terms you need to know to understand this chapter include the following:

Root: a base to which prefixes and suffixes can be added
Prefix: a letter or syllable added to the beginning of a word to form a new word
Suffix: a letter or syllable added to the end of a word to form a new word

26A   Spelling Roots

Some of the most difficult spelling rules have to do with the vowel sounds in our language. The following rules explain how certain vowel sounds are spelled. See Chapter 23 for definitions of **vowel, vowel sound,** and **consonant.**

A silent *e* at the end of a one-syllable word makes the previous vowel long.

Examples: tap   tape
            cut   cute
            hat   hate

Ordinarily, *ie* is used to spell the *e* sound.

Examples: achieve   retrieve
            relief   believe

Exceptions: seize   weird
            either   neither
            protein   caffeine
            codeine   sheik

Usually, *ei* is used after *c* to spell the *e* sound.

Examples: receive   receipt
            deceive   conceive

Exceptions: Sometimes, *ei* spells the *a* sound, as in *freight,*
            weight, neighbor.

A traditional jingle that covers most of the examples in these last two rules goes like this:

I before *e*
Except after *c*
Or when sounded like *ay,*
As in *neighbor* and *weigh.*

Practice 26–1 In the reading selection at the beginning of this unit, list one example of each of the first two rules.
Practice 26–2 According to the rules in 26A, list any long vowels in the following words.

1. rape   5. flaw   9. pine
2. make   6. ate   10. bat
3. mute   7. toe
4. grid   8. pose

Practice 26–3 Rewrite the following words, filling in *ie* or *ei* according to the rules in 26A.

1. rec___pt   4. w___gh   7. conc___t
2. ___ther   5. r___gn   8. n___ce
3. misch___f   6. rel___f   9. kerch___f

203

26B   Prefixes

The following rule can help you add syllables (called **prefixes**) to the front of words.

When a prefix is added to a word, no changes are made in either part of the word.

Examples: dis + similar   = dissimilar
           under + rated   = underrated
           mis + spell   = misspell
           un + natural   = unnatural
           dis + appear   = disappear
           un + imaginable = unimaginable

Practice 26–4 For the rule about adding prefixes, make up two words that show how it works.

Practice 26–5 According to the rule in 26B, rewrite the following words, adding the prefixes indicated here.

1. un + natural
2. dis + associate
3. un + imaginative
4. ir + regular
5. co + operate
6. dis + satisfy

26C   Suffixes

A few common problems exist when we add **suffixes** to roots. They involve plurals, doubled letters, and roots ending in vowels. The following rules explain how to avoid these problems when adding suffixes.

26C(1) Plurals

The most regular way to form plurals is to add an -*s* to the singular form of a word. The following rules show how most plural forms are based on this fundamental principle, with slight variations.

Most singular words form their plurals by adding -s. Never add an apostrophe to make a plural; apostrophes are used only for contractions and possessive forms.

Examples: book   books
          magazine   magazines
          eye   eyes
          lamp   lamps

Singular words ending in -s, -sh, -ch, -x, and -z form their plurals by adding -es.

Examples: bus   buses
          wish   wishes
          church   churches
          box   boxes
          topaz   topazes

When a vowel comes before a final -y in a singular noun, the word forms its plural by adding -s.

Examples: monkey   monkeys
          play   plays
          key   keys

When a consonant comes before a final -y in a singular noun, the word forms its plural by changing the y to i and adding -es.

Examples: army   armies
          lady   ladies
          body   bodies

The singular form of a noun ending in -f or -fe forms its plural by dropping the -f or -fe and adding -ves.

Examples: self   selves
          leaf   leaves
          life   lives

205

An -*s* is usually added to the main word of a hyphenated word to make it plural.

Examples: brother-in-law   brothers-in-law
           passer-by   passers-by
           attorney-at-law   attorneys-at-law

Most singular words that end in -*o* form their plurals by adding -*es*, but some add only -*s*. If you are unsure about which ending to use, a dictionary can help you determine whether a particular word takes -*es* or -*s*.

Examples: veto   vetoes
           mosquito   mosquitoes
           buffalo   buffaloes
           volcano   volcanoes
           silo   silos
           cameo   cameos
           radio   radios
           dynamo   dynamos

Some singular nouns require no changes to form their plurals.

Examples: deer   deer
           sheep   sheep
           shrimp   shrimp
           fish   fish

Some plural spellings do not follow these rules but make irregular changes to form their plurals.

Examples: man   men
           woman   women
           child   children
           mouse   mice
           ox   oxen
           tooth   teeth

Practice 26–6 In the reading selection at the beginning of this unit, list the plural forms.

Practice 26–7 According to the rules in 26C(1), write the plurals of the following words.

1. flower	8. attorney-at-law	15. goose
2. craze	9. potato	16. series
3. deer	10. radio	17. library
4. mouse	11. sister-in-law	18. elf
5. match	12. life	19. class
6. moose	13. childhood	20. plant
7. tomato	14. tax	21. watch

26C(2) Doubled Letters

Doubling letters means repeating the same letter in a word. The following rules explain when to double letters before suffixes.

When a word consists of one syllable ending in one consonant after one vowel, the last letter in the word is doubled before a suffix beginning with a vowel.

Examples:	fit	fittest
	dim	dimmest
	strip	stripping

When a word has more than one syllable and ends in an accented syllable with a single consonant and vowel before it, the consonant is doubled before a suffix beginning with a vowel.

Examples:	begín	beginning
	commít	committed
	forgót	forgotten
	occúr	occurred

When a word has more than one syllable and ends in an unaccented syllable with a single consonant and vowel before it, the consonant is not doubled before a suffix beginning with a vowel.

Examples: cáncel   canceled
           bénefit   benefiting
           prófit   profited
           stámmer   stammering

Exceptions: This rule applies most of the time, but *canceled, traveler,* and *kidnaper* are sometimes spelled *cancelled, traveller,* and *kidnapper.* However, the single-consonant spelling is preferred.

   When the last letter of a root and the first letter of a suffix are the same, both letters are written.

Examples: tail + less   = tailless
           partial + ly   = partially
           sudden + ness = suddenness

Practice 26–8 According to the rules in 26C(2), rewrite the following words, adding the endings indicated here. Double the consonant before the ending if necessary.
1. snap__ed   4. fat__est   7. hit__ing
2. grip__ing   5. jump__ing   8. harsh__ness
3. swim__ing   6. hid__en   9. cut__ing

Practice 26–9 According to the rules in 26C(2), rewrite the following words, adding the endings indicated here. Double the consonant before the ending if necessary.
1. occur__ed   6. equal__ed
2. forfeit__ed   7. utter__ance
3. offer__ed   8. consider__ing
4. develop__ed   9. disturb__ance
5. forget__ing   10. begin__ing

Practice 26–10 According to the rules in 26C(2), rewrite the following words, adding the endings indicated here.
1. head + less   4. open + ness
2. barren + ness   5. mental + ly
3. natural + ly   6. final + ly

26C(3) Roots Ending in Vowels

The following rules explain how suffixes are added to roots ending in vowels.

When a word ends in *-y* and the letter before the *-y* is a consonant, the *y* is changed to *i* before a suffix beginning with a vowel—but not before the *-ing* ending.

Examples:
cry	cried
cry	crying
noisy	noisiest
study	studying

In general, the final *-e* of a word is kept before a suffix beginning with a consonant, such as *-ment*, *-ness*, *-ly*, *-less*, and *-ful*.

Examples:
arrange	arrangement
humane	humaneness
sincere	sincerely
care	carefully

Exceptions:
true	truly
argue	argument
judge	judgment

The final silent *-e* is dropped before a suffix beginning with a vowel.

Examples:
dine	dining
retire	retiring
desire	desirable
mine	mined

Practice 26–11 In the reading selection at the beginning of this unit, find all the examples of suffixes added to roots ending in vowels.

Practice 26–12 Rewrite the following words, according to the rules in 26C(3), adding the endings indicated here.

1. beauty + ful   4. phony + ly   7. fly + er
2. fry + ed   5. fly + s   8. funny + er
3. phony + ness   6. say + s   9. sunny + er

Practice 26–13 According to the rules in 26C(3), rewrite the following words, adding the endings indicated here.

1. fine + ly   4. harm + ful   7. confine + ed
2. sample + ing   5. care + less   8. compare + able
3. achieve + ment   6. regret + able 9. trample + ing

Review

A. Our spelling rules are derived from our English phonic system.
B. The spelling rules in this chapter are grouped as follows: spelling roots, adding prefixes, and adding suffixes.

Review Practice 26–1 According to the spelling rules in Chapter 26, identify any spelling mistakes you find in the following paragraph.

Moondale and the surrounding citys had suffered through hurricanes before, but none had been as serious as this one. The lifes of the inhabitantes had been in trouble in the past, and by this time many fictiones had been started about the hexs that were on these principalitys. On this particular day, the passer-bies who had not yet found shelter were frantic in their actions and expressions. All radioes were turned up full-blast so that the announcer on the emergency station could be heard for blocks. In basments toothes chattered, and the childrens cryed aloud. Though sometimes dimer than at other times, the messages concerning the danger of the inhabitantes were clearly transmited through the radio waves. Begining at noon that day, all busyness had stoped and people began puting resources designed for emergencys to work. Some unecessary activitys were caused by excessive nerveous energy. Soon, there were roofs full of debri throughout the area, and the wind was striping the buildings of their walls and foundations. Branches were hurled across entire blockes as the citys gradualy tumbled to the ground and the people sought refuge on the ege of the next town. Doors flew off their hinges as the violent whirlwinds attacked their marks. Parents bodyly tryed to retreive their childrens and seize them from the oncomeing holocaust. The instincts of the parents were absolutely correct when they sealled their childrens into rooms and bared them from further activitys. This time, the storm past over the area without takeing any lifes. The people appeared—almost gracfully—from their hideing places. But they have never forgoten the drudgery and tragedys that destroyed their solitude at the end of the summer that year.

Review Practice 26–2 Notice how hard it is to read a passage containing multiple spelling errors. Correct the spelling errors you found in Review Practice 26–1 by rewriting the paragraph with corrections. Above each word that you change, indicate whether the rule applies to the root, prefix, or suffix of the word.

27 Spelling Problems

The words in our language that do not adhere to any of the spelling rules discussed in Chapter 26 must be considered by themselves. One way to broaden your vocabulary and also to avoid looking up certain common words in the dictionary is to develop your own way of remembering them. In other words, develop your associations with words that cause you trouble.

A number of troublesome words and some associations (or mnemonic devices) that people have made to remember the spellings of these words are listed here. Most of these associations have been with us for quite a while. But it is worthwhile to develop associations based on your own experience so that you can remember words that are troublesome to you. It does not matter whether your memory devices seem absurd to others, as long as they help you spell difficult words.

A good technique for eliminating spelling errors from your writing is to keep a list of all the words you misspell on papers you write in college. Spell the words correctly on your list and develop an association for each word; review the list as often as possible. (Then, you can develop this into a vocabulary list, as suggested in Unit IV—see page 274.) With this method, you are unlikely to misspell the same word twice.

Word Associations

across	Across has *a cross* in it.
adviser	Even an adviser may *err*.
athlete	An athlete has as many *e*'s as arms (not ath*e*lete).
bargain	Bargain has a *gain* in it.
buses	Buses have many *uses*.
calendar	Think of calendar *art*.
capitol	A capitol is a building with a dome, round like an *o*.
compliment	Compliments flatter the ego—or the *I*.
costumes	Costumes *cost* money.
courtesy	Courtesy is important when *court*ing.
definite	Definite comes from *finite*.
desert	A desert is barren and has only one *s*.
dessert	Dessert has *two s's*, as in strawberry shortcake.
embarrass	Embarrass has *two r's* and *two s's*.
February	February asks *R U* ready for spring.
forty	Forty soldiers held the *fort*.

friend	A friend stays to the *end*.
holiday	Holiday comes from *holy* and therefore has only one *l*.
hypocrisy	Hypocrisy can produce a *crisis*.
imminent	Imminent means something might happen any *min*ute.
occurrence	Occurrence has most of the word *current* in it, as in current event.
peculiar	Look at it this way: *pecu liar*.
principal	The school principal was a *pal* (sometimes).
principle	Principle refers to ru*le* and both end in *le*.
separate	Separate has *a rat* in it.
stationary	Stationary means stay where you *a*re.
stationery	Stationery has an *er* in it, as in pap*er*.
their	Their rhymes with *heir* and has a *the* in it.
there	There has a *here* in it.
tragedy	Tragedy has a *rage* in it.

For your reference, a list of the most commonly misspelled words in the English language is included here.* You might want to mark the words that are especially troublesome for you and then make some personal associations to help you remember how to spell those particular words. Also, in Unit IV on pages 246–258 is a list of words that are often confused with one another.

absence	amateur	appearance
accidentally	among	arctic
accommodate	analysis	argument
accumulate	analyze	arithmetic
acquaintance	annual	ascend
acquitted	apartment	athletic
advice	apparatus	attendance
advise	apparent	balance

*Adapted from Watkins-Dillingham-Martin: PRACTICAL ENGLISH HANDBOOK, 5th edition. Copyright © 1978 by Houghton Mifflin Company. Used by permission. (Boston: Houghton Mifflin, 1978). Pp. 129-131.

battalion
beginning
believe
benefited
boundaries
Britain
business
calendar
candidate
category
cemetery
changeable
changing
choose
chose
coming
commission
committee
comparative
compelled
conceivable
conferred
conscience
conscientious
control
criticize
deferred
definite
description
desperate
dictionary
dining
disappearance
disappoint
disastrous
discipline
dissatisfied
dormitory

eighth
eligible
eliminate
embarrass
eminent
encouraging
environment
equipped
especially
exaggerate
excellence
exhilarate
existence
experience
explanation
familiar
fascinate
February
fiery
foreign
formerly
forty
fourth
frantically
generally
government
grammar
grandeur
grievous
height
heroes
hindrance
hoping
humorous
hypocrisy
hypocrite
immediately
incidentally

incredible
independence
inevitable
intellectual
intelligence
interesting
irresistible
knowledge
laboratory
laid
led
lightning
loneliness
lose
maintenance
maneuver
manufacture
mathematics
may
maybe
miniature
mischievous
mysterious
necessary
Negroes
ninety
noticeable
occasionally
occurred
omitted
opportunity
optimistic
parallel
paralyze
pastime
performance
permissible
perseverance

personnel	recommend	succeed
perspiration	reference	successful
physical	referred	supersede
picnicking	repetition	surprise
possibility	restaurant	studying
practically	rhyme	temperamental
precede	rhythm	tendency
precedence	ridiculous	their
preference	sacrifice	thorough
preferred	sacrilegious	to
prejudice	salary	too
preparation	schedule	tragedy
prevalent	secretary	tries
privilege	seize	truly
probably	separate	tyranny
professor	sergeant	unanimous
pronunciation	severely	undoubtedly
prophecy	shining	until
prophesy	siege	usually
quantity	similar	village
quiet	sophomore	villain
quite	specifically	weather
quizzes	specimen	weird
recede	stationary	whether
receive	stationery	writing
recognize	statue	

Review

A. You should develop memory devices to help you remember words that are difficult for you.
B. Making your own associations with words can help you spell troublesome words correctly.

Review Practice 27–1 Develop and write down your own associations for the following words.

1. a lot	7. conscience	13. misspelling
2. accurate	8. counsel	14. necessary
3. advice	9. its	15. parallel
4. advise	10. it's	16. studying
5. all right	11. loose	17. succeed
6. already	12. lose	18. they're

Review Practice 27–2 Develop and write down your own associations for ten difficult words from the reading selection listed on page 217.

Reading Tasks

Comprehension

To check your comprehension, answer the following questions about the reading selection on remembering and forgetting at the beginning of this unit. Refer to the selection when necessary.

1. What physical change takes place when we learn something?
2. Which events do old people remember best: present events or past events?
3. What happens when memories interfere with one another?
4. Explain three methods for getting more out of your studying.
5. According to this article, what does it mean to be an "active" learner?

For more comprehension exercises, turn to the Unit III Appendix Selection.

The reading selection at the beginning of this unit contains a few difficult words. These words are difficult either to spell or to understand.

remembering	prevent	repeat
psychologists	experience	demonstration
physical	determine	advised
exceptions	unpleasant	categories
explanations	improve	inventing

childhood   resembles   mnemonics
interfere   studying
displaces   overlearning

Roots

As you know from this chapter, **roots** are the bases of all words; every word has a root. Roots have meanings of their own and can also be expanded into other words. If you know the meanings of some roots and can find them in words that are unfamiliar to you, then you might be able to determine the meanings of those unfamiliar words.

6. List the roots of the words listed here. Then, look the roots up in an unabridged (not condensed) dictionary and record the meanings of the roots only.
7. List the roots of the words listed at the end of the appendix selection. Then, look the roots up in an unabridged (not condensed) dictionary and record the meanings of the roots only.

Context Clues

The **context** of a word is the sentence, paragraph, or passage in which the word appears. Sometimes this context contains clues that can help you figure out the meanings of unfamiliar words and phrases. The following examples are from the reading selection at the beginning of this unit.

Comparison clue: *Remembering* is closely linked to learning.
Contrast clue: In general, people are apt to forget things that are *unpleasant* or upsetting and remember things that are pleasant.
Definition clue: In order to remember something you are studying, it helps to go over the material a number of times, even after

	you have mastered it. This is called *overlearning*.
Example clue:	In studying the French Revolution, a student might invent such *categories* as "causes," "major events," "important figures," and "results."

8. For ten words from page 217, list the words or phrases in the reading selection that give you clues to their meanings. Then, record the meanings of those words based on their contexts.

9. For ten words from those at the end of the appendix selection, list the words or phrases in the reading selection that give you clues to their meanings. Then, record the meanings of those words based on their contexts.

Discussion/Writing Assignments

The following questions are based on the reading selection at the beginning of this unit and the Unit III Appendix Selection. Follow your instructor's directions for discussing and/or writing on the topics here. All discussion and written work should be in complete sentences.

10. According to the selection at the beginning of this unit, how are remembering and learning related? Explain your answer in detail.

11. Have you ever used one of the study methods described in the selection at the beginning of this unit? If so, explain how it did or did not help you.

12. What study methods have you learned or developed that are not described in the selection at the beginning of this unit? Describe them in detail.

13. What type of information (numbers, ideas, dates, places, explanations, and the like) do you best remember from the appendix selection? Why do you think you remember this type of information best?

219

Unit III Appendix Selection

Learning and Memory

(1)   Brains can learn different kinds of tasks. Better developed brains can learn more complicated tasks. In the simplest brains, learning is very crude. Humans show the greatest learning abilities. Among all animals, only humans can learn verbal (speaking, writing) behavior.

(2)   *Memory.* How and where does the brain store the information that we call memory? That is an easy question to ask, but very difficult to answer. In the human brain, areas of the cortex appear to be involved. When these areas are excited by a weak electrical current, the person "relives" past experiences. Apparently these electrical stimuli force the brain to reproduce experiences that are stored within it from the past. It is also known that injury to certain areas will result in loss of memory.

(3)   But this does not mean that these are the places in the brain where the information is stored. Nor does it tell us anything about the way information is stored. Some scientists think that memory storage is chemical in nature. That is, they think that individual nerve cells have chemically coded information within them. Other scientists believe that memory is a result of some permanent change in the structure of the nerve—in the dendrites, for example.

. . . .

Research on Brains

(4)   Today scientists in many countries are studying the brain of man and other animals. In recent years electronic equipment has been developed that lets scientists observe the tiny electrical signals produced by nerve cells. These signals provide much important information about the operation of the brain. Other instruments

permit experimenters to use tiny amounts of electricity to stimulate or prevent activity in certain parts of the brain. These methods have been used to trace pathways through the brain, to discover the connections between cells, and to see how signals are sent from one center to another. These experiments also tell us what functions are served by different areas of the brain.

Nevertheless, we have only begun to uncover (5) the basic processes going on within the brain. As more and more of our questions about the brain are answered, the number of unanswered questions becomes larger. The brain is the most complicated of all organs. And it will continue to be a challenge to scientists as long as man wonders about the workings of the living body.

George P. Moore, "Brains, Human." From THE NEW BOOK OF KNOWLEDGE, vol. 2, 1979, © Grolier Incorporated. (Danbury, Conn.: Grolier, 1979.) P. 369. Reprinted by permission of the publisher.

Difficult words in this selection:

complicated	information	operation
simplest	storage	instruments
verbal	chemical	permit
behavior	individual	electricity
memory	scientists	activity
involved	permanent	discover
apparently	equipment	functions
stimuli	observe	uncover
reproduce	produced	processes

To check your comprehension, answer the following:

1. Which animals have verbal skills?
2. How does the brain store information?
3. What kinds of equipment do scientists have for studying the brain?
4. What brain research is going on at present?
5. What is the most complicated organ of a living being?

221

Unit IV

Diction

Diction refers to choice of words. Diction is the words and phrases you choose to make your sentences and paragraphs. Knowing why you select certain words and phrases will help you develop a style of your own. Since style is an individual, creative part of your writing, you should be in control of its development. If you do not control your own words, they have a way of controlling you. This unit offers some suggestions and guidelines you can follow to develop an awareness of your diction and to learn some methods of improving it. The unit begins with an explanation of word choice and moves to a discussion of phrases and sentences.

Before you begin this unit, read the following selection about digging into the past. Look closely at the way particular words and phrases work to get the author's message across. Various exercises in this unit will ask you to return to this passage to find examples of certain rules you will be studying.

(1)   Archaeology, in its short life of about seventy years, has made familiar thousands of years of human history which a hundred years ago were a total blank. But this is not all. The old histories, resting principally on written documents, were largely confined to those events which at every age

writers thought most fit to record—wars, political happenings, the chronicles of kings. The digger may produce more written records, but he also brings to light a mass of objects illustrating the arts and handicrafts of the past, the temples in which men worshiped, the houses in which they lived, the setting in which their lives were spent; he supplies the material for a social history of a sort that was never before possible. Up to the time when Heinrich Schliemann dug at Mycenae, in Greece, and Sir Arthur Evans in the Mediterranean island of Crete, no one guessed that there had been a Minoan civilization. Yet now we can trace the rise and fall of the ancient Minoan power and can see again the splendors of the Palace of Minos. The whole history of Egypt has been recovered by archaeological work and that in astonishing detail; I suppose we know more about ordinary life in Egypt in the fourteenth century before Christ then we do about that of England in the fourteenth century A.D. To the spade we owe our knowledge of the Sumerians and the Hittites, great empires of the Near East whose very existence had been forgotten. It is a fine list of achievements.

Why is Everything Underground?

. . . .

    How does it come about that things get buried (2) and have to be dug up? The articles found in graves were put underground deliberately and have remained there; but how do houses and cities sink below the earth's surface? They do not sink; the earth rises above them, and, though people do not recognize the fact, it is happening all around them every day. Go no farther than London. How many steps does one have to go down to enter the Temple Church? This twelfth-century building stood originally at ground level but is now five feet or so lower. The mosaic pavements of Roman Londinium lie twenty-five to thirty feet below the streets of the modern city. Wherever a place has been continuously occupied the same thing has happened. In old times the street was the natural place for refuse, and the street level gradually rose with accumulated filth; if it was repaved, the new cobbles were laid over the old dirt, at a higher level, and you stepped down into the houses on either side. When a house was pulled down and rebuilt, the site would be partly filled in and the new ground floor set at or above street level.

(3)   In the Near East, the rate of rise is faster. The commonest building material is mud brick, and mud brick walls have to be thick; when they collapse, the amount of debris is considerable. The carting away of rubbish is expensive, so the simplest course is to level the surface of the ruins and build on the top of them. In Syria and in Iraq, every village stands on a mound of its own making, and the ruins of an ancient city may rise a hundred feet above the plain.

How Do You Know Where to Dig?

(4)   There are generally some surface signs to guide the digger. In the Near East, no one could possibly mistake the great mounds or "tells," which rise above the plain to mark the sites of ancient cities. In Mesopotamia, the highest mound will probably conceal the ziggurat, or staged tower, attached to the chief temple; sometimes a low-lying patch will betray the position of the temple itself. The famous Greek historian, Herodotus, visiting Egypt in the fifth century B.C., remarked that the temples there always lay in a hollow; the reason was that while the mud-brick houses of the town were short-lived, the temples, built of stone and kept always in good repair, outlived many generations and remained at the same level throughout. On an Egyptian site, therefore, a square depression ringed about by mounds of crumbling gray brick gives the

excavator an obvious clue. Earthworks, too, are enduring, and the site of a Roman camp in Britain can nearly always be traced by the low grass-clad lines of its ramparts.

Sir Leonard Charles Wooley, "The Archaeologist: His Work and His Rewards." Reprinted by permission from OUR WONDERFUL WORLD: A YOUNG PEOPLE'S ENCYCLOPEDIC ANTHOLOGY, Grolier Incorporated. (Chicago: Spencer Press, 1957.) Pp. 25–26. Reprinted by permission of the publisher.

28   Language

Written and spoken English consist of several levels of **usage.** Just as a social situation often dictates your behavior, so your audience dictates your language. In a job interview, for example, you would use mostly formal and informal English, probably being careful not to use any slang. Later on, when you tell your friends about the interview, you might talk more informally, with or without slang. Your ultimate goal in either situation is to say what you mean as precisely and clearly as possible.

The levels of usage, which will be discussed in this chapter, can be divided into five major categories.

Informal: words or phrases that are appropriate in informal writing and speaking; labeled "informal" or "colloquial" in a dictionary

Formal: words or phrases that are appropriate in formal writing and speaking; listed in a dictionary without usage labels

General: words or phrases that are appropriate in both formal and informal writing and speaking; listed in a dictionary without usage labels

Standard: all general, informal, and formal words or expressions

Nonstandard: words or expressions that are not considered part of the standard English vocabulary;

225

labeled in a dictionary as "archaic,"
"obsolete," "illiterate," "slang,"
"nonstandard," or "substandard"

28A Informal or Colloquial Language

Informal or **colloquial English** consists of words used in everyday speaking and writing. These words are labeled "informal" or "colloquial" in a dictionary and are considered part of our standard English vocabulary.

> Informal: They tried to *pull off* the prank but failed when the dean *got wise* to their plans.
> Informal: She thinks she can *make a go of it.*

Practice 28–1 List any informal or colloquial words or expressions in the following sentences. Consult a dictionary when necessary.
1. I figure he's bound to give out on the eighteenth lap.
2. What did you get away with this time?
3. Things are looking up now.
4. I know you can take it, but why don't you give it to him?
5. They would like to get to know you, but you tend to put people off.

28B Formal Language

Formal English is standard English that is unlabeled in a dictionary. It is used in writing for such purposes as business correspondence, reports, or school assignments, all of which are meant to reach a varied audience. Contractions are not acceptable in formal English. Neither is the indefinite *you* when you mean *one* or *a person* or *people*. The following examples show how the informal sentences from 28A can be rewritten in formal English.

> Informal: They tried to *pull off* the prank but failed when the dean *got wise* to their plans.

Formal: They tried to *perform* the prank but failed when the dean *discovered* their plans.

Informal: She thinks she can *make a go of it.*
Formal: She thinks she can *succeed.*

Practice 28–2 Rewrite the sentences in Practice 28–1, changing to formal English any informal words or expressions that you identified.

28C Slang

Slang words are considered nonstandard and are the most changeable words in English. They vary from year to year, from region to region, and from generation to generation. They are appropriate only when you are speaking and, even then, only when your audience understands the words. Actually, slang words are often colorful and interesting. But they are just as often vague and imprecise, because many slang words have several different meanings (see the list of slang words that follows). Since slang words often arise when a particular group gives new meaning(s) to an old word (such as *bad,* meaning "good" in the late 1970s), slang generally accomplishes very little except to announce that the speaker or writer is a member of a particular group. Formal and informal diction are preferred because they are more precise than slang and communicate to a wider audience. A person does not have to be a member of a group to understand formal or informal diction. Therefore, avoiding slang in your writing is safest unless you are trying to prove a point or to write dialogue.

Some current slang words and expressions include the following:

turn on	dynamite	out of sight
the pits	right on	jazzed

turkey	jive	bummer
boogie	reefer, joint	busted
smashed, stoned,	sharp	rags
wasted	pop, soda	groove
crash	lightweight	man
dude	junkie	mellow out
cool		

Practice 28–3 Add five slang words or expressions of your own to this list of current slang.

Practice 28–4 List any slang words or expressions in the following sentences.

1. Give me five so I can jive on over to Sue's for dinner.
2. Hey, brother, what made you streak across campus when you were wasted?
3. I want to go home and, like, crash.
4. Did you see that dynamite dude who just walked by?
5. You'd better mellow out or you're going to spend the rest of the evening with the other turkeys, you know?

Practice 28–5 Rewrite each sentence in Practice 28–4 in standard written English.

28D   Jargon or Technical Language

Jargon is technical or trade language. Most occupations or professional fields have their own languages, which—like slang—are usually meaningless to anyone outside a special group. For instance, the following sentence could be understood only by people who had studied medicine:

> Jargon: Ten minutes after the bee sting, generalized *pruritus, urticaria,* sneezing, *rhinorrhea, edema,* coughing, and wheezing occurred.

To address an audience that is not trained in medicine or biology, the speaker or writer should rework this statement. Notice the changes when standard English replaces technical language:

> Standard: Ten minutes after the bee sting, *itching, hives,* sneezing, *a runny nose, swelling,* coughing, and wheezing occurred.

The drug subculture has also developed a language of its own.

> Jargon: Where did you *score* that number before you got *busted?*
> Standard: Where did you *get* that *marijuana cigarette* before you were *arrested?*

You might have noticed that most of your college courses have specialized vocabularies, which are also forms of jargon. In fact, most academic subjects, professions, sports, and subcultures have developed their own unique vocabularies or technical languages. The wisest practice is to keep jargon at a minimum no matter how specialized your audience so that you can communicate to a wide range of people. If you must use jargon that your audience is unlikely to understand, you should define it.

Practice 28–6 List five examples of jargon or technical language connected with the following activities or fields. Then use each technical word in a sentence.

1. football
2. nursing
3. art
4. tennis
5. science

28E Regional Language

Regional language consists of words or phrases characteristic of a certain area of the country. These words are usually understood only by the people from that region.

Including these words in your written work is unwise, because someone who is not from your region might not understand you. These regional words or expressions are also called "localisms," "provincialisms," and "dialects." Notice the regionalisms in the following examples.

> Regional: Don't be waiting on me.
> Regional: You may be book read, but you ain't got no sense to go fetch the doctor when need be.
> Regional: My mother she is not home.

Practice 28–7 Rewrite the following sentences in standard written English.
1. I ain't got no desire to die.
2. He's a-scared of frosts.
3. Why you be so late all the time?
4. Pa shore whupped me when I fibbed to the neighbor lady.
5. She hit the dog upside the head.

28F Nonstandard Language

Nonstandard English is labeled in a dictionary as "archaic," "obsolete," "illiterate," "slang," "nonstandard," "substandard." You should avoid this level of language in your writing, because it is usually sloppy and inexact and, therefore, often misread.

> Nonstandard: I *ain't* never heard such a loud group.
> *They's* going home for the holidays.
> Standard: I *have* never heard such a loud group.
> *They are* going home for the holidays.

28G Flowery Language

Flowery language refers to the unnecessary use of fancy (ornate) words or expressions in written English. You should avoid such language because it calls the reader's attention to the words on the page and distracts the reader from the ideas being presented. In addition, it can result in padded sentences, which sound artificial and pompous.

You should not, for example, choose a three-syllable word when a one-syllable word will do. In other words, do not write *utilize* when *use* will do.

Ornate: She *tripped* through the *babbling* brook and the *meandering* hills until she arrived at my *abode*.
Standard: She *walked* through the brook and the hills until she arrived at my *house*.

Euphemisms, which are a delicate but roundabout way of saying something, should also be avoided in your writing. Americans are particularly fond of euphemisms for death and for anything related to sex or bodily functions.

Ornate: She *passed away* and was *laid to rest* within twenty-four hours.
Standard: She *died* and was *buried* within twenty-four hours.

Practice 28–8 Write five examples of flowery language. Then use each example in a sentence.

Review

A. There are five general categories of usage in English: informal, formal, general, standard, and nonstandard.
B. Informal or colloquial English consists of words used in everyday speaking and writing.
C. Formal English is standard English that is used in writing for such purposes as business correspondence, reports, or school assignments, all of which are meant to reach a varied audience.

D. Slang words or expressions are considered nonstandard and are appropriate only when you are speaking.
E. Jargon is technical or trade language that should be kept to a minimum and, if essential, defined.
F. Regional language consists of words or phrases that are characteristic of a certain area of a country; they should not be used in your written work.
G. Nonstandard English, which is labeled in a dictionary "archaic," "obsolete," "illiterate," "slang," "nonstandard," or "substandard," should be avoided.
H. Flowery language, fancy words or expressions, should be avoided in written English.

Review Practice 28–1 Label the following italicized words and expressions "informal," "formal," "slang," "jargon," or "regional."
1. The seashore is *loaded with* shells that are ours *for the taking*.
2. That class was a real *trip,* but I don't feel sure of the new material that the instructor *threw at us*.
3. If you're *fixing* to go out tonight, you'd better *get moving*.
4. I have a strong feeling that my future is going to be *worthwhile*.
5. What do you know about *deictic semantic differences?*
6. Just *keep on trucking* and you just might *make a success of yourself*.
7. His *reaction* was *anticipated* by the participants.
8. He *belayed* the ropes to set sail.
9. I *ain't about* to help you now.
10. It is *only natural* for you to wonder about this *stupid* state of affairs.

Review Practice 28–2 Rewrite the sentences from Review Practice 28–1 in standard written English. Not all sentences require rewriting.

Review Practice 28–3 Develop the following thoughts into complete sentences written in standard English (informal and formal). Avoid slang, jargon, regional language, nonstandard English, and flowery language.

1. my hair
2. the dorm that I live in
3. Dad's energy level
4. the band that I play in
5. my grandmother's house
6. the American stories of cowboys and Indians
7. driving a truck
8. my roommate's problems in chemistry
9. as soon as I get out of class
10. Saturday nights

Review Practice 28–4 Compose a letter of inquiry according to the following skeleton. Fill in the blanks with as many words of explanation as you like, concentrating on the use of formal written English.

Your address
City, State

Date

Name of business or firm
Address
City, State

Dear _____:

    I am writing to inquire about your job opening in __
_____.

    I would like to apply for this position on the basis of my qualifications, which are _____
_____.

    In addition, the following people are willing to write you on my behalf, recommending my work to you: _____
_____.

Thank you for your _____.

                       Sincerely,

                       Your name

Review Practice 28–5 Why is the reading selection at the beginning of this unit a good example of standard written English? Does it contain slang, jargon, or regional language? Explain your answer by applying what you learned about usage in this chapter to certain words, phrases, and sentences in the selection.

29   Exactness

This chapter discusses how to choose the exact word or words to express a certain thought. Its goal is to help you be as precise as possible in your use of language. Because there are several considerations in the choice of a word, it is often difficult to find the word you want. This chapter explains each consideration separately.

29A Good and Bad Usage

Certain words that have crept into our language are currently considered incorrect. The following examples show some of the most common of these words in sentences:

Wrong: I *ain't* ready to take the test.
Right: I *am not* ready to take the test.

Wrong: *Most* everyone you know will be at the party
              Saturday night.

Right: *Almost* everyone you know will be at the party Saturday night.

Wrong: We have *alot* of time left.
Right: We have *a lot* of time left.

Wrong: *Being as (how)* he's sick in bed, he can't come to the movie with us.
Right: *Because* he's sick in bed, he can't come to the movie with us.

Wrong: They *should of* called before they dropped by.
Right: They *should have* called before they dropped by.

Wrong: Your answer is *different than* mine.
Right: Your answer is *different from* mine.

Wrong: The athlete was *enthused* about his scholarship.
Right: The athlete was *enthusiastic* about his scholarship.

Wrong: *Everywheres* I look, I see crime.
Right: *Everywhere* I look, I see crime.

Wrong: He bought *hisself* a new sweater.
Right: He bought *himself* a new sweater.

Wrong: Your grades are *inferior than* mine.
Right: Your grades are *inferior to* mine.

Wrong: *Irregardless* of the situation, I want to help.
Right: *Regardless* of the situation, I want to help.

Wrong: They must be *sort of* tired.
Right: They must be *somewhat* tired.

Wrong: There is hope for me *somewheres*.
Right: There is hope for me *somewhere*.

Wrong: Jeff's basketball is *superior than* mine.
Right: Jeff's basketball is *superior to* mine.

235

Wrong: You were *suppose* to meet me at noon.
Right: You were *supposed* to meet me at noon.

Wrong: As far as I'm concerned, they can fare for
        theirselves.
Right: As far as I'm concerned, they can fare for
        themselves.

Wrong: He *use* to jog.
Right: He *used* to jog.

Wrong: I need to know *where* you're *at.*
Right: I need to know *where* you are.

Practice 29–1 After consulting a dictionary to check any words in this chapter that are unfamiliar to you, choose one of the two words or phrases to fill the blank in each of the following sentences.

1. You <u>(should of, should have)</u> seen *Cabaret.*
2. <u>(A lot, Alot)</u> of people used to call General Patton "Old Blood and Guts."
3. I can't attend the party <u>(because, being as)</u> I will be out of town.
4. <u>(Where at, Where)</u> is the aspirin?
5. Julio is <u>(different than, different from)</u> Julia.
6. My friends are <u>(sort of, somewhat)</u> demanding.
7. <u>(Most, Almost)</u> everyone is invited to Melvin's Halloween party.
8. I feel as if my work follows me <u>(everywheres, everywhere)</u>.
9. Ted has to make this decision for <u>(hisself, himself)</u>.
10. <u>(Somewhere, Somewheres)</u> there's a place for us.
11. Your grades are <u>(superior than, superior to)</u> mine.
12. Some people get really <u>(enthused, enthusiastic)</u> about grammar.

29B   Denotation and Connotation

Most words in English have both a **denotation** (*de* [of] + *nota* [note] + *-ion* [process] = the process of noting the meaning of a word) and a **connotation** (*com* [together with] + *nota* [note] + *-ion* [process] = the process of adding notes or meanings to a word). It is important to take both of these levels of meaning into consideration when you are choosing words in your written work.

The denotation of a word is its actual meaning as defined in the dictionary.

Face:	the front part of the head, including the eyes, cheeks, nose, mouth, forehead, and chin
Car:	a vehicle that moves on wheels
Work:	exertion of strength or faculties to accomplish something
Parent:	one who brings forth offspring

Practice 29–2 Write the denotations, or the dictionary definitions, of five words from the list on page 221 that is taken from the selection at the beginning of this unit.

Practice 29–3 Write the denotations of the following words. Then use each in a sentence.

1. yellow
2. institution
3. rational
4. court
5. astrology
6. liberal
7. progress
8. religion
9. motorcycle
10. dog

The connotation of a word is what it suggests or implies in addition to its standard dictionary definition. The connotation of a word includes emotions and feelings that most people associate with the word.

Face:	looks, appearance
Car:	mobility, prestige
Work:	discipline, unemployment
Parent:	conflict, misunderstanding, love

237

Some words that have similar dictionary definitions have different connotations, to which you should give special attention. All the following words mean *overweight*, but each has a slightly different connotation:

fat	heavy	gross
overweight	plump	chunky
obese	chubby	

All the following words mean *laugh*, but each has a slightly different connotation:

laugh	snicker	chuckle
cackle	twitter	snigger
giggle	guffaw	

Practice 29–4 Write the connotations, or the suggested meanings, of the five words you chose in Practice 29–2.

Practice 29–5 Write the connotations of the words in Practice 29–3.

Practice 29–6 Arrange the following words from most positive connotation to least positive connotation. Then, use each word in a sentence. Consult a dictionary when necessary.

unique	unheard of
exclusive	different
singular	peculiar
strange	weird
exceptional	odd

Practice 29–7 Arrange the following words from most negative connotation to least negative connotation. Then, use each word in a sentence. Consult a dictionary when necessary.

obscene	indelicate	vulgar
immoral	indecent	dirty
filthy	improper	bawdy

29C   General and Specific Words

The more specific (particular, definite, precise) your choice of words, the better your writing will be, because you will communicate exactly what you mean and will run very little risk of being misread. Specific references are easier to understand, more precise, and usually more vivid than general words (words that name an entire group or class).

> General: The *food* tastes *good.*
> Specific: The *vegetables* taste *fresh.*
> More
> Specific: The *green beans* taste *home grown.*

The words in your writing should be as specific as the words in the right-hand column.

General	Specific	More Specific
garment	clothing	jacket
food	meat	hamburger
education	course	physics

Practice 29–8 List the ten most specific words in the reading selection at the beginning of this unit.

Practice 29–9 In the following sentences, replace the italicized general words or phrases with specific words or phrases.

1. *Sports* help me *build my body.*
2. *Fashions* are changing for both men and women.
3. *My job* keeps me *busy.*
4. The roof is *sagging.*
5. *Music relaxes* me.

Practice 29–10 Rewrite the following general statements, developing them by adding specific details to each.

> Example: Pollution is a problem today.
> Details: *Air* pollution is a *major industrial* problem today, *especially on the West Coast.*

239

1. TV can be fun.
2. Things grow better in our backyard than in yours.
3. I like some sports.
4. My astrological sign is revealing.
5. Wine is good with food.

29D Concrete and Abstract Words

Concrete words name things that can be touched, seen, tasted, smelled, or heard *(car, person, hair, desk, book, jeans)*. Concrete words bring clear images to a reader's mind. **Abstract words** name ideas and concepts that are not related to material things *(love, hate, understanding, democracy, courtesy, insanity)*. Abstract words do not bring a clear image to a reader's mind, because they do not appeal to any of the five senses.

Using more concrete words than abstract will make your writing exact and vivid. When you do include abstract words, you should be sure to explain them with concrete examples.

> Abstract: Their *exchange of feelings* took place on December 30.
> Concrete: Their *wedding* took place on December 30.

Practice 29–11 List ten concrete words in the reading selection at the beginning of this unit.

Practice 29–12 In the following passage, identify each of the italicized words as "abstract" or "concrete."

> Our *trip* was fairly *successful* in that we accomplished what we set out to do. I dreamed of this day for a long time, and my *dream* finally came true. *Lake Anderson* in British Columbia is beautiful this *time* of year, and we had great *fun* with the *canoes*, the *motor boats*, and the *water skis* that were available at the *dock*. The *sun* shone clearly every

morning when we got up, and the days were warm and balmy. The *natural sights* in the surrounding area were breathtaking—especially the *waterfalls* that poured into the *lake*. Our *days* were spent basking in *nature*. Returning *home* was a physical and mental *shock*.

Practice 29–13 Rewrite the following abstract statements, developing them by adding concrete explanations to each.

Example: I used to feel inferior.
Concrete: I used to feel inferior *to my lab partner in chemistry until he spilled a beaker of food coloring on his shoe.*

1. I like to dream.
2. Basketball makes me feel free.
3. He says classical music is a way for him to escape.
4. It takes time to be sensitive to others.
5. He is a patient person.

29E Figurative Language

A **figure of speech** is a word or series of words used in an imaginative—rather than a literal (matter-of-fact)—way. Figurative language is valuable in writing because it focuses on concrete explanations and exact relationships between things. Two main types of figurative language are **similes** and **metaphors.** Each is effective in written English when supplying an explanation.

29E(1) Simile

A simile is a comparison between two unlike things that is introduced by *like* or *as.*

Simile: His bald head was *as bare as a snowless ski slope.*

241

29E(2) Metaphor

A metaphor is an implied comparison between two things that is not introduced by *like* or *as*.

Metaphor: Life is *a tale told by a madman.*

Practice 29–14 Make up one simile and one metaphor from the contents of the article at the beginning of this unit by completing the following statements:

Simile: Finding civilizations underground must be *like*

_____

_____ .

Metaphor: Archaeologists look underground for the past
             because the past is _____

_____ .

Practice 29–15 Rewrite the following sentences, completing each by using a vivid figure of speech: a simile or metaphor.

1. These capsules look as if <u>(simile)</u>.
2. I felt as content as <u>(simile)</u>.
3. You are <u>(metaphor)</u>.
4. The tape recorder looks as if <u>(simile)</u>.
5. The novel is as funny as <u>(simile)</u>.

Practice 29–16 Find the similes and metaphors in the paragraph here, and explain how they work.

> Now here comes the sad part of the story, at least my family says it's sad, but I don't think it's so sad myself. The store's pretty empty, it being Thursday afternoon, so there was nothing much to do except lean on the register and wait for the girls to show up again. The whole store was like a pinball machine, and I didn't know which tunnel they'd come out of. After a while, they come around out of the far aisle, around the light bulbs, records at discount of the Caribbean Six or Tony

Martin Sings or some such gunk you wonder they
waste the wax on, sixpacks of candy bars, and
plastic toys done up in cellophane that fall apart
when a kid looks at them anyway. Around they
come, Queenie still leading the way and holding a
little gray jar in her hand. Slots Three through
Seven are unmanned, and I could see her
wondering between Stokes and me, but Stokesie
with his usual luck draws an old party in baggy
gray pants who stumbles up with four giant cans
of pineapple juice (what do these bums *do* with all
that pineapple juice? I've often asked myself) so
the girls come to me. Queenie puts down the jar,
and I take it into my fingers icy cold. Kingfish
Fancy Herring Snacks in Pure Sour Cream: 49¢.
Now her hands are empty, not a ring or a bracelet,
bare as God made them, and I wonder where the
money's coming from. Still with that prim look she
lifts a folded dollar bill out of the hollow at the
center of her nubbled pink top. The jar went heavy
in my hand. Really, I thought that was so cute.

John Updike, "A & P," *Pigeon Feathers and Other Stories* (New
York: Alfred A. Knopf, 1952), p. 346. © 1952 by Alfred A.
Knopf, Inc. Reprinted by permission of the publisher.

Review

A. Certain words that have crept into our language are
   currently considered incorrect.
B. Words have denotation and connotation:
   1. Denotation is a word's dictionary definition.
   2. Connotation is what the word suggests or implies in
      addition to the dictionary definition.
C. Specific words are more precise than general words in
   your writing.
D. Concrete words are more interesting than abstract
   words in your writing.
E. Figures of speech are words that are used in an imaginative way; they include similes and metaphors.

243

Review Practice 29–1 Rewrite the following sentences, filling in the following blanks with a concrete, specific word or phrase that fits into the sentence. Use figurative language when you can.

1. I am constantly _____ my major social responsibilities.
2. "_____," the woman said into the microphone.
3. Kathy approached the cat with _____.
4. Please double-check my work so that I don't _____ any of our major problems.
5. While I was memorizing the entire chart for the biology exam, I _____.
6. Why is everything _____?
7. Her life is as uninteresting as _____.
8. I will _____ the problem by outlining it in detail.
9. Authorities _____ that in the 1960's female suicides in our country increased by two thousand and male suicides by one thousand.
10. Ethnicity is an awareness of _____.

Review Practice 29–2 Rewrite and complete the following letter to the editor of a local newspaper, filling in the blanks. Be aware of both the denotation and connotation of each word that you choose, and concentrate on finding specific, concrete words for each blank in the letter.

Local newspaper
Address

Date

Dear Newspaper Staff:

I am writing this letter to call to your attention the inadequate coverage of _____. I feel that the coverage of _____ is very _____.

I am in my _____ year at _____. Living

here in the _____, I read _____ any chance I get. After years of living here, I have the impression your paper simply does not want to acknowledge the fact that _____ .

Do you people feel that just because _____ _____ the volume of newsworthy stories would be uninteresting? If this is the case, then I feel you are in great error. If you would just look a bit closer, you would find that _____ .

Therefore, I feel that if your paper does not improve its coverage of _____ you are guilty of _____ .

In closing, I would like to say that _____ depends a great deal on public interest and acceptance, which can be aided by you and others in the news media.

Thank you for your consideration.

Sincerely,
Your Name
Address

Review Practice 29-3 Explain why ten nouns from the selection at the beginning of this unit are especially well chosen. Show how they fit well into their sentences by comparing them to similar words and by discussing what you know about *denotation/connotation*, *general/specific*, and *concrete/abstract*. Discuss each word separately.

Example: *Spade* is better than *shovel* in the second-to-last sentence of the first paragraph: "To the *spade* we owe our knowledge of the Sumerians and the Hittites, great empires of the Near East whose very existence had been forgotten."

Denotation/connotation: The denotation of the two words is the same—a digging tool. But *spade* implies something sharp and something often taken on scientific expeditions.

General/specific: The word *spade* refers to a kind of shovel and is more specific than the word *shovel*, which also refers to snow shovels, grain shovels, steam shovels, and the like.

Concrete/abstract: *Spade* is a concrete word,

245

because it can be seen; it brings a clear image to mind.

30   Frequently Confused Words

Many words in English are similar in sound, spelling, or meaning, so it is easy to confuse them in your writing. This confusion is usually marked on your papers by "wrong word" (abbreviated as *ww*), a phrase that means that you have the sound, spelling, or meaning of one word mixed up with that of another. This fault is easy to correct by consulting a dictionary or taking a careful look at this chapter. To help you recognize and correct your own problems of this kind, the following list explains frequently confused words.

a/an: A is the indefinite article used before words beginning with a consonant sound: all letters except *a, e, i, o,* and *u*. (Exception: many words beginning with *u* actually begin with a consonant sound: *a uniform, a united front.*) *An* is the indefinite article used before words beginning with a vowel sound: *a, e, i, o,* and *u*. (Exception: *an* is sometimes used before words beginning with *h* if the *h* is not pronounced: *an hour, an honor,* but *a hospital.*)

Article: Marilyn bought *a* plant.
Article: Is there *an* error in your work?

accept/except: Accept is a verb meaning "to receive." *Except* is a preposition meaning "not included."

Verb: Yvonne walked up to *accept* her award.
Preposition: The hardware store is open every day *except* Sunday.

advice/advise: Advice is a noun meaning "counsel" or

"information." *Advise* is a verb meaning "to counsel" or "to inform."

Noun: Tom went to his counselor for *advice*.
Verb: Tom's counselor is glad to *advise* him.

affect/effect: Affect is a verb meaning "to influence." *Effect* is either a verb meaning "to bring about" or "to achieve" or a noun meaning "the result."

Verb: The weather often *affects* my moods.
Verb: The committee met to *effect* a change in policy.
Noun: The *effect* of the new policy could be severe.

already/all ready: Already is an adverb meaning "at or before the specified time." *All ready* is an adverb *(all)* and an adjective *(ready)* meaning "completely ready."

Adverb: Is it *already* time for midterms?
Adverb/adjective: Greg and his friends were *all ready* to leave.

altar/alter: Altar is a noun meaning "a table used for ritual." *Alter* is a verb meaning "to change."

Noun: Frank isn't ready to meet me at the *altar*.
Verb: A lack of sleep may *alter* your awareness.

altogether/all together: Altogether is an adverb meaning "completely." *All together* is an indefinite pronoun *(all)* and an adjective *(together)* meaning "in a group."

Adverb: I'm not *altogether* sure when the bus leaves.
Pronoun/adjective: The track team arrived *all together*.

among/between: Among is a preposition used when referring to three or more items. *Between* is a preposition used when referring to two items.

Preposition: Let's go sit *among* the wildflowers.
Preposition: Do we have time for lunch *between* classes?

amount/number: Amount is a noun that refers to bulk or mass. *Number* is a noun that refers to objects capable of being counted.

Noun: What is the *amount* of your deposit?
Noun: The *number* of applicants was surprising.

are/our/or: Are is a present-tense form of the verb *to be*. *Our* is a possessive pronoun. *Or* is a conjunction indicating alternatives: "this or that."

Verb: They *are* planning to see a movie.
Pronoun: The roof of *our* house leaks.
Conjunction: Shall we swim *or* play tennis?

awhile/a while: Awhile is an adverb referring to a short time span. *A while* is an article *(a)* and a noun *(while)* referring to a short time span.

Adverb: Stay here *awhile*.
Article/noun: Stay here for *a while*.

beat/win: Beat is a verb that, when meaning "to surpass," is followed by living objects only. *Win* is a verb meaning "to surpass" that is usually followed by objects that are not living.

Verb: Elaine *beat* Robert at tennis.
Verb: Elaine knew she would *win* the match.

beside/besides: Beside is a preposition meaning "at the side of." *Besides* is a preposition or adverb meaning "in addition to" or "as well."

Preposition: The old dog lay *beside* the fireplace.

Preposition: I work part-time *besides* going to school.
Adverb: *Besides*, I'm tired.

chance/change: Chance is a verb meaning "to happen" or a noun meaning "luck" or "risk." *Change* is a verb meaning "to make or become different" or a noun meaning "difference."

Verb: I *chanced* upon a good source.
Noun: I caught the bus by pure *chance*.
Noun: Take a *chance* now and then.
Verb: I had to *change* the lock on my door.
Noun: Meeting Tom made a *change* in my life.

choose/chose: Choose is the present tense form of the verb *to choose*. *Chose* is the past tense form of the verb *to choose*.

Verb: It was hard to *choose* which play to see.
Verb: We *chose* the play by Tennessee Williams.

complement/compliment: Complement is a verb meaning "to complete" or a noun meaning "something that completes." *Compliment* is a verb meaning "to express praise" or a noun meaning "praise."

Verb: The red scarf *complemented* Jean's outfit.
Noun: The red scarf was a *complement* to Jean's outfit.
Verb: Dave *complimented* Jean on her scarf.
Noun: Dave's remark about Jean's scarf was quite a *compliment*.

conscience/conscious: Conscience is a noun meaning "a feeling of right and wrong." *Conscious* is an adjective meaning "awake" or "aware."

Noun: My *conscience* told me to stay home and study.
Adjective: Were you *conscious* when the telephone rang?
Adjective: Are you *conscious* of your bad habits?

249

continual/continuous: Continual is an adjective meaning "steadily recurring"; recurrences are very close together, with only small breaks coming between them. *Continous* is an adjective meaning "continuing without interruption."

Adjective: Jeff's tardiness was *continual.*
Adjective: The *continuous* chiming of the bells distracted me.

council/counsel: Council is a noun meaning "an official group." *Counsel* is a verb meaning "to give advice" or a noun meaning "advice."

Noun: The student *council* met at 4:00.
Verb: I had to *counsel* my brother concerning his new job.
Noun: My brother paid no attention to my *counsel.*

desert/dessert: Desert is a noun (singular or plural) meaning "a dry, barren region," a noun (plural) meaning "reward," or a verb meaning "to withdraw from." *Dessert* is a noun meaning "a course served at the end of a meal."

Noun: We went walking in the *desert.*
Noun: Did you receive your just *deserts?*
Verb: The soldiers *deserted* the village.
Noun: A chocolate *dessert* will complete the meal.

disinterested/uninterested: Disinterested is an adjective meaning "having no personal interest." *Uninterested* is an adjective meaning "not interested."

Adjective: A *disinterested* judge would be able to help us reach a fair decision.
Adjective: He was completely *uninterested* in hearing my excuse.

does/dose: Does is the present tense form of the verb *to do. Dose* is a verb meaning "to prescribe or give medicine" or a noun meaning "a certain amount of medicine."

Verb: On weekends, Anna *does* her laundry.
Verb: The veterinarian *dosed* my sick dog.
Noun: That *dose* of cough syrup helped my cough.

dominant/dominate: Dominant is an adjective meaning "controlling" or "superior." *Dominate* is a verb meaning "to control" or "to rule." (Note: a similar distinction applies to the words *predominant* and *predominate.*)

Adjective: The guest speaker was the *dominant* figure at the meeting.
Verb: The guest speaker *dominated* the meeting.

emigrate/immigrate: Emigrate is a verb meaning "to leave one place in order to reside in another place." *Immigrate* is a verb meaning "to come to reside in a place of which one is not a native."

Verb: My grandparents *emigrated* from England.
Verb: They *immigrated* to America.

explicit/implicit: Explicit is an adjective meaning "clearly expressed." *Implicit* is an adjective meaning "understood but not expressed; implied."

Adjective: The book's message was *explicit.*
Adjective: Although she said nothing, Teresa's meaning was *implicit.*

farther/further: Farther is an adverb referring to physical distance. *Further* is an adverb referring to additional time, degree, or quantity.

Adverb: The library was *farther* away than I thought.
Adverb: After doing the outline, I went a step *further* and wrote a rough draft.

fewer/less: Fewer is an adverb referring to numbers of

251

elements that can be counted. *Less* is an adverb referring to value, degree, or amount.

Adverb: There were *fewer* people present than I had expected.
Adverb: My coat cost *less* than Paula's coat.

formally/formerly: **Formally** is an adverb meaning "according to a specific accepted custom." *Formerly* is an adverb meaning "previously."

Adverb: You must dress *formally* for the wedding.
Adverb: Dean was *formerly* head of the association.

hear/here: **Hear** is a verb meaning "to perceive by ear." *Here* is an adverb meaning "in this place."

Verb: I didn't *hear* what you said.
Adverb: What time did you get *here?*

imply/infer: **Imply** is a verb meaning "to suggest." *Infer* is a verb meaning "to draw a conclusion."

Verb: Your tone of voice *implied* that you were in trouble.
Verb: From what I heard, I *inferred* that you were in trouble.

its/it's: **Its** is the possessive form of the pronoun *it.* *It's* is a contraction of *it is* or *it has.*

Pronoun: My car looks great with *its* new paint job.
Contraction: *It's* a shame we couldn't go with them.
Contraction: *It's* been a long time since we saw them.

later/latter: **Later** is an adverb or an adjective meaning "at a time after an earlier specified time." *Latter* is an adjective meaning "the last mentioned of two items." (If more than two things were mentioned, the appropriate adjective for the most recently named item would be *last.*)

Adverb: The concert began *later* than usual.
Adjective: The *later* hour would be more convenient.
Adjective: Of the two alternatives offered, I chose the
            latter.

lay/lie: Lay is a transitive verb meaning "to place." *Lie* is an intransitive verb meaning "to be in a horizontal position." (*Lie* is also a verb meaning "to tell an untruth" and a noun meaning "an untruth.") See also 7G.

Verb: Marie wanted to *lay* the book down.
Verb: There *lies* my shoe in the middle of the floor.

learn/teach: Learn is a verb meaning "to gain knowledge or understanding." *Teach* is a verb meaning "to guide the studies of" or "to instruct."

Verb: I hope to *learn* a lot about literature from you.
Verb: I'll *teach* you all I know about the job.

life/live: Life is a noun meaning "a state that is vital and alive." *Live* is a verb meaning "to remain in a state that is vital and functioning" or "to reside."

Noun: My *life* seems complicated at times.
Verb: Does that drooping plant still *live?*
Verb: I *live* on the east side of town.

loose/lose: Loose is an adjective meaning "free" or "not tight" or a verb meaning "to release." *Lose* is a verb meaning "to misplace" or "to cease having."

Adjective: Since I gained weight, my clothes are no longer
            loose.
Verb: He *loosed* the balloons, and they flew off over
            the roofs of the city.
Verb: Be careful not to *lose* any more weight.

253

many/much: Many is an adjective referring to quantity. *Much* is an adjective or an adverb referring to amount.

Adjective: He has *many* friends.
Adjective: The argument resulted in *much* difficulty.
Adverb: He wanted to come along very *much*.

passed/past: Passed is the past tense form and the past participle of the verb *to pass. Past* is a noun meaning "a former time," an adjective meaning "earlier," or a preposition meaning "beyond" or "by the side of."

Verb: He *passed* me slowly, his head down.
Verb: The days of inexpensive living have *passed*.
Noun: In the *past,* I was not very responsible.
Adjective: Over the *past* month, I have learned a lot.
Preposition: Can you reach *past* me?

precede/proceed: Precede is a verb meaning "to come in front of." *Proceed* is a verb meaning "to continue."

Verb: Page 4 *precedes* page 5.
Verb: *Proceed* to the next book in the series.

principal/principle: Principal is an adjective meaning "chief" or "most important" or a noun meaning "chief official of a school" or "money used as capital." *Principle* is a noun meaning "a rule or basic truth."

Adjective: My *principal* worry is that we might run out of gas.
Noun: The *principal* of my high school was very young.
Noun: If you invest this *principal,* you might make a considerable profit on it.
Noun: Humanism was an important *principle* during the Renaissance.

quiet/quite: Quiet is an adjective meaning "not noisy" or "peaceful." *Quite* is an adverb meaning "very" or "entirely."

Adjective: I spent a *quiet* evening at home reading.
Adverb: I was *quite* exhausted after the long drive.

raise/rise: Raise is a transitive verb meaning "to lift" or "to cause to get up." *Rise* is an intransitive verb meaning "to get up."

Verb: It's almost time to *raise* the curtain for the show.
Verb: I must *rise* early tomorrow for school.

sensible/sensitive: Sensible is an adjective meaning "reasonable." *Sensitive* is an adjective meaning "having feeling."

Adjective: It's important to be *sensible* about study habits.
Adjective: Ralph is very *sensitive* to criticism.

set/sit: Set is a transitive verb meaning "to put in a position of rest." *Sit* is an intransitive verb meaning "to put oneself in a sitting position." See also 7G.

Verb: I'll help you after I *set* my books down.
Verb: If you're tired, *sit* down and rest in that chair.

stationary/stationery: Stationary is an adjective meaning "in a fixed position" or "not moving." *Stationery* is a noun meaning "writing paper and envelopes."

Adjective: The overhead light in my kitchen is *stationary*.
Noun: The letter must be typed on official *stationery*.

than/then: Than is a subordinating conjunction used in comparisons. *Then* is an adverb referring to time other than the present.

Conjunction: Paul is more energetic *than* I am.
Adverb: I didn't know you very well back *then*.

255

their/there/they're: Their is the possessive form of the pronoun *they. There* is an adverb referring to place; it is also used as an expletive. *They're* is a contraction of *they are.*

Pronoun:	*Their* new house is painted yellow.
Adverb:	My new plant is over *there.*
Expletive:	*There* are many people here.
Contraction:	*They're* always busy at night.

through/threw: Through is an adjective or an adverb meaning "complete" or "finished"; it is also an adverb or a preposition meaning "from one side to the other." *Threw* is the past tense form of the verb *to throw.*

Adjective:	Katie is *through* with the exercise.
Adverb:	We will see the ordeal *through.*
Preposition:	I ran *through* the building because I was late.
Verb:	I *threw* the paper into the wastebasket.

to/too/two: To is a preposition meaning "toward"; it is also used to form infinitives. *Too* is an adverb meaning "also" or "excessively." *Two* is the numeral following the numeral *one. Two* is also used as an adjective.

Preposition:	Cynthia went *to* her friend for help.
Preposition:	I want *to* go home.
Adverb:	I bought a new car *too.*
Adverb:	I was *too* cold to go swimming.
Numeral:	Three and *two* make five.
Adjective:	The *two* friends were not speaking to each other at the time.

wander/wonder: Wander is a verb meaning "to move about aimlessly." *Wonder* is a verb meaning "to feel curiosity or surprise" or a noun meaning "marvel" or "astonishment."

Verb:	I'll just *wander* through the museum.

Verb: Do you *wonder* what will happen next?
Noun: It's a *wonder* that we got here safely.

want/what: Want is a verb meaning "to need" or a noun meaning "need." *What* is a relative or interrogative pronoun and an adjective that inquires about the nature of something.

Verb: I *want* to fix my car tomorrow.
Noun: Those people are in severe *want*.
Pronoun: I know what I want.
Pronoun: Good grief, *what* on earth is that ahead of us?
Adjective: Your new rug is *what* color?

weather/whether: Weather is a noun meaning "condition of the atmosphere" or a verb meaning "to endure." *Whether* is a conjunction meaning "if."

Noun: If the *weather* is nice, we'll go to the beach.
Verb: Martha certainly didn't *weather* the storm too well.
Conjunction: Rich didn't know *whether* Mark would be angry.

were/where: Were is a past tense form of the verb *to be*. *Where* is an adverb, a conjunction, or a pronoun referring to place.

Verb: Roberta and Jo *were* not at home.
Adverb: Oh, *where* did you put my glasses?
Conjunction: I'm going home, *where* I can get some peace.
Pronoun: *Where* did you spring from?

who's/whose: Who's is a contraction of *who is* or *who has*. *Whose* is the possessive form of the pronoun *who*.

Contraction: Who's going to buy the groceries?
Contraction: I don't know *who's* been here.
Pronoun: *Whose* groceries are those?

257

your/you're: Your is the possessive form of the pronoun *you. You're* is a contraction of *you are.*

Pronoun: I knew I'd find you in *your* room.
Contraction: *You're* going to your room?

Review

A. Many words are similar in sound, spelling, or meaning and are easily confused.
B. This confusion is often marked on your papers by the notation *ww,* meaning "wrong word."

Review Practice 30–1 In the reading selection at the beginning of this unit, identify ten correctly used words from the list in this chapter, and explain why they are used correctly.

Review Practice 30–2 Choose the correct word to complete each sentence.

1. I don't mind the financial loss; ___(its, it's)___ the ___(principal, principle)___ of the matter that bothers me.
2. Your friends were hoping for a ___(chance, change)___ in your attitude.
3. Who did your ___(conscience, conscious)___ tell you to ___(choose, chose)___ in the last election? Did that person ___(beat, win)___ the election?
4. Agnes always carries her ___(loose, lose)___ change in a pocket.
5. Though speaking no words, the two women had an ___(explicit, implicit)___ understanding of the problem.
6. My dog's death really ___(affected, effected)___ me.

7. Time _(passed, past)_ slowly on the day that Cheryl and Randy were arguing.

8. Why don't you _(set, sit)_ those books down and make yourself at home.

9. I'm convinced that the confusion is not _(your, you're)_ fault; _(its, it's)_ mine.

10. _(A lot, Alot)_ depends on how my mother feels.

11. If you can figure out _(who's, whose)_ purse this is, _(then, than)_ you will uncover more details in the mystery.

12. _(Their, There, They're)_ house is going up for sale because _(their, there, they're)_ falling behind in _(their, there, they're)_ house payments.

13. _(Precede, Proceed)_ to the next door for the surprise of _(your, you're)_ life.

14. _(Its, It's)_ only _(through, threw)_ his intuition that he got this far in _(life, live)_ .

15. Thanks to the waiter's _(advice, advise)_, we ordered a bottle of wine that was really a _(complement, compliment)_ to the meal.

Review Practice 30–3 From the choices in the following paragraph, choose the correct word for each blank.

I _(hear, here)_ that your sister is the _(dominant, dominate)_ force in _(your, you're)_ family. Is that the case? Does _(your, you're)_ sister's strength _(affect, effect)_ you one way _(are, our, or)_ the other? I sure wish someone would _(accept, except)_ the leadership role in _(are, our, or)_ family. For _(awhile, a while)_, I made a lot of decisions when Mom and Dad _(were, where)_ getting divorced. Then, I had a (chance, change) to go back to school, and my (conscience, conscious) told me to take advantage of that opportunity. I (wander, wonder) if I (chose, choose) the right course to follow because such a decision can make a difference (later, latter) on in (life, live).

Review Practice 30–4 Write ten sentences using similar groups of words. Underline the words that are often confused with others.

---

31 Idioms

An **idiom** is a phrase whose meaning as a unit is different from the combined definitions of its individual words (for example, *catch one's eye, get hold of*). Every language has idiomatic expressions that are peculiar to that language and cannot be translated word for word into another language.

Idiom: give me a break
Idiom: step on it
Idiom: hit the road
Idiom: cut it out
Idiom: little does he know
Idiom: on sale
Idiom: for sale

Right: Zelga is *tired of* sitting in the sun.
Right: Zelga is *tired from* sitting in the sun.
Right: Can you *put up with* us for a whole quarter?
Right: Did they *settle for* the cheaper chair?
Right: I *agree with* the previous statement.

Idioms are often difficult for nonnative speakers of English to grasp, but their meanings can always be checked in a dictionary. For example, under the word *agree* in a dictionary, the idiom *agree with* is listed like this: "Used with *with*: *Spicy food does not agree with him.*"*

Review

A. An idiom has a meaning of its own as a unit.
B. Idioms mean something different from the dictionary definitions of their individual words.

Review Practice 31–1 List five idioms from the reading selection at the beginning of this unit.

Review Practice 31–2 Write five sentences, each including at least one idiom not listed here.

Review Practice 31–3 List the idioms in the following sentences.

1. It is up to you to adjust.
2. Tennis is very beneficial to your health.
3. He has a mind to play basketball today.
4. In contrast to Frank, you're a master mechanic.
5. Rosa's dress was on sale.
6. Hold your tongue.
7. We're going to take off for Hawaii next week.
8. The history instructor was responsible for arranging the details for the party.
9. The fact remains that she hit him.
10. Don't get upset; I'm just putting you on.

Review Practice 31–4 Rewrite the following sentences, filling in the missing parts of the idioms.

1. The kittens were prone _____ act _____ instinct.

The American Heritage Dictionary (Boston: Houghton Mifflin, 1979), p. 26.

2. Ralph is putting his car up _____ sale.
3. I thought you used _____ like the way I wore my hair.
4. His fortune says that he is going to _____ the dust at an early age.
5. His dog performed its stunt _____ command.
6. I hope this plan will meet _____ the family's approval.
7. I agree _____ his plan but not _____ his strategy.
8. You had better quit fooling _____ and get down to work.
9. I can easily identify _____ the main character of the story.
10. Any ghetto tends _____ affect the thinking of the people who live there.

32 Clichés

A **cliché** is a phrase that has been overused through the years and, therefore, lacks it original appeal and force (for example, *sly as a fox, busy as a bee*). Because these expressions have been worn out in speaking and writing, they are uninteresting and trite.

Politics and advertising tend to wear expressions out quickly.

> Cliché: by popular request
> Cliché: your chance of a lifetime

Because they communicate nothing interesting or new, clichés are not desirable in your writing. Instead you should write fresh, original expressions of your own.

Cliché: Don is as sly *as a fox.*
Original: Don is as sneaky *as a rat in tennis shoes.*

Cliché: I am *flat broke.*
Original: I am *so broke that my wallet just went on strike.*

Review

A. A cliché is a trite, overused phrase that has lost its appeal.
B. To avoid clichés you must create fresh, original expressions of your own.

Review Practice 32–1 Furnish fresh, original expressions for the following overused phrases. Then use each original expression in a sentence.
1. as dry as a bone
2. when in Rome, do as the Romans do
3. hot as hell
4. better late than never
5. happy as a clam
6. as drunk as a sailor
7. pitch black
8. as hard as a rock
9. don't give up the ship
10. as free as a bird

Review Practice 32–2 List any clichés you detect in the following sentences.
1. You scared me to death.
2. I can tell by her looks that she is as sharp as a tack.
3. I am dead tired after that last run down the slopes.
4. Beverly will be madder than a hornet when you tell her the news.
5. You were as drunk as a skunk last Saturday night.

Review Practice 32–3 Rewrite the sentences in Review Practice 32–2 so that they no longer contain clichés.

33 Wordiness

In your writing, every word should count. More specifically, every word in your sentences should have a reason for being there and should add something to what you are saying. All unnecessary words and useless repetitions should be eliminated from your writing. Because being concise in your writing is as important as being precise, you should also avoid rambling aimlessly.

> Wordy: *It is my own personal opinion* that *the reason for which* we have come together *at this point in time* is to consider *among ourselves* the consequences of the first agenda item.

This type of writing is sometimes called "gobbledygook." A more concise version of the same sentence follows:

> Better: *I think* we have come together *now* to consider the consequences of the first agenda item.

33A Unnecessary Words

Whenever possible, you should restructure a sentence to eliminate unnecessary words **(wordiness).**

> Wordy: *There is* a desperate need for a child-care center *that would be* on our campus.
> Better: Our campus desperately needs a child-care center.

Certain phrases and constructions that are wordy and awkward can easily be corrected.

Wordy	Concise
in view of the fact that	because, since
on account of the fact that	because, since

Wordy	Concise
due to the fact that	because, since
in a sloppy manner	sloppily
she is a woman who	she
he is a man who	he
with regard to	about
kind of	slightly
sort of	slightly
true facts	facts
free gift	gift
yellow in color	yellow
large in size	large
two in number	two

Just as certain phrases are always wordy, so are certain constructions. A sentence in the passive voice is almost always wordier than a sentence in the active voice: see 7E.

Passive: The dog *was run over* by a truck. [8 words]
Active: The truck *ran over* the dog. [6 words]

Similarly, a negative statement is almost always wordier than a positive statement.

Negative: He *did not* like me. [5 words]
Positive: He *disliked* me. [3 words]

33B Repetition

You should also avoid needless repetition of words or ideas.

Repetitious: *Each and every single one* of us should subscribe to the magazine to win a *free gift*.

Better: *Each* of us should subscribe to the magazine to win a *gift*.

Repetitious: After a strenuous day of work, I like watching situation comedies on TV. I *enjoy watching TV* especially when I'm tired.

Better: When I'm tired after a strenuous day of work, I enjoy watching situation comedies on TV.

Review

A. Every word in your writing should add something to what you are saying.
B. To be concise, you must eliminate unnecessary words and useless repetition from your written work.

Review Practice 33–1 Rewrite each of the following sentences, correcting any awkward wordiness or repetition.

1. I am convinced that I don't have any reason in the world at all to be angry with you.
2. He promised her that she was his one and only single love.
3. There should be available a child-care center on our very own campus.
4. How does this new decision seem to you in your own mind?
5. There is little need in this world for people that are pompous and arrogant.
6. The reason that I can't go scuba diving with you is that I'm going home this very same weekend.
7. Why is it that you like sports so very much?
8. Thelma doesn't ever like anybody at all getting in her way.
9. I think I like this story. In fact, I like the story a lot. I even like it enough to read it again.
10. Cycling is an exciting sport, an exciting way to spend a Sunday. And I enjoy it most for its exciting nature.

Review Practice 33–2 Rewrite the following paragraph, correcting any awkward wordiness.

I myself have never really actually seen a real U.F.O., but I strongly believe that U.F.O.'s really do exist. One reason I believe U.F.O.'s exist is that Uncle Walt told me he himself saw one single U.F.O. just last month while he was hauling a load of dried corn up to the top of the hill behind his farm in Kentucky. My uncle has never ever lied, and when he says he saw a real live U.F.O., I really do believe him! He told my sister and me that he was just about at the top of the hill when a funny, oddly shaped object came over the hill and tried to capture him. It tried to take him prisoner, but he shot at it with his very own rifle, and the U.F.O. disappeared. Ever since Uncle Walt told me this very story, I have actually really believed in U.F.O.'s, and I never ever leave my house without my sling shot.

34   Omission of Necessary Elements

In order to prevent confusion in your writing, you should be careful not to omit any words that are necessary to the meaning of your sentences. Some important items that are often left out of sentences are explained in the following rules and examples.

34A   Pronouns and Articles

Necessary pronouns and articles are not omitted in writing.

> Incomplete: The house was robbed was mine.
> Complete: The house *that* was robbed was mine.

267

34B Conjunctions

Necessary conjunctions (subordinating and coordinating) are not omitted in writing.

Incomplete: You want me to run away with you, then you must want me to live with you.

Complete: *If* you want me to run away with you, then you must want me to live with you.

34C Prepositions

Necessary prepositions are not omitted in writing.

Incomplete: I never drove that type car before.

Complete: I never drove that type *of* car before.

34D Verbs and Helping Words

Necessary verbs and helping words are not omitted in writing.

Incomplete: I been here before.

Complete: I *have* been here before.

34E Complete Constructions

Incomplete constructions with *so, too,* and *such* are informal and inexact. These words are not synonyms for *very.* They simply suggest the degree of an action or feeling (*so* happy, *too* nervous) and require a phrase or clause to complete their meanings.

Incomplete: I am so happy.
Complete: I am *so* happy *that I'll buy your dinner tonight.*

34F Complete Comparisons

Incomplete comparisons are inexact. Logically, comparisons involve at least two things. Incomplete comparisons leave the reader wondering exactly what the second half of the comparison is.

Incomplete: My dog likes me more than my cat.
Complete: My dog likes me more than my cat *likes me.*
Complete: My dog likes me more than *he likes my cat.*

Incomplete: Dentoshine is better for your teeth.
Complete: Dentoshine is better for your teeth *than Brand X.*

Review

A. Necessary pronouns and articles are not omitted in writing.
B. Necessary conjunctions are not omitted in writing.
C. Necessary prepositions are not omitted in writing.
D. Necessary verbs and helping words are not omitted in writing.
E. Incomplete constructions with *so, too,* and *such* are inexact.
F. Incomplete comparisons are inexact.

Review Practice 34–1 Rewrite the following sentences, adding any words that are needed to complete them.
1. She will graduate college next summer.
2. They been on the road since August.
3. My niece enjoys flying kites more than my nephew.

4. We all know flamenco dancing originated in Spain and is so disciplined.
5. I wish I were more athletic.
6. I'm ready, then I'll come pick you up.
7. If I could, I like to help you move.
8. Our prices are cheaper.
9. The term-paper assignment is not too hard, but I only have two more days to work on it.
10. Our toothpaste makes your mouth sexier.

Reading Tasks

Comprehension

To check your comprehension, answer the following questions about the reading selection on digging into the past that appears at the beginning of this unit. Refer to the selection when necessary.

1. How many years of human history have archaeologists uncovered?
2. What is the main difference between history and archaeology?
3. Why do archaeologists look underground to find traces of the past?
4. Why does the earth rise faster in the Near East?
5. How do archaeologists know where to dig?

For more comprehension exercises, turn to the Unit IV Appendix Selection.

The following list consists of difficult words from the reading selection at the beginning of this unit.

archaeology	recovered	attached
principally	astonishing	betrayed
documents	deliberately	generations
confined	recognize	depression
chronicles	originally	excavator
produce	mosaic	obvious
illustrating	accumulated	enduring
splendors	considerable	ramparts

Vocabulary Aids

A **dictionary** furnishes information about the meaning, pronunciation, part of speech, origin, and use of words. The best way to see how a dictionary works is to look at some sample entries with the various parts labeled. Some entries from *The American Heritage Dictionary* with explanations of various elements appear on page 273.

6. Using your dictionary, furnish the following information for ten words on the list of words (page 271) taken from the article at the beginning of this unit: syllable marks, accent marks, part of speech, usage label (if no usage label is given for a word, classify the word as "general"), definition (according to the use of the word in the reading selection).
7. Using your dictionary, furnish the following information for ten words on the list after the appendix selection: syllable marks, accent marks, part of speech, usage label (if no usage label is given for a word, classify the word as "general"), definition (according to the use of the word in the reading selection).

A **thesaurus** furnishes synonyms for many words. Each synonym has a slightly different meaning, so you should consider each word carefully in order to choose the one that suits your purpose. To be as accurate as possible, you should use a dictionary along with a thesaurus. Also, to make sure you can distinguish the subtle differences between words, you should work with words that are already in your vocabulary.

A thesaurus is usually organized in one of two ways: by subject or in alphabetical order. The first type of thesaurus is organized around an alphabetical subject index in the back of the book. In this case, each word has several page references in the back. Each of these references represents a group of words associated with the orig-

All word entries are listed alphabetically.

At·ti·ca (ăt′ĭ-kə). **1.** The hinterland of Athens in ancient Greece. **2.** An administrative division of modern Greece. Population, 2,058,000. Capital, Athens.

All the meanings of a word are listed, with the standard meanings placed first.

Pronunciation, syllable division, and accents for each word are given directly after the entry. Occasionally a word has more than one acceptable pronunciation.

at·tire (ə-tīr′) *tr.v.* **-tired, -tiring, -tires.** To dress, especially in elaborate or splendid garments; clothe. —*n.* **1.** Clothing; array. **2.** *Heraldry.* The antlers of a deer. [Middle English *attiren*, from Old French *atirier*, to arrange into ranks, put in order : *a-*, from Latin *ad-*, to + *tire*, order, rank (see **tier**).]
At·tis (ăt′ĭs). *Phrygian Mythology.* A god of fertility, the consort of Cybele.
at·ti·tude (ăt′ə-tōōd′, -tyōōd′) *n.* **1.** A position of the body or manner of carrying oneself, indicative of a mood or condition: *"men . . . sprawled alone or in heaps, in the careless attitudes of death"* (John Reed). **2.** A state of mind or feeling with regard to some matter; disposition: *"My attitude towards historicism is one of frank hostility"* (Karl Popper). **3.** *Aviation.* The orientation of an aircraft's axes relative to some reference line or plane, such as the horizon. **4.** *Aerospace.* The orientation of a spacecraft relative to its direction of motion. **5.** *Ballet.* A position in which a dancer stands on one leg with the other bent backward. [French, from Italian *attitudine*, disposition, from Late Latin *aptitūdō*, faculty, fitness, from Latin *aptus*, fit, **APT**.] —**at′ti·tu′di·nal** (ăt′ə-tōōd′n-əl, -tyōōd′n-əl) *adj.*

Some definitions will be further explained by illustrations or quotations.

Verb tense, alternative spellings, and plural and comparative forms are also shown.

at·torn (ə-tûrn′) *intr.v.* **-torned, -torning, -torns.** *Law.* To acknowledge a new owner as one's landlord. [Middle English *attournen*, from Old French *atorner*, to turn to, assign to : *a-*, from Latin *ad-*, to + *torner*, to turn, from Latin *tornāre*, to turn on a lathe, from *tornus*, lathe, from Greek *tornos* (see **ter-²** in Appendix*).] —**at·torn′ment** *n.*
at·tor·ney (ə-tûr′nē) *n., pl.* **-neys.** *Abbr.* **at., att., atty.** A person legally appointed or empowered to act for another; especially, an attorney at law. See Synonyms at **lawyer.** —**by attorney.** By proxy. [Middle English *attourney*, from Old French *atorne*, "one appointed," past participle of *atorner*, to appoint, **ATTORN**.] —**at·tor′ney·ship′** *n.*

Word derivations are often given. These include the language(s) from which a word originally came and its earliest meaning.

Phrases including an entry are explained separately.

Special usage labels tell how a word is used.

at·to·tes·la (ăt′ō-tĕs′lə) *n.* *Physics. Abbr.* **aT** One-quintillionth (10⁻¹⁸) of a tesla.
at·tract (ə-trăkt′) *v.* **-tracted, -tracting, -tracts.** —*tr.* **1.** To cause to draw near or adhere. **2.** To draw or direct to oneself by some quality or action: *sugar attracts insects.* **3.** To evoke interest or admiration in; to allure. —*intr.* To possess or use the power of attraction; be magnetic or alluring. [Middle English *attracten*, from Latin *attrahere* (past participle *attractus*) : *ad-*, toward + *trahere*, to draw (see **tragh-** in Appendix*).] —**at·trac′ta·ble** *adj.* —**at·trac′tor, at·trac′ter** *n.*
at·trac·tion (ə-trăk′shən) *n.* **1.** The act or capability of attracting. **2.** The quality of attracting; allure; charm. **3.** A feature, characteristic, or factor that attracts: *Money was not the least of her attractions.* **4.** A public spectacle or entertainment.

Examples of usage can help clarify the meaning of the word.

All grammatical uses of a word are recorded as abbreviations.

at·trib·ute (ə-trĭb′yōōt) *tr.v.* **-uted, -uting, -utes.** To regard or assign as belonging to or resulting from someone or something; ascribe. —*n.* (ăt′rə-byōōt′). *Abbr.* **attrib. 1.** A quality or characteristic belonging to a person or thing; a distinctive feature: *"Travel has lost the attributes of privilege and fashion"* (John Cheever). **2.** An object associated with and serving to identify a character, personage, or office: *Lightning bolts are the attribute of Zeus.* **3.** *Grammar.* An adjective or a phrase used as an adjective. —See Synonyms at **quality.** [Latin *attribuere* : *ad-*, to + *tribuére*, to allot, grant (see **tribute**).] —**at·trib′ut·a·ble** *adj.* —**at·trib′ut·er, at·trib′u·tor** (-yōō-tər) *n.*
Synonyms: attribute, ascribe, impute, credit, assign, refer. These verbs mean to declare as belonging to an owner, time, class, or other source. *Attribute* and *ascribe*, often interchangeable, have the widest application: *a saying attributed* (or *ascribed*) *to Jefferson; a distrust of big business attributed* (or *ascribed*) *to his father's failure in Wall Street. Impute* is often

Cross-references provide supplementary information.

Spelling, grammar, and suggestions for usage are furnished in usage notes.

Synonyms are usually listed in a paragraph following the definition.

inal word. You should check all the references before de-
ciding which word best explains your thought.

The second type of thesaurus, like a dictionary, offers
listings in alphabetical order. In this case, a list of possible
synonyms follows each entry.

8. Record two synonyms for each of the ten words you
   studied in question 6.
9. Record two synonyms for each of the ten words you
   studied in question 7.

Another aid that can help you develop your vocabulary skills requires you to keep a list of your own. In one
type of word list, which you were encouraged to begin on
page 212, you record certain features of new or troublesome vocabulary words as you encounter them in writing,
reading, or listening to class lectures. One helpful feature
of this list is the context (phrase or sentence) in which you
encountered each word. So the only definition you record
is the meaning of the word in that particular context. A list
of this kind can help you improve your spelling and expand your vocabulary.

10. Begin your own vocabulary list here by recording at
    least five words that caused you trouble in the selec-
    tion at the beginning of this unit. In your list, include
    their contexts, pronunciations, your own associations
    with their spellings, definitions, synonyms, and any
    other details from the dictionary that can help you re-
    member the words.
11. Add to your vocabulary list five words from the ap-
    pendix selection that caused you trouble.

Discussion/Writing Assignments

The following questions are based on the reading selection
at the beginning of this unit and the Unit IV Appendix

Selection. Follow your instructor's directions for discussing and/or writing on the topics here. All discussion and written work should be in complete sentences.

12. Why do you think people dig up past civilizations?
13. How could we of the twentieth century benefit from understanding the symbols on the Rosetta Stone (see appendix selection)?

Unit IV   Appendix Selection

It has taken many a pick and shovel to prove (1) to the unbelieving world that the history of Greece went back long before the year 776 B.C., the year with which historians used to begin it. But with Egypt, the case has been different. The magic spades of archaeology have given us the whole lost world of Egypt. We know more about the vanished Egyptians than we know about the early Greeks and Romans, whose civilization died just yesterday. We know nearly everything there is to know. And one of the reasons is climate.

Egypt is the archaeologist's paradise—dig and (2) you shall find. In Egypt, almost nothing rots, nothing spoils, nothing crumbles away. Dig up the most delicate carving, the finest substance, and you will find it fresh and perfect after thousands of years of lying in the sand, as though it had just come from the artist's hand. The dry desert soil keeps everything forever.

For nearly fifty centuries, the Egyptians kept (3) depositing in the all-preserving soil everything their great civilization produced—food, dishes, clothing, furniture, jewelry, statues, ornaments, books—together with the bodies of their dead. Is it any wonder that we have a complete record of their civilization? It has been estimated that in

275

those 4,700 years, something like 731,000,000 persons received burial, each with all the trappings his family could afford. Egypt is one vast cemetery out of which have come the richest treasures ever found by man. Even today, when so much has already been found, you may put your spade in any virgin soil and have a good chance of bringing something to light.

(4)   Before Napoleon went down to Egypt for his campaign, he made plans to study the country as no one else had done, because he had been so impressed with its monuments. Along with his army, he arranged to bring to Egypt a number of scholars whose business would be to tell the world about the wonders of the land. And then came a discovery which raised excitement to a pitch and sent thousands of curiosity seekers scurrying to Egypt.

(5)   The discovery which caused all this excitement was made in the year 1799 by one of Napoleon's soldiers. He was digging a trench when his spade struck something hard. He dug carefully all around the object and pulled it out. It was a flat stone, about the size of a sheet of an opened newspaper, and had curious writing on it. He wiped it off, but he could not make head or tail of the writing. However, he could recognize that some of the characters were like the mysterious symbols inscribed on the obelisks and tombs. The soldier decided it was something important. He had no idea that before his eyes was one of the greatest treasures ever found by man.

(6)   This stone—which we call the Rosetta Stone because it was found near the Rosetta arm of the Nile—was the magic key for which scholars had been sighing for centuries. Nothing had intrigued them like the hieroglyphics. If they could only get to the bottom of those curious symbols, the curtain of time would roll back, and they would be able to read all the forgotten history of the Egyptians, learn all the manners and customs and thoughts of

that once-mighty people. But though they had puzzled and puzzled till they were weary, they seemed no nearer the solution than when they began.

There seemed to be no getting at the hieroglyphics. Snakes, geese, lions, heads, owls, hawks, beetles, bees, fish, palm leaves, lotus flowers, people squatting on their haunches, people with their hands raised over their heads, triangles, half-moons, knots, loops—not one of them could be made out. One scholar after another had been obliged to come to the conclusion that he was beaten. There was just one way of solving the riddle—they must get hold of something written in both hieroglyphics and a language already known and compare the two. (7)

And now, here was the Rosetta Stone, answering the description exactly, a priestly decree written in Greek, in hieroglyphics, and in ancient Egyptian business script! The scholars were filled with joy, and, when in 1801 the stone was ceded to England and placed in the British Museum, they fell to work on the inscription immediately. Getting to the bottom of the hieroglyphics was a much harder job than any of them had anticipated, however. One after another was forced to give up in despair. But the French scholar Jean François Champollion refused to be defeated. Stubbornly, he stuck to the task he had set for himself. (8)

He employed the method of working through proper names. Some of the signs on the Rosetta Stone were set off in a little frame. When he looked at the corresponding place in the Greek inscription, he saw written there the name of a pharaoh—Ptolemy. The natural thing to conclude was that in the Egyptian writing, the word in the frame was likewise Ptolemy. The signs, he decided, stood for letters. (9)

He little knew that he was only at the beginning of his difficulties. The Egyptians had used letters only for writing names. Other words (10) they had written in various ways. Some signs stood for whole words, some for syllables, some for letters. The only path open to Champollion was to keep on working with names, and this he did, searching the monuments for cartouches, as the little frames were called. It was slow, slow work, and, twenty-three years after the Rosetta Stone was found, he had worked out only one hundred and eleven of the thousands of symbols. But it was a beginning, and already the mystery of Egypt was giving way before it. Victory over the whole was just a question of time.

Anne Terry White, "A Key to the Past," in *Lost Worlds* (New York: Random House, 1941). © 1941 by Random House, Inc. Reprinted by permission of the publisher.

Difficult words from the appendix selection:

archaeology	mysterious	decree
vanished	inscribed	script
civilization	obelisks	ceded
paradise	intrigued	anticipated
substance	hieroglyphics	despair
desert	curious	corresponding
depositing	mighty	pharaoh
impressed	obliged	difficulties
pitch	conclusion	cartouches
scurrying	priestly	victory

To check your comprehension, answer the following questions:

1. Why is Egypt the archaeologist's paradise?
2. For how many years did the Egyptians bury their possessions?
3. What discovery caused so much excitement in 1799? Why did it cause this excitement?
4. How many years did it take Champollion to figure out 111 of the thousands of Egyptian symbols?

Unit V

Effective Sentences

Although writing grammatically correct sentences is important, not all grammatically correct sentences are also **clear** or **effective.** This unit explains how to make correct sentences clear and precise. Right and wrong usages are not described here, but methods are suggested for making effective statements in some frequently encountered situations. In these situations, certain modes of expression simply get your point across better than others do.

Before you begin this unit, read the following selection about biology. Look closely at the way the sentences work to get the author's message across. Various exercises in this unit will ask you to return to this passage to find examples of certain rules you will be studying.

Since the very beginning of human history, (1) men have taken an interest in what they saw, particularly in everything that moves or grows and can be called alive. *Biology* is the name given to this study of living things. Much of the study has been, and still is, simply a process of looking at what can be seen and thinking about it. This activity may be broadened by carefully dissecting (taking apart) living things so that more internal (inside) structure can be seen. The study may also be broadened by use of a lens or a microscope. And since all living things are active in some ways, the action may be interfered with; that is, the action may be experimented with, just as one can experiment with any piece of working machinery to discover what stops it or changes the manner in which it works.

Great Biologists of the Ancient World

(2) All we know of ancient efforts to study the nature of living things comes from the records made by the early biologists. Unfortunately, only some of those records survived to later times. What is now known is mainly the work of Aristotle, who lived in Greece about 2,300 years ago. Aristotle observed the world of nature, thought about it, taught about it, and left records. And he was undoubtedly one of the best naturalists of all time. He described in a remarkably accurate manner the animal life that was familiar to him and attracted his atten-tion—particularly the habits of fishes, the breeding habits of octopuses, the behavior of bees, and the nature of whales, dolphins, and porpoises. All are still being studied by biologists today. Aristotle also attempted to analyze the nature of reproduction, heredity, and sex, with which biologists are still deeply concerned. Aristotle, in fact, represents the climax of the great intellectual adventure of the ancient Greeks. For nearly 2,000 years afterward, no one really tried to improve on his ideas concerning the nature of life.

(3) We have a record of only one other important biologist of ancient times. This is Galen, a Greek who spent most of his active life in Rome during the second century A.D. Aristotle was an observer who saw things as they were and thought about their nature. Galen was outstanding for his skill and inventiveness in making experiments. He paid much attention to the flow of blood in the body. He was also much concerned with the effect of injuries to the spinal nerve cord with regard to

paralysis and death. Galen stands for the second period of biology.

After Galen, biology ceased to be an active (4) science. It made no progress throughout the Dark Ages and most of the Middle Ages. It came to life again only as part of the general reawakening of scientific interest during the Renaissance.

Biology During the Renaissance

The Renaissance, which means "rebirth," was (5) the great surge of intellectual activity that came into full force during the 1500's. It showed itself in art, science, and exploration. Biological science has its roots in all three of these activities.

This was a time of great painters and (6) sculptors, such as Botticelli, Leonardo da Vinci, Dürer, and Michelangelo. All of them were greatly interested in the exact portrayal of animal and plant forms, as well as the structure of the human body. These artists needed also to be scientists because they were intensely curious about the real nature of what they were attempting to portray on canvas or in stone. For the first time in ages men began to look at plants and animals as they really were, rather than studying old drawings and descriptions.

At the same time, the discovery of the New (7) World and of the Far East took place. Explorers brought home accounts of an exciting variety of strange forms of life.

All of this happened at the same time as the (8) invention of printing and of reproducing drawings by means of wood engravings. So it became an easy step for other students of nature to produce the first biological textbooks of this new period of biology. In Germany, the first books of this sort dealt with plants. In Italy, at the University of Padua, great advances in the study of the human body were made by Vesalius and Fabricius. And somewhat later, another great advance was made

281

by William Harvey, an Englishman who had been a student under Fabricius at a time when Galileo was also present at Padua. In 1628 Harvey published his demonstration that blood circulates through the body, a fact previously unknown.

. . . .

(9) *Advances with the Microscope.* Although he was not concerned with biology, Galileo worked out and described the construction of the compound microscope; in it a system of two or more lenses was employed. It gave biologists a means of seeing what had previously been invisible.

(10) During the second half of the 1600's, the great pioneers in the use of the microscope were at work. The most important of these men were Robert Hooke in England, Anton van Leeuwenhoek and Jan Swammerdam in Holland, and Marcello Malpighi in Italy. All contributed to the growth of the new biology, each in his own way. Malpighi, for instance, saw and described the circulation of the blood in the fine capillary vessels in the lung of a frog. Swammerdam's magnificent book called the *Bible of Nature* is probably the finest collection of microscopic observations ever published and is still used. Leeuwenhoek drew attention to the complexity and beauty of microscopic structure in plant and animal tissues. Hooke showed that plant material is made up of small units enclosed by cell walls. Thus began *microscopy,* which is the name given to the use of microscopes generally; *histology,* which is the study of tissues; and *cytology,* which is the study of cells. However, little headway was made in those fields for another 150 years. Then, in the early 1800's, important improvements in microscopes made more rapid advances possible. Meanwhile, biology had been divided into *botany* (the study of plants) and *zoology* (the study of animals). And it had made progress in various ways.

Biology in Our Century

Twentieth-century biology has developed (11) along several major lines. All are related to the work that went on before.

In physiology the greatest advance has been in (12) our understanding of the nervous system. Today we view nerve cells as systems capable of transmitting electrical and chemical signals in a number of ways. We see the patterns of pathways and centers in the brain and spinal cord. And we can relate all this and also the nature of sense organs to the behavior of animals.

. . . .

The nervous system is now known to be in (13) direct or indirect control of all that goes on in the body: for example, the action of sweat glands in the skin, the nutrition of muscles, the mechanism of childbirth, and so on. Brain and body are now seen to be so closely interrelated that neither can be understood by itself. How do mental states influence the body? How does body chemistry influence the mind? These questions are among the most important being investigated. Great efforts are also being made to analyze and understand the working of the brain itself: How is the brain related to sensation, action, thought, memory, feeling, and both consciousness and sleep?

Progress in any branch of biology depends to a (14) great extent on advances in methods and instruments. This has been true of *biochemistry*. This science deals with the chemical analysis of the processes occurring in the living cell and in the organism as a whole. Knowledge of microscopic cell structure has grown continually as microscopes have improved or changed. Some of the most important advances in cytology (the study of cells) were made toward the end of the 1800's. They were made through improvements in various techniques of staining and in the use of the microscope. As a result, the fine detail of the mechanism of cell division was observed. It was observed both of the cell as a whole and of the nucleus with its chromosomes. Division of the nucleus was seen to be so exact that each resulting nucleus was the image of the parent nucleus.

. . . .

(15) Biology has now reached a critical stage in its own development. Rapid advance is being made along many separate approaches that appear to be coming together. As the various lines merge, our understanding of the nature of life and our capacity to control life will take a great leap forward.

(16) See also Biochemistry; Cell; Darwin, Charles Robert; Evolution; Fermentation; Fossils; Genetics; Harvey, William; Medicine, History of; Microbiology; Pasteur, Louis; Photosynthesis; Taxonomy.

N. J. Berrill, "Biology." From THE NEW BOOK OF KNOWL-EDGE, vol. 2, 1979, © Grolier Incorporated. (New York: Grolier, 1979.) Pp. 187–196. Reprinted by permission of the publisher.

35 Pronoun Reference

Every pronoun in a sentence must refer to some noun. That noun is the pronoun's antecedent. An antecedent gives a pronoun meaning since a pronoun has none of its own. In effective writing, the noun that each pronoun refers to should be clear.

35A Unclear Reference

The two types of pronoun references that are most mis-leading to a reader are references that are either unclear or far away from their nouns. The misuse of pronouns at the beginning of a theme can also cause unnecessary trouble for a reader.

35A(1) Two References

References of a pronoun to either of two nouns are unclear.

Unclear: Alvin beat Willy in Scrabble. *He* is like that sometimes. [Does *he* refer to Alvin or to Willy?]
Clear: Alvin beat Willy in Scrabble. *Alvin* is like that sometimes.

35A(2) Placement of Pronouns

Pronouns are placed as close as possible to their antecedents.

Unclear: Transcendental *meditation* is a method of rest. *It* involves reciting a mantra.

Clear: A method of rest is transcendental *meditation. It* involves reciting a mantra.

35A(3) Pronouns and Titles

A pronoun is not used at the beginning of a theme to refer to a noun in your title.

Title: Learning How to Design Cut Glass
Unclear: When I started to learn *this,* I found that I was fascinated by *it.*
Clear: When I started to learn *how to design cut glass,* I found that I was fascinated by *the technique.*

35B   Broad Reference

Confusion in your writing can result from the use of pronouns to refer to ideas, unstated thoughts, and *everyone* and *someone.* This confusion is caused by making pronouns refer to broad concepts rather than to specific words.

35B(1) General Ideas

A pronoun does not refer to the general idea of a previous clause or sentence. *This, that, it,* and *which* are the pronouns most commonly misused this way.

Unclear: Some students think that cramming for exams is the most effective way to study. *That* is not true.
Clear: Some students think that cramming for exams is the most effective way to study. *Cramming* is not effective.

If the pronoun used to refer to a general idea is *this* or *that,* the problem can often be solved simply by adding a noun after the pronoun: instead of *this,* write *this claim* or *this fact;* instead of *that* (as in the example above), write *that technique* or *that habit.*

35B(2) Unstated Thoughts

A pronoun cannot refer to a word or thought that is not stated in a sentence.

Unclear: When I took swimming lessons last summer, I wanted my instructor to think *this* was easy for me.
Clear: When I took swimming lessons last summer, I wanted my instructor to think *the backstroke* was easy for me.

35B(3) The Pronouns *You* and *It*

The pronouns *you* and *it* do not mean *everyone, someone,* or *something.*

Unclear: When *a person* learns how to water ski, *you* should bend your knees and let the rope pull *you* up.
Clear: When *a person* learns how to water ski, *he or she* should bend *his or her* knees and let the rope pull *him or her* up.

Clear: When *you* learn how to water ski, *you* should bend your knees and let the rope pull *you* up.

Of the last two sentences, the first is an example of formal writing. The second is informal unless directed to a specific audience, as in a letter.

Unclear: In the driver's manual, *it* says to allow 225 feet to stop when traveling at 55 miles per hour.
Clear: *The driver's manual* says to allow 225 feet to stop when traveling at 55 miles per hour.

Review

A. The particular noun that each pronoun in your writing refers to should be clear.
   1. References of a pronoun to either of two nouns are unclear.
   2. Pronouns are placed as close as possible to their antecedents.
   3. A pronoun cannot be used at the beginning of a theme to refer to a noun in your title.
B. Confusion in your writing can result from using pronouns to refer to general elements in your sentences.
   1. A pronoun cannot refer to the general idea of a previous clause or sentence.
   2. A pronoun cannot refer to a word or thought that is not stated in a sentence.
   3. The pronouns *you* and *it* do not mean *everyone, someone,* or *something.*

Review Practice 35–1 List the pronouns in the first paragraph of the reading selection at the beginning of this unit. Then, to the right of each pronoun, name each pronoun's antecedent.
Review Practice 35–2 In the following sentences, list the pronouns that do not have clear antecedents.

1. The fibula and the tibia extend from the knee. It is a small bone.
2. Chalk lines keep ants away. They are effective.
3. According to your records, it says that you are a science major.
4. They promised to be here in time for dinner, which proves that they must like our cooking after all.
5. Taxpayers might not have to file a federal income tax return if you make only $2,000 a year.
6. Mark gave someone special a hand-tooled leather belt for his birthday. He was excited.
7. In your letter you said you were sorry, but now you are contradicting that.
8. Pillow fights are still common in the dorms. They don't hurt anyone.
9. The explorer shivered and pulled his parka around him. When they put in the zipper, they had used weak thread.
10. After meeting her parents, who were strict people, I realized why it was very difficult for her.

Review Practice 35–3 Rewrite each sentence in Review Practice 35–2 so that the reference of each pronoun is clear.

Review Practice 35–4 Write a short (one-paragraph) character sketch of someone who has played an important role in your life. Explain your relationship with this person and the role the person has played in your life. Then underline each pronoun and draw arrows to each pronoun's antecedent. Finally, reread your paragraph and correct any grammar errors that you find.

36 Misplaced and Dangling Modifiers

Most sentences in English depend on word order for their meaning. Therefore, the position of all parts of a sentence, including the modifiers, is important. Modifiers are words that describe, limit, or further explain other parts of a sentence; see Chapter 8. They should be as close as possible to the words they describe. If they are not close to the words they modify, they are called **misplaced modifiers.** A **dangling modifier** is a phrase that does not refer clearly to any word in its sentence. Usually a reader can eventually figure out your meaning when you insert misplaced or dangling modifiers. But both of these problems interrupt the process of communication while your reader tries to understand your meaning or—even worse—laughs at what you have written. Either reaction will interfere with your attempt to get your message across clearly and efficiently.

36A Misplaced Modifiers

Misplaced modifiers are words or phrases of description that are not as close as possible to the words they modify. Modifiers that are easily misplaced are adjectives, adverbs, prepositional phrases, and some clauses.

36A(1) Adjectives and Adverbs

Adjectives and adverbs are usually placed before and as close as possible to the words they modify.

Misplaced: The decision was considered by the committee *carefully.*

Clear: The decision was *carefully* considered by the committee.

Misplaced: She was so happy that she forgot *almost* to get her award.

Clear: She was so happy that she *almost* forgot to get her award.

Notice how the meanings of the following sentences change when the modifiers are shifted from one place to another.

Only José is a son.

I am *just* asking for a settlement.

José *only* is a son.

I am asking *just* for a settlement.

José is *only* a son.

I am asking for *just* a settlement.

José is an *only* son.

I am asking for a *just* settlement.

Practice 36–1 Place the words on the left in the sentences provided at the point where the words make the most sense or give the stress that you want.

1. only   I am going to ask you once.
2. carefully The problem was diagnosed by the physician.
3. even   They know the answer.
4. nearly   I lost the race.
5. hardly   I am so busy that I have time to eat.

36A(2) Prepositional Phrases

Prepositional phrases are usually placed immediately after the words they modify or at the beginning or the end of a sentence.

Misplaced: Students were surprised to find out that Aristotle was respected *in high school.*

Clear: Students *in high school* were surprised to find out that Aristotle was respected.

Misplaced: He swept his date off her feet *with a hello.*

Clear: *With a hello,* he swept his date off her feet.

Practice 36–2 Revise any unclear sentences that follow by putting the prepositional phrases as close as possible to the words they modify.

1. At the age of one, my parents put me in a nursery school.
2. The instructor explained why plagiarism is wrong on Friday.
3. We offered champagne to the guests in paper cups at the wedding.
4. When you pick up your mail, let me know if you get the check on Monday.
5. He talked about his trip to the sixth grade.

36A(3) Clauses

Clauses are placed near the words they modify.

> Misplaced: The forest protected the couple, *which furnished shade.*
>
> Clear: The forest, *which furnished shade,* protected the couple.

Practice 36–3 Revise any unclear sentences that follow by putting the misplaced clauses as close as possible to the words they modify.

1. Ethel promised when she got home that she would call me.
2. They advertised the motorcycle in today's paper which is fairly new and in good condition.
3. We bought some food in an all-night store which came to $5.30.
4. In most states it is illegal to carry liquor in a car that is opened.
5. A gun in the house that is loaded is dangerous.

36A(4) "Squinting" Modifiers

Constructions in which modifiers can refer to the material either before or after them are unclear and should be avoided.

Unclear: The student left school *sadly* heading for home.

Clear: *Sadly* the student left school, heading for home.

Clear: The student left school, *sadly* heading for home.

Practice 36–4 Rewrite each of the following sentences, showing whether the modifier in italics belongs with the first or the last part of the sentence.
1. While you were taking a shower *in the bathroom* I was waiting for you.
2. The people walked the streets *unhappily* out of work.
3. He sent a letter *hoping* for attention.
4. I decided *yesterday* I would apply for the job.

36B   Dangling Modifiers

Dangling modifiers are phrases that have nothing to modify. They are usually verbal phrases at the beginning of sentences. Since no subject exists in these phrases, they must be attached to the subject of the main clause that follows. When they do not modify the subject of the main clause that follows, they are said to dangle.

36B(1) Phrases

Phrases are placed as close as possible to the words they modify.

Dangling: *Writing his girlfriend,* the tent collapsed.

Clear: *Writing his girlfriend,* he felt the tent collapse.

In this case, the word that the phrase modifies (*he*) has been added to the sentence and placed as close as possible to the phrase.

Practice 36–5 List the dangling phrases in the following sentences. Not all sentences need correction.

1. Running to the store, my bicycle was stolen.
2. While eating lunch at the corner greasy spoon, my bus passed.
3. Tracking down the rabid dog, the problem was under control.
4. To add to the excitement of their wedding, the bride and groom slid down the bannister at their reception.
5. To fill out the application, his past academic record had to be found.
6. The roof fell in sitting all by himself.
7. The yard work was done wearing his blue shirt.
8. After running out of gas, the concert began before we arrived.
9. The party turned out to be pretty good, drinking soft drinks and eating popcorn.
10. While eating his breakfast, the cat got out and the dog bit the mail carrier.
11. While shopping downtown, my car hit a fire hydrant.
12. Reading must be done to write well.

36B(2) Unstated Subjects

When the subject and verb of a clause are not stated, the subject of that clause is the same as the subject of the main clause.

> Dangling: *When just a child,* my teacher took me to Yellowstone National Park.
> Clear: *When just a child,* I went to Yellowstone National Park with my teacher.

Practice 36–6 Rewrite the following sentences so that each clause has a clear subject or is clearly attached to a word in the main clause.

1. When done, his blue shirt was dirty.
2. Once made, discard the chicken bones.

3. You can stop adding soap when pale blue.
4. Until certain, we will hold his seat.
5. Until thawed, do not turn the heat down.

Review

A. Misplaced modifiers are words or phrases of description that are not as close as possible to the words they modify.
   1. Adjectives and adverbs are placed as close as possible to and usually before the words they modify.
   2. Prepositional phrases are usually placed immediately after the words they modify or at the beginning or the end of a sentence.
   3. Clauses are placed near the words they modify.
   4. Constructions in which modifiers can refer to the material before and after them are unclear.
B. Dangling modifiers are usually verbal phrases at the beginning of sentences.
   1. Phrases are placed as close as possible to the words they modify.
   2. When the subject and verb of a clause are not stated, the clause's subject is the same as the subject of the independent clause.

Review Practice 36–1 For each group of words, place the words or phrases in the list into an order that makes a logical, clear sentence. Use all the words that are listed in each case.

1. of your Cessna No. 105
   I
   detect
   in the engine
   a
   clearly
   problem

2. argued
   after
   Harold
   the
   with
   meeting
   Marge

3. to give
   your
   time
   to the cause
   at hand
   consistently
   are
   you
   and
   willing
   energy
4. while filing
   decided
   one
   for divorce
   more
   happily
   the
   to give
   try
   couple
   their
   marriage
5. on
   raspberries
   I
   to
   the
   day
   agreed
   pick
   following
6. scalp
   one thousand
   hairs
   exist
   per square inch
   on a human

7. have found
   quite
   the
   bottle-return plan
   well
   ecologists
   that
   in Oregon
   is working
8. churning
   at night
   River Queen
   the
   its
   noisily
   wheel
   the
   travels
   water
9. for the game
   on time
   had
   at 7:00
   to be
   we
   to break up
   the party
10. for a job
    you
    a
    formal
    must submit
    letter
    in applying

Review Practice 36–2 Correct the sentences that contain misplaced and dangling modifiers by rewriting them. The arrows show which words each modifier now modifies. Not all sentences require revision.

1. To find an answer, the problem was discussed with great care.

2. Skirting the globe, the Indian Ocean is the third largest ocean in the world.

3. Once heard, you must carry out the orders.

4. After walking for awhile, it began to rain.

5. Wanting to be a top competitor, his body is like a finely tuned machine.

6. You should add paint to the mixture until bright green.

7. While searching for peace, confusion reigned.

8. Being completely out of money, tongue depressors make good shoe horns.

9. As a friend in times of trouble, it is important for me to be there.

10. To grow cotton successfully, the weather should be favorable.

Review Practice 36–3 Write down five phrases that describe your bedroom (or dorm room). Then work these five phrases into a paragraph, making sure that each phrase is as close as possible to the word or words it modifies. Finally, reread your paragraph and correct any grammar errors that you find.

37 Parallelism

In geometry, when two or more lines are *parallel,* they run side by side with an equal distance between them at all points. In grammar, we call words, phrases, or clauses *parallel* when they are in a series of two or more— especially when they are also connected by coordinating conjunctions. Writers emphasize the parallel elements in a sentence by placing them in parallel grammatical form. The following guidelines about **parallelism** are designed to help you write logical sentences.

One way to make your writing logical is to concentrate on parallel structures in your sentences. When you write and revise your work, remember that words are balanced with words, phrases with phrases, and clauses with clauses.

37A Words

Words are balanced with words in a sentence, so they should be the same parts of speech. This rule applies to words connected by coordinating conjunctions; see 1G(1).

Awkward: He is ⎰ married [adjective]
and   ✕
a father. [noun]

Parallel: He is ⎰ a husband [noun]
and   ‖
a father. [noun]

Awkward: He is ⎰ indifferent [adjective]
and   ✕
feeling sad. [verb and adjective]

Parallel: He is ⎰ indifferent [adjective]
and   ‖
sad. [adjective]

Awkward: I worry about not only ⎰ what has [dependent
passed   clause]
but also   ✕
the future. [noun]

```
                                      ⎡ the past    [noun]
        Parallel:    I worry about not only—⎨ but also        ‖
                                      ⎣ the future. [noun]
```

Practice 37–1 In the following sentences, bracket any words that seem to form series. Then rewrite these sentences with the bracketed words in parallel form.

1. Gwenn had to run to the store to get bananas, bread, and is also buying some fruit.
2. I feel neither angry nor warmth toward my new friend at college.
3. Since when do you enjoy soccer or playing tennis?
4. Kiss me but you should also hug me.
5. His suit for the dance was chosen with time and care and because it was in style.

37B Phrases

Phrases are balanced with phrases in a sentence, so they should be the same type of phrases—prepositional, verbal, and so on. This rule applies to phrases connected by coordinating conjunctions; see 1G(1).

```
                      ⎡ for fun        [prepositional phrase]
        Awkward:  I travel—⎨ or                  ✕
                      ⎣ working.       [participle]

                      ⎡ for fun        [prepositional phrase]
        Parallel:    I travel—⎨ or                  ‖
                      ⎣ for work.      [prepositional phrase]
```

Practice 37–2 In the following sentences, bracket any phrases that seem to form a series. Then rewrite these sentences with the bracketed phrases in parallel form.

1. Frustration is renting an apartment and to find that its windows leak air.
2. I feel tired but also having energy.

3. This exclusive and privately used dining room is available only to government officials.
4. I hope the plane is on schedule and going to San Francisco.
5. "I promise to love her and that I will cherish her till death do us part."

37C   Clauses

Clauses are balanced with clauses in a sentence, so they should be of the same type—independent or dependent—and should begin with the same parts of speech. This rule applies to clauses connected by coordinating conjunctions; see 1G(1).

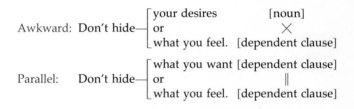

Practice 37–3 In the following sentences, bracket any clauses that seem to form a series. Then rewrite these sentences with the bracketed clauses in parallel form.

1. You have a party of ten or more or if you are serving a large amount of food, it's a good idea to use the basement.
2. I am certain that I have met you somewhere before or recognizing your car.
3. We know what we see is not always that which we get.
4. The nut bread that Mark and Susan baked for their party and hoping that everyone would like it was a sensation.

5. Although Christmas is near and school being out, you still have a paper due when you return in January.

Review

A. Words, phrases, and clauses should be parallel in grammatical form if parallel in thought.
B. Words are balanced with words in a sentence.
C. Phrases are balanced with phrases in a sentence.
D. Clauses are balanced with clauses in a sentence.

Review Practice 37–1 In paragraphs 2 and 10 of the reading selection at the beginning of this unit, list in groups all the words, phrases, and clauses that are in parallel form. Use the coordinating conjunctions *(and, but, or, nor, for, so, yet)* in these paragraphs as your clues. Write your answers following the examples used in this chapter.

word	phrase	clause
‖	‖	‖
word	phrase	clause

Write only the parallel parts of the sentences.
Review Practice 37–2 In the following sentences, bracket any words, phrases, or clauses that are not parallel with each other.
1. Because of inflation and that I'm out of money, let's watch TV tonight.
2. Autumn is a beautiful season—damp, cool, and being very colorful.
3. Employers forced me to wait patiently and sometimes even worried about being selected.
4. Encyclopedias are a source of knowledge and reading.
5. Either for reservations or to ask questions, call 324–INFO.

6. Are the clauses in these sentences balanced and in good style?
7. Both to be on time and being prepared are different matters.
8. I like to sing, to dance, and jogging.
9. Why are you grouchy and are you also difficult to please?
10. Please put down your books and will you help us with dinner?

Review Practice 37–3 Rewrite the sentences in Review Practice 37–2 so that their words, phrases, and clauses are properly balanced with one another.

Review Practice 37–4 Respond to the instructions below by writing complete sentences in which the words, phrases, or clauses are properly balanced with one another.

1. Name three things you enjoy doing.
2. Name four interesting places to which you have traveled.
3. List the three most important pieces of advice your mother, father, coach, minister, or teacher has given you.
4. What three things would you do first if you won a million-dollar lottery?
5. What are the two most important hints you would give a high school senior on how to succeed in college?

Review Practice 37–5 Make a list in parallel grammatical form of the things you do in the morning on a typical school day.

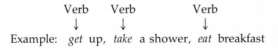

Then develop the items on this list into a paragraph describing your morning activities. Use parallel construction in at least two cases in your paragraph. Finally, reread your paragraph and correct any grammar errors that you find.

38   Misleading Shifts

Unnecessary **shifts** can be misleading to a reader and can make your writing difficult to follow.

When describing a series of events, you should be consistent (avoid shifts) in tense, voice, mood, person, and number.

38A   Tense

Unnecessary shifts in verb tense can be misleading. Keeping to the same time (present, past, or future) while describing a series of actions is important to the coherence of your writing. The most common error is a shift from the present to the past or vice versa. See 7B for more information on tense.

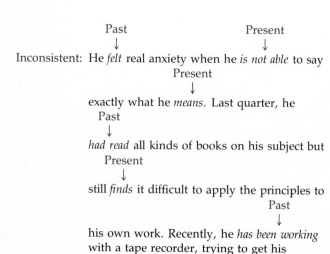

Past   Present
↓   ↓

Inconsistent: He *felt* real anxiety when he *is not able* to say
Present
↓
exactly what he *means.* Last quarter, he
Past
↓
had read all kinds of books on his subject but
Present
↓
still *finds* it difficult to apply the principles to
Past
↓
his own work. Recently, he *has been working* with a tape recorder, trying to get his

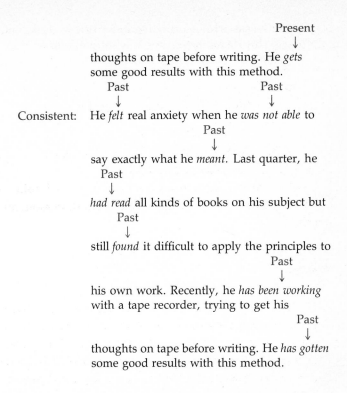

Present
↓

thoughts on tape before writing. He *gets* some good results with this method.

Past   Past
↓   ↓

Consistent: He *felt* real anxiety when he *was not able* to

Past
↓

say exactly what he *meant*. Last quarter, he

Past
↓

had read all kinds of books on his subject but

Past
↓

still *found* it difficult to apply the principles to

Past
↓

his own work. Recently, he *has been working* with a tape recorder, trying to get his

Past
↓

thoughts on tape before writing. He *has gotten* some good results with this method.

Practice 38–1 Explain how the tenses are consistent in one paragraph taken from the reading selection at the beginning of this unit. List all the verbs first; then label each "present," "past," or "future."

Practice 38–2 Rewrite the following paragraph, correcting any shifts in tense.

I found a key under the door mat, but I don't know if it opens this particular door. I fumbled with a flashlight as I try to make my way into the cabin. But the night's darkness and silence catch me by surprise. I lit a candle and let myself blend in with the noiselessness. The key works, so I move stealthily through this house that is unfamiliar to me. But the suspense ended quickly when a booming voice came down the stairway and asks who is prowling in his house. I ran, and to this day, I never knew who that was on the stairs of the deserted house.

38B Voice

Unnecessary shifts in voice can also be misleading. In the active voice, the subject performs the action (for example, *Esther* hit Mary); in the passive, the subject receives the action (Mary was hit *by Esther*). Once you begin to describe a series of actions in one voice, you should not suddenly shift to the other. One reason that a shift in voice can be confusing is that it usually also involves an unnecessary shift in subject. In the example that follows, notice how the subject awkwardly shifts from *I* to *the paper*. See 7E for more information on voice.

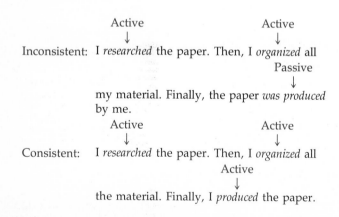

Active   Active
↓   ↓
Inconsistent: I *researched* the paper. Then, I *organized* all
                              Passive
                              ↓
my material. Finally, the paper *was produced* by me.

Active   Active
↓   ↓
Consistent: I *researched* the paper. Then, I *organized* all
                              Active
                              ↓
the material. Finally, I *produced* the paper.

Practice 38–3 Explain how the voices of the verbs are consistent in one paragraph taken from the reading selection at the beginning of this unit. List all the verbs first; then label each "active" or "passive."

Practice 38–4 Rewrite the following sentences, correcting any shifts in voice.

1. The poem was analyzed by the instructor, and then he read it to the class.

2. I have been asked to the party by a friend, and I accepted.
3. The jacket was washed three times. Then, I dried it.
4. His hair was styled by an expert, and then the expert combed it to perfection.
5. The explanation is easily made by the scientist. The scientist usually finds that he has to explain his theories.

38C Mood

Unnecessary shifts in mood can be misleading. Verbs have three moods: (1) the indicative, which is used for factual statements and questions; (2) the imperative, which is used for giving commands or making requests; and (3) the subjunctive, which is used to express doubt, condition, wishes, and the like (in short, anything not strictly factual). If you mix these moods—especially within a single sentence—your reader may become confused about the overall intent of your statement, not knowing whether you are expressing a fact, a command, or a wish. Once you begin to explain a series of events in one mood, you should be consistent throughout your explanation. See 7F for more information on mood.

Subjunctive
↓
Inconsistent: If I *were* honest with you, we probably
Indicative
↓
will have a better relationship.
Subjunctive
↓
Consistent: If I *were* honest with you, we probably
Subjunctive
↓
would have a better relationship.

Practice 38–5 Explain how the moods of the verbs are consistent in one paragraph taken from the reading selection at the beginning of this unit. List the verbs first; then label each "indicative," "imperative," or "subjunctive."

Practice 38–6 Rewrite the following sentences, correcting any shifts in mood. Not all sentences require revision.

1. I request that you will join me for dinner and be on time.
2. When there is a full moon, surgical patients would bleed more.
3. He could be kind, but he sure is aggressive.
4. If you can read this sign, you didn't go to Harding Elementary School.
5. Go study for your midterm, and you should close the door after you.

38D Person

Unnecessary shifts in person can also be misleading. There are three persons in English: (1) the first person is the person speaking *(I, me; we, us)*; (2) the second person is the person spoken to *(you*—singular and plural); and (3) the third person is the person or thing spoken about *(he, him; she, her; they, them; it;* indefinite pronouns; and nouns). In an explanation of a series of events, your references to person should be consistent in your sentences. If you start a sentence in the first person *(I)* and then, while still talking about yourself, shift to the second person *(you)*, you will undoubtedly confuse your readers about whether you are referring to yourself or to them.

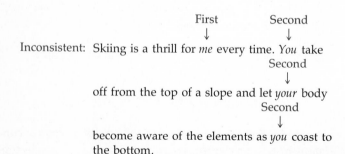

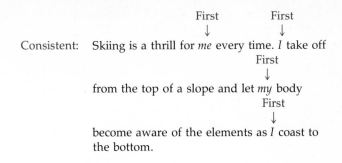

Consistent: Skiing is a thrill for *me* every time. *I* take off from the top of a slope and let *my* body become aware of the elements as *I* coast to the bottom.

Practice 38–7 Pick a paragraph from the reading selection at the beginning of this unit, and explain how the person of the pronouns in each sentence is consistent. List the pronouns in each sentence; then, label each pronoun "first person," "second person," or "third person."

Practice 38–8 Rewrite the following sentences, correcting any shifts in person.

1. I know that one has to finish the exam in an hour.
2. They will soon find out that he needs to back themselves.
3. When you camp, you commune with nature and understand your uniqueness. I really appreciate that.

38E Number

Unnecessary shifts in number can also be misleading. Number refers to a word's being singular or plural. Pronouns in your sentences must agree in number with the words they refer to. You should choose singular pronouns to refer to singular nouns and plural pronouns to refer to plural nouns.

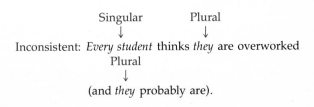

Inconsistent: *Every student* thinks *they* are overworked (and *they* probably are).

307

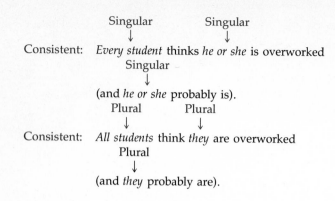

Shifts in number seem to occur most frequently after singular indefinite pronouns that appear, at first glance, to be plural; see 1C.

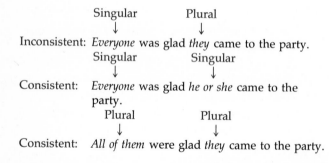

The same principle of matching the number of a pronoun to the number of a noun applies to demonstrative adjectives and the nouns to which they refer.

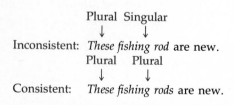

Practice 38–9 Pick a paragraph from the reading selection at the beginning of this unit, and explain how pronouns

agree in number with their nouns. List the pronouns in the paragraph first; next, draw an arrow from each pronoun to the noun it refers to; then, label each noun and pronoun "singular" or "plural."

Practice 38–10 Rewrite the following sentences, correcting any shifts in number.

1. Each person knows they are responsible for the success of the program.
2. I think a college athlete should get tutors if they want it.
3. I find it difficult to follow these lecture.
4. The lawyer didn't recognize this particular clients.

Review

Unnecessary shifts in the following features of your sentences can be misleading:

A. tense (present, past, future)
B. voice (active, passive)
C. mood (indicative, imperative, subjunctive)
D. person (first, second, third)
E. number (singular, plural)

Review Practice 38–1 Rewrite the following sentences, correcting any unnecessary shifts.

1. I am having fun at the party today, so I didn't want to leave.
2. The papers were returned by the instructor, and then she put the class grades on the chalkboard.
3. I was doing my chemistry reading when I heard a person who is calling my name outside my bedroom window.
4. I went to the coast and it was found to be great fun by me, especially when you relax and spend some time watching the breakers come in to the shore.
5. If I were disciplined, I will finish my psychology paper tonight.

6. When I play in the snow, you feel the freedom a child feels.
7. If I owned that bike, I will drive in the city only.
8. What type of car will you buy if you could choose any kind you wanted?
9. I saw heavy air pollution, and sorrow was felt by me.
10. If you are my boss, I wouldn't like you.

Review Practice 38–2 Rewrite the following paragraph, correcting any unnecessary shifts.

> The moon was full when the werewolf's head was raised in the still of the night. The cry of the wild comes from afar and the werewolf set out in search of their prey. You could always tell a werewolf by the wicked glare in his eyes and their snarl that would be heard on moonlit nights. Werewolfs are often being ruled by the brute urge to kill.

Review Practice 38–3 Write a one-paragraph description of a recent sports event from an observer's point of view. Keep tense, voice, mood, person, and number consistent throughout the paragraph. Finally, reread your paragraph and correct any grammar errors that you find.

39   Subordination

Subordination is the process of combining dependent and independent clauses. A subordinate clause contains a subject and a verb but is introduced by words that make its meaning dependent on the rest of the sentence. Subordination can help you relate thoughts in a logical manner and place emphasis on a single idea.

Subordination: *Because* we won the game today, we should celebrate.

Coordination, the process of combining independent clauses, is used to give ideas equal emphasis.

> Coordination: I watched the game, *but* I'm not sure who won.

Long sentences are not always better than short sentences. Longer sentences, however, are often better than short sentences when the short sentences are closely related. When related sentences remain short, they can be boring and their relationship is not always clear to a reader. Subordination can clarify these relationships.

Subordination can be used to connect a related series of thoughts, to clarify the logical relationships of those thoughts, and to emphasize the main clause.

39A · How to Subordinate

Writing subordinated sentences involves placing the main idea in an independent (or main) clause and the other ideas in dependent (or subordinate) clauses.

Choppy:	Esther got mad.
	She hit me.
Illogical subordination:	*When* Esther hit me, she got mad.
Logical subordination:	*When* Esther got mad, she hit me.

Sometimes the decision about which idea to put in the independent clause is more difficult than this, because the decision is based solely on which idea you want to stress.

Choppy:	We lost the case.
	We're not sure where we went wrong.
Logical subordination:	*Although* we lost the case, we're not sure where we went wrong.
Logical subordination:	*Although* we're not sure where we went wrong, we lost the case.

311

39B Combining Short Sentences

Subordination can be used to combine a series of short, related sentences. To combine sentences, choose one of them as the main clause, and then relate all the others to that clause by adding subordinating conjunctions or relative pronouns.

Choppy: I took the garbage out.
          I noticed our neighbors.
          The neighbors have a new car.
          The car is a sports car.
Subordination: *When* I took the garbage out, I noticed *that* our neighbors have a new sports car.

Choppy: We are invited to dinner.
          The dinner is tonight.
          The dinner is a potluck dinner.
          We are supposed to bring a tossed salad to the dinner.
Subordination: We are supposed to bring a tossed salad to the potluck dinner we are invited to tonight.

Practice 39–1 Combine the following short, choppy sentences into longer, properly subordinated sentences.

1. I like the class.
   I'm making very good grades.
2. I washed my hair.
   I went out.
3. I couldn't get a reservation on the flight.
   The flight was to Houston.
   I took a bus to Houston.
4. I was late.
   There was a problem.
   The problem was at work.
   I settled the problem.
5. I am lonesome.
   I still like being alone.

6. I get paid on Friday.
   We can go to a movie.
   You can choose the movie.
7. The exam will take three hours.
   I explained the length of the exam.
   People were still confused.
8. She plays tennis.
   She hits the ball hard.
   She wants to win.
9. I bought this book
   I didn't know it was a best seller.
   I like it.
   I recommend it to you.
10. I'll bring the potato salad and meat.
    You bring the baked beans and the buns.
    We'll have a picnic.

39C Coordinating Conjunctions

Coordinating conjunctions *(and, but, or, nor, for, so, yet)* should not connect ideas that should be subordinated.

Some sentences should be coordinated because they contain information that is of equal weight.

> Effective coordination: A father helped his son get a job, *but* the son didn't appreciate the favor.

Other sentences, however, contain one main idea and one or more related ideas. In these cases, the related ideas should be connected to the main idea with carefully chosen subordinating—rather than coordinating—words. Excessive and awkward coordination most often becomes a problem when a writer gives in to the temptation to string together a series of sentences with *and*'s, not taking the time to think out the precise relationships among the ideas in order to subordinate some of them.

Example:	I enjoyed the picnic. I didn't want to go home. It was getting dark.
Awkward coordination:	I enjoyed the picnic, *and* I didn't want to go home, *but* it was getting dark.
Effective subordination:	*Because* I enjoyed the picnic, I didn't want to go home *even though* it was getting dark.

Example:	The play was entertaining. I especially liked the scenery. The music was also unique.
Awkward coordination:	The play was entertaining for me, *and* I especially liked the scenery, *and* the music was also unique.
Effective subordination:	The scenery and music of the play were unique, which made the play entertaining for me.

Practice 39–2 Revise the following sentences, subordinating any ideas that are connected by awkward coordination.
1. I bought this car, and it had a reasonable sticker price.
2. I found the key, and I went in.
3. I repaired the damages from the earthquake, so we had another one.
4. You must have seen the special, for you watched TV last night.
5. He went to bed, for he couldn't sleep.

Review

A. Writing subordinated sentences involves placing the main idea in an independent (or main) clause and the other ideas in dependent (or subordinate) clauses.
B. Subordination can be used to combine a series of short sentences that are related, to spell out the logical relationships among those sentences, and to place emphasis on one of them.

C. Coordinating conjunctions should not connect ideas that should be subordinated.

Review Practice 39–1 Explain the use of subordination and coordination in the first paragraph of the reading selection at the beginning of this unit.

Review Practice 39–2 Read the following sentences.

Abraham Lincoln was the sixteenth President of the United States.
Abraham Lincoln's parents were almost completely illiterate.
Abraham Lincoln didn't have much formal education.
Abraham Lincoln loved to read.
Abraham Lincoln practiced law in Illinois.
Abraham Lincoln was fond of the Bible and Shakespeare.
Abraham Lincoln was elected President of the United States in 1860.
Abraham Lincoln opposed the Confederacy.
The Confederacy was made up of the Southern slave states.
Lincoln's stand led to the Civil War.

1. Choose any one of these sentences about Lincoln as your main clause. Then, add to it the information from two of the other sentences.
2. By changing the position of words and phrases, write three other versions of the sentence you composed in 1. Make your sentences logical.
3. Choose a different sentence from the list as your main clause. Now, add to it the information from three of the other sentences. (You can use sentences you have already used in 1.)
4. By changing the position of words and phrases, write five other versions of the sentence you composed in 3. Make your sentences logical.

315

Review Practice 39–3 Eliminate all illogical subordination and awkward coordination in the following sentences by rewriting each sentence with proper subordination and coordination.

1. I bought a small rug, and my feet were cold while I got up in the morning.
2. I like the course itself, and the lab is too long.
3. I was hungry, since I ate dinner.
4. I enjoy making bread, so I have a lot on my mind.
5. I went to the doctor's, although I felt worse than I did yesterday.

Review Practice 39–4 Eliminate all illogical subordination and awkward coordination in the following paragraph by rewriting it with proper subordination and coordination.

> After I went to buy some material for transplanting, I couldn't find the type of soil I wanted. But I asked the clerk in the garden shop of a large department store. I asked him, and I saw what I needed. For I looked for some interesting pots to put the cuttings in. So I didn't want the plain pots everyone gets and something new or different. Although I was still waiting for help, I found some coasters to protect the table tops from the dampness of plants. Before all I need are some attractive hangers to hold some of my plants from the ceiling. At long last, I located everything I wanted, for I returned home to begin my new project.

Review Practice 39–5 Write a paragraph describing how to do something (for example, how to assemble a model plane). Begin by listing the steps that someone must follow. Then, develop this list into a paragraph, using effective subordination. Finally, reread your paragraph and correct any grammar errors that you find.

40 Variety

Varying the structure and length of your sentences can make your compositions effective. **Variety** in writing is also helpful in holding a reader's interest. This chapter will discuss certain methods of achieving variety in your sentence structure.

You can achieve variety in sentence structure by paying close attention to the order of the words in your sentences, the combination of different types of phrases and clauses in your sentences, the length of your sentences, and the types of sentences you write.

40A Varied Beginnings

Avoiding a series of sentences that begin in the same way can give your writing variety. In other words, you should vary the first words of your sentences.

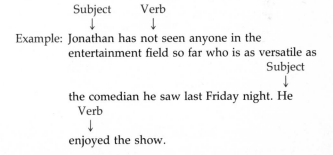

Notice the different ways you can relay the information in this example by changing the beginning of the first sentence:

Adverb
↓

Varied: *So far,* Jonathan has not seen anyone in the entertainment field who is as versatile as the comedian he saw last Friday night. He enjoyed the show.

Prepositional Phrase
↓

Varied: *In the entertainment field,* Jonathan has not seen anyone so far who is as versatile as the comedian he saw last Friday night. He enjoyed the show.

Verbal Phrase
↓

Varied: *Enjoying the show* made Jonathan realize that he has not seen anyone in the entertainment field so far who is as versatile as the comedian he saw last Friday night.

Subordinating
Conjunction
↓

Varied: *Since* he has not seen anyone in the entertainment field so far who is as versatile as the comedian he saw last Friday night, Jonathan enjoyed the show.

Participial Phrase
↓

Varied: *Not having seen anyone in the entertainment field so far who is as versatile as the comedian he saw last Friday night,* Jonathan enjoyed the show.

Sentence 2   Sentence 1
↓   ↓

Varied: Jonathan enjoyed the show, *for* he has not seen anyone in the entertainment field so far who is as versatile as the comedian he saw last Friday night.

In your attempts to vary the beginnings of your sentences, be sure to avoid writing misplaced and dangling modifiers; see Chapter 36.

Practice 40–1 Using the guidelines in 40A, explain how the author varies the beginnings of sentences in paragraphs 9 and 10 of the reading selection at the beginning of this unit.

Practice 40–2 Rewrite each of the following sentences according to a different pattern, selected from the examples in 40A. Add or subtract words when necessary.

1. Since I got caught in a mud slide on my way to school today, my shoes need cleaning and polishing.
2. I got new glasses because my prescription was outdated. My eyes had changed, and I was not seeing well.
3. Although I didn't understand everything that went on in class today, I have hopes that the textbook will clear up my uncertainties.
4. I saw an excellent comedy special on television last night. It was hosted by my favorite comedian.
5. If you use a dictionary religiously to find words in your reading that give you trouble in pronunciation or in meaning, you will naturally increase your vocabulary.

40B Varied Structure

Avoiding ineffective compound sentences can also give your writing variety.

Independent Clause

Example: The streets were covered with fresh snow at

Independent Clause

night, and they were plowed by morning.

To avoid this problem, you can choose one of the following solutions:

Prepositional Phrase
↓

Varied: *With the streets covered with snow at night,*

Independent Clause

the plows worked to clear them by morning.

Compound Verb
↓

Varied: The streets *were covered with snow but were plowed by morning.*

Participial Phrase   Independent Clause
↓

Varied: *Covered with snow*, the streets were plowed by morning.

Dependent Clause
↓

Varied: *Although the streets were covered with snow,*
Independent Clause

they were plowed by morning.

Practice 40–3 Rewrite each of the following sentences, eliminating ineffective compound sentences.

1. My jogging clothes really were dirty, and they are in the laundry.
2. She is going to the movies, but she still may stop by later.
3. I sympathize with you, and I know what it means to be lonely.
4. I'll save enough money to go by plane, or I'll have to forget the entire trip.
5. I don't know how the thief got in my window, and I don't want to know.

40C   Varied Length

Avoiding a series of short, simple sentences can also give your writing variety. A series of short, simple sentences is choppy, lacks emphasis, fails to relate ideas to each other, and can bore readers. Vary the length of your sentences by using all four clause combinations: (1) simple, (2) compound, (3) complex, and (4) compound-complex. See 4E for more information about these clause combinations.

Simple

Example: I was glad to get a lunch break.

Simple   Simple

I ate lunch fast today. I was busy.

Simple

I had to finish my research on a biology paper.

Simple

I also had to write a short political science paper

for tomorrow.

Simple

Varied: I was glad to get a lunch break.

Complex

But I ate lunch fast today *because* I was busy.

I had to finish my research on a biology paper

Simple with a Compound Verb

and write a short political science paper.

In the varied example, related thoughts are connected by appropriate transitions, including subordinating conjunctions and transitional words and phrases; see 1G(2) and 43C(2). In this way, the relationships among the thoughts in the sentences are made clear, and main ideas are emphasized.

Practice 40–4 Using the guidelines in 40C, explain how the author varies the length of sentences in paragraphs 7 and 8 of the reading selection at the beginning of this unit.

Practice 40–5 Vary the length of the sentences in the following paragraph by combining sentences when possible.

The card catalog in the library is a useful source of reference. It can help you find material on any subject in any discipline. Most card catalogs offer three separate listings for each book in the

321

library. These listings are (1) subject, (2) title of book, and (3) author. First, a person should locate the books needed in the catalog. Then, he or she should carefully copy the call number from the catalog card. Next, the person should locate each call number on a map of the library. Then, the person should be able to find the book or books on the shelves themselves. The periodical or magazine sources are listed separately in the library. They are also usually kept in a separate, designated area of the library.

40D Varied Types

Varying the types of sentences can also give your writing variety. The four types of sentences are shown here:

Statement: I like all kinds of soup.
Exclamation: Soup again!
Command: Eat your soup.
Question: What kind of soup is this?

See 4F for a description of each type of sentence.

Practice 40–6 Rewrite each of the following sentences according to a pattern from the examples in 40D other than the one it follows. That is, rewrite a statement as an exclamation, a command, or a question; or rewrite an exclamation as a statement, a command, or a question; and so on. You can repeat a pattern more than once.
1. I went roller skating for the first time yesterday.
2. When did you last see your wallet?
3. They still don't understand why I dress the way I do.
4. Go away and leave me alone.
5. No! You locked yourself out of your house?

Review

You can vary the structure and length of your sentences in any of the following ways:

A. by avoiding a series of sentences that begin in the same way
B. by avoiding ineffective compound sentences
C. by avoiding a series of short, simple sentences
D. by varying the types of your sentences

Review Practice 40–1 Rewrite the following sentences, varying the order of the elements, the structure, the length, or the type.

1. I have no idea why my friend yelled at me during dinner.
2. Sometime today I lost the necklace I was wearing.
3. Go to the meeting; then, come to my house for a late dinner.
4. When will you be turning in your paper in our Contemporary Drama 102 course?
5. I should wax my car before we start out on our trip across the country.
6. Get out of here! I've heard enough of your complaining!
7. Yes! I would love to go on a cruise with you.
8. The first step in writing a paper on any subject is collecting a list of books and articles on your topic.
9. Did someone in your family knit the sweater you have on?
10. Sharpen your pencils before you go to the testing session.

Review Practice 40–2 Rewrite the following paragraph, varying sentence structure, length, type, and order of sentence elements.

I found a hundred-dollar bill in the street today. I wasn't quite sure what to do. I remember my grandmother telling me to turn in any money that I ever found, but I didn't know where to turn it in. I wasn't sure I really wanted to turn it in, anyway. So I held onto the bill. I walked around for a while and thought about my dilemma. I finally decided to let my friends know that I had found the money, hoping these people would locate the real owner of the hundred-dollar bill. Otherwise, I would give it a good home in my wallet.

Review Practice 40–3 Write a paragraph narrating an important event that has recently occurred in your life. Vary your sentence structure throughout the paragraph. Finally, reread your paragraph and correct any grammar errors that you find.

41   Unity and Logic

Related ideas and clear thinking are valuable features in your writing because they help your readers follow your train of thought. This chapter discusses how to write clear sentences and develop your ideas logically.

41A   Unity

Unity in writing involves producing clear sentences that contain only related material. The word *unity* comes from *unite,* which means "to combine so as to form a whole." Therefore, writing with unity means that the writing forms one coherent whole because it is about a single subject. A unified sentence, then, contains only related thoughts. All unrelated material should be put into another sentence.

> Unrelated: The movie, which is at the corner drive-in and will probably be there another week, unless, of course, the downtown theatre shows it next week, is stimulating and full of suspense.
>
> Related: The movie at the corner drive-in is stimulating and full of suspense. It will probably be there another week if the downtown theatre doesn't show it next week.

Practice 41–1 Examine the sentences in paragraph 14 of the reading selection at the beginning of this unit. Explain how the ideas in each sentence relate to the other ideas in that sentence.

Practice 41–2 Rewrite the following sentences so that each contains only related ideas. Add words or put ideas in separate sentences when necessary.

1. Yesterday, Maggie lost her French book and cut herself on the wire fence around the soccer field.
2. This month's best-selling novel, which sells for $3.95 in hardcover at Semaphore's Bookstore, is a real thriller.
3. Becky got a tutor in political science, and her work hours were keeping her from studying.
4. My friend sent me flowers, which were arranged like a Japanese fan, because I was in a car accident.
5. I wonder what I'll find if I go on this treasure hunt sponsored by the League of Women Voters, whose members all have a message to get across.

41B Logic

Unity is concerned with whether or not sentences are related, but **logic** is concerned with how well they are related. Logically related sentences support what you are saying with relevant details. By contrast, illogical sentences are based on inadequate or irrelevant details.

41B(1) Sufficient Evidence

Logically sound sentences furnish sufficient support for your generalizations (broad claims).

> Faulty: I had a car accident last year, and the police didn't arrive for twenty minutes. The police are never available when needed.

This example demonstrates a generalization without enough examples to support it. The writer could not really conclude that, because the police did not arrive at the scene of an accident for twenty minutes in one case, they are never there when they are needed.

A better way to write generalizations is to avoid such words as *never, always, all, none* and instead to qualify these statements by adding *sometimes, often, many,* or *some.* Qualifiers like these make your generalizations more believable because they help to tailor your generalizations to fit the details (or evidence) you have to support those generalizations.

> Better: I had a car accident last year, and the police didn't arrive for twenty minutes. The police are *sometimes* not available when needed.

41B(2) Facts

Well-chosen evidence to support a generalization is factual. In general, you can consider something a fact if it can be (or has been) confirmed by one of the five senses or by statistics.

Generalization:	Smoking causes many deaths.
Weak support:	Smoking is bad for the lungs. It might even cause cancer.
Strong support (factual):	This year alone smoking will kill more than 300,000 Americans, six times as many as the number of American deaths in the years of fighting in Vietnam.

Practice 41–3 In paragraph 10 of the reading selection at the beginning of this unit, does the author give factual examples and details to support the general statements? Explain your answer in detail.

Practice 41–4 Rewrite the following generalizations so that they are qualified with the appropriate modifiers (such as *sometimes, often, many, some,* and the like). Also, be prepared to discuss the evidence you might use to support each generalization.

1. All young people want to leave home.
2. Smoking marijuana does not lead to using hard drugs.
3. Everyone in the East goes to Florida for the winter.
4. All students are unmotivated.
5. Inflation has hit every phase of our lives.

41B(3) Logical Conclusions

Logically sound statements follow logical steps and do not present false conclusions from unstated assumptions. This rule applies especially to cause-effect relationships in your writing.

Illogical: The vegetable garden in the back of their house shows that they are health food freaks.

Logical: The vegetable garden in the back of their house shows that they probably like fresh vegetables.

In this example, the corrected statement explains the relationship of the elements in the sentence logically to avoid hidden assumptions and unsupported generalizations.

Practice 41–5 In paragraph 14 of the reading selection at the beginning of this unit, does the author draw logical conclusions from sound statements? Explain your answer in detail.

Practice 41–6 Correct the following false conclusions by rewriting the sentences so that they include assumptions and conclusions that are related and logical.

327

1. Jake took his umbrella to work. I guess it's going to rain today.
2. Mom and Dad are late tonight. They must have run into trouble on the highway.
3. He is good looking. He certainly won't get good grades in college.
4. They enjoy reading. They probably don't like sports.
5. She's not eating lunch. She must be upset over her grade on the philosophy midterm.

Review

A. A unified sentence contains only related thoughts.
B. Logically sound sentences furnish sufficient support or evidence for your generalizations.
C. Well-chosen evidence to support a generalization is factual.
D. Logically sound statements follow logical steps and do not present false conclusions from unstated ideas.

Review Practice 41–1 Using the guidelines in this chapter, explain why paragraphs 6 and 8 of the reading selection at the beginning of this unit are logical and unified. Answer the following questions in your explanation.

1. Are the ideas in each sentence related to the other ideas in that sentence? Give examples.
2. Does the author give examples and details to support the general statements in these paragraphs? Explain your answer in detail.
3. Are the examples and details in these paragraphs factual? Explain your answer in detail.
4. Do the conclusions in these paragraphs develop logically from sound statements? Explain your answer in detail.

Review Practice 41–2 Rewrite the following paragraphs, eliminating irrelevant material or opinions and adding appropriate explanations to the generalizations.

The physiology of nutrition involves the study of how the body's tissues use and get rid of certain materials. It is the study of the food, which can taste good, bad, and mediocre, that the body, which is complex, processes. I became interested in nutrition when my grandmother moved to a nursing home that had well-insulated rooms and good service. But nursing homes never have good food. My grandmother didn't like it at all. She always complained.

One fact I learned from watching the dietician plan my grandmother's meals is that a constant supply of protein is necessary to sustain life. All dieticians agree, in addition, that fats and carbohydrates are secondary to protein. Carbohydrates, which I always get cravings for, yield energy in their combustion to CO_2 and H_2O, and they save large amounts of protein material as sources of energy. My grandmother won't eat potatoes. She must not like carbohydrates. Fats, on the other hand, are simply stored for future use when energy is needed. Some people really show where they store their fats in their bodies. But everyone underestimates the value of fats.

Review Practice 41–3 Write a unified theme on one of the following topics.
1. My Favorite Pet
2. Returning to School [after the summer or a break of some sort]
3. The Necessity of Good Study Habits
4. The Advantages [or Disadvantages] of Working While Going to School
5. Why Go to College?

Reading Tasks

Speed

Bad reading habits can hinder your reading. Following are some hints about bad habits that you ought to look for in yourself. The discussion then describes each problem and explains how you can correct it.

Your speaking rate reaches a maximum of only 150 words per minute. If you are mouthing the words that you read, you are holding your reading to this rate or less—depending on how fast you can talk. According to research, when you do not move your lips, you can eventually increase your reading rate to 900 words per minute with a high degree of comprehension.

To stop your lips from moving when you are reading, you should touch your mouth with your hand every now and then to make sure your lips are not moving. Also, concentrate and use your will power to avoid moving your lips. Moving only your eyes will give you a chance to improve your overall reading speed.

1. Read paragraphs 1, 2, 3, and 4 of the reading selection at the beginning of this unit and see if you move your lips as you read. If you do, work on correcting this habit now by rereading those paragraphs. Read them two or three times until you no longer move your lips.

Using your voice while you read slows your reading time down, too, because, as you move from word to word, your eyes must wait for you to say each word with your vocal cords.

To keep from using your voice, you should put your hands on your throat and check your vocal cords as you read. If you stop using your voice, your reading speed will begin to increase naturally, and you can then practice other speed-reading skills.

2. Read paragraphs 5, 6, 7, and 8 of the reading selection at the beginning of this unit and see if you use your voice while you read. If you do, work on correcting this habit now by rereading those paragraphs. Read them two or three times until you no longer use your voice.

Fast reading is not always efficient reading. The key to successful reading is adjusting your reading rate to your purpose. If, for example, you had to prepare an oral report on a particular article, you would have to read the article slowly and carefully at least two or three times to make sure that you had not missed any important information and that the details you had taken from the article were accurate. If, on the other hand, you were working on a term paper, you would have to read all the related material quickly in search of specific information.

By moving your eyes faster or slower, you can adjust your reading speed to your reason for reading the material. You can always gain speed later. For now, if you adjust your speed to different types of reading material—that is, vary the movement of your eyes—you will accomplish your purpose for reading more easily and efficiently.

3. Read paragraphs 9 and 10 of the reading selection at the beginning of this unit and experiment with your reading rate, moving your eyes to speed up or slow down your rate. Read these paragraphs two or three times until you are comfortable with your speed and are sure you understand what you are reading.

The habit of going back with your eyes and picking up lines and sentences that you think you have missed will definitely slow down your reading time. It will also decrease your understanding of the material. As a result, you should try never to backtrack. You will find that your mind will fill in the material that you miss as you read. If you still do not understand what you are reading without going back over it, then slow down your reading rate. You can pick up speed as you gain an understanding of the subject.

To keep yourself from backtracking, place a ruler or a tablet of paper at the top of each page and then move it down the page as you read, covering each line that you have read so that you cannot go back to it. This exercise can help your concentration whether you have this specific problem or not.

4. Read paragraphs 11 and 12 of the reading selection at the beginning of this unit and see if you backtrack with your eyes as you read. If you do, work on correcting this habit now by rereading those paragraphs. Read them two or three times with a ruler or a tablet until your eyes become accustomed to moving through the paragraphs without backtracking.

Reading one word at a time is a hindrance to your speed and to your comprehension. First, you do not think a word at a time; you think in ideas and phrases, so that is the way you should read. Second, most material is written not word by word but in groups of words, or phrases, which give words the most meaning.

Reading groups of words is one of the most important keys to faster reading, especially with textbooks and other school assignments. Forcing your eyes to pick out phrases can improve your reading speed and your comprehension.

To begin with
you should see
each phrase
as a single unit.
Then read
each phrase
in one
eye movement

and consider each
as a single thought.
Read the phrases
as rapidly as possible.
    The following example,
paragraph 13
from the reading selection
at the beginning of this unit,
demonstrates
the sweeping movements
your eyes should make
as you read.

       The nervous system   is now   known to be
in direct or indirect control   of all   that goes on
in the body: for example,   the action
of sweat glands   in the skin,   the nutrition
of muscles,   the mechanism   of childbirth,
and so on.   Brain and body   are now seen
to be   so closely interrelated   that neither
can be understood   by itself.   How do
mental states   influence the body?   How does
body chemistry   influence the mind?
These questions   are among   the most important
being investigated.   Great efforts
are also being made   to analyze and understand
the working   of the brain itself:
How is   the brain   related to sensation,
action,   thought,   memory,   feeling,
and both consciousness and sleep?

Berrill, ''Biology,'' p. 196.

Reading in phrases is a bit like tennis or golf, in that
you should not think too hard about what you are doing,
but rather you should build up an easy rhythm, in this
case, with your eyes. An understanding of the structure of
phrases and clauses (Chapters 2 and 3) is especially important to successful phrase reading, so that your eyes naturally pick up key words, such as verbs, important nouns,

and the words around them. But this understanding of sentence structure should be second nature to you and not the focus of your attention. Your concentration should be on gaining a thorough understanding of what you are reading by moving your eyes through the reading material in a rhythmic fashion.

5. Practice phrase reading on paragraphs 14 and 15 of the selection at the beginning of this unit, concentrating on moving your eyes in a sweeping fashion. Read these paragraphs two or three times, trying to improve your speed each time.

Summary

Problem	Solution
Moving your lips	Keep your lips still
Voicing the words on the page	Keep your vocal cords still
Reading everything at the same speed	Adjust your reading speed to difficulty and purpose
Repeating lines or sentences	Use a ruler or tablet to cover each line after you read it
Reading one word at a time	Read by phrases

6. Time yourself as you read the entire reading selection at the beginning of this unit, concentrating on correcting these five bad reading habits as you read. After writing down your finishing time, answer questions 7 through 13 without looking back at the selection. Then, figure out your reading rate. Begin timing yourself now by recording your starting time.

Starting time: _____
Finishing time: _____

7. Define *biology*.
8. What did Aristotle contribute to the field of biology?
9. What inventions and discoveries happened at the same time in the Renaissance?
10. How did the inventions and discoveries you discussed in question 9 affect the study of biology?
11. Name one pioneer in the use of the microscope and explain what he accomplished.
12. Into what two fields was biology divided during the Renaissance?
13. Name and explain one important discovery connected with biology in the twentieth century.

Now figure out your reading rate according to the following formula: count the number of words you read; divide by the number of seconds it took you to read them, and multiply by sixty. The result equals words per minute. For example, if it took you 288 seconds to read the paragraph, you would compute the rate like this:

$$\frac{1,441}{288} \times 60 = 300 \text{ words per minute}$$

Now try to improve your speed and comprehension by reading the Unit V Appendix Selection and answering the questions that follow the selection. Calculate your reading rate after answering the questions.

Discussion/Writing Assignments

The following questions are based on the reading selection at the beginning of this unit and the Unit V Appendix Selection. Follow your instructor's directions for discussing and/or writing on the topics here. All discussion and written work should be in complete sentences.

14. At the end of the article on biology at the beginning of this unit is a list of related subjects. Choose one

subject; look it up in an encyclopedia, science magazines, and other related sources. Then, explain how that subject is related to the study of biology (based on what you read in the selection).

15. Based on the information in the appendix selection, write a letter to your senator or representative, suggesting several ways of controlling the major pollution problems in your area.

Unit V Appendix Selection

Time yourself as you read this selection.

Starting time: _____

(1) At one time it was believed that the oceans were so vast that pollution of them would never become a problem. But human use of the oceans has increased greatly. For example, much oil is now transported from one country to another in ships. Oil leaking or spilled from tankers has caused some serious pollution. Many people are becoming concerned about the amount of such pollution and its effects on marine life. Much of the world's population is dependent upon marine life for food, and this dependency is likely to increase as the demand for food increases. Also, much of the biosphere's* oxygen is produced by plants in the oceans.

(2) The coastline near Santa Barbara, California, has long been considered an example of natural beauty. In 1969 oil began seeping from cracks in the ocean floor near an offshore oil well. A giant oil slick spread over hundreds of square kilometers,

336   *biosphere:* that portion of the earth where life of any sort is evident.

covering Santa Barbara's coastline. Birds and fish were destroyed, and once-beautiful beaches were covered with a gooey mess of crude oil. Of course, oil pollution is not limited to the coast of California. It has occurred in oceans and seas throughout the world.

Oil, however, is not the only cause of water (3) pollution. People have dumped trash, raw sewage, and industrial wastes directly into the oceans, lakes, rivers, and streams for years. Fresh water that was once considered fit for humans is now becoming unfit for any form of life. Few cities have water that can be used without first being treated in purification plants.

Many cities are now faced with another kind (4) of pollution—pollution of their air. Smoke, fumes, and dust are the common offenders. The term *smog* originally referred to a mixture of fog and smoke given off by factories and automobile engines. Today "smog" is used to refer to many kinds of visible air pollution. Smog sometimes becomes so dense that a person's eyes "burn" continuously. When it is thick enough—and it often rises above the danger levels established by public health officials—it can cause illness.

The pollution problem least understood by (5) many people is the action of ozone, a colorless, toxic gas. On the surface of the earth, ozone and other visible air pollutants are produced by *photochemical* reactions of ultraviolet (UV) radiation (a normal part of sunlight) with various pollutants, mainly those given off by automobile exhaust. Therefore ozone levels are highest on warm, sunny days.

Even at low levels, ozone is highly toxic. It can (6) irritate the eyes, nose, throat, and lungs. When ozone levels reach a certain point, ozone alerts are issued. People are warned to stay indoors as much as possible. Ozone alerts are on the increase in Chicago, Denver, and many other cities.

Ozone also interferes with photosynthesis. (7) **337**

Leaves lose their green color. Trees and other plants in many parts of the U.S. are slowly being killed by the action of ozone.

(8)   Yet, life benefits from a layer of ozone in the stratosphere about 30–45 kilometers above the surface of the earth. This layer absorbs most UV radiation from the sun. If all of the UV radiation reached Earth, most forms of life would not survive. Thus, while ozone at the earth's surface is a hazard, ozone in its proper place in the stratosphere is of great benefit to all life.

(9)   Many scientists believe that chemicals used in aerosol spray cans, along with certain other pollutants, are escaping from the earth's surface and could destroy at least a part of the ozone layer in the stratosphere. If the scientists are correct, even a small increase in UV radiation reaching the earth could result in an increase of skin cancer and other diseases. This is why many spray cans now have hand-operated pumps or contain nontoxic chemicals. Action has been taken to avoid further danger.

(10)   Areas having damp, poorly circulated air tend to develop worse pollution problems than areas with well-circulated air. Residents of Los Angeles, Chicago, and New York City, for example, have lived with smog for a long time. Denver, Colorado, used to be considered an ideal place because of its clean air. Today Denver also faces a serious smog problem. All large cities produce air pollution, which tends to rise in the atmosphere above; then it may spread for hundreds of kilometers. Some scientists think such pollution may be causing changes in the temperature of the earth's atmosphere—changes that could have long-range effects on life.

(11)   For many years automobiles have been made to operate with ethyl gasoline, which contains a lead compound. Thus tiny particles of poisonous

lead have been spewed into the atmosphere daily.
Now cars are made to run on lead-free gasoline,
but it will be several years before the older cars are
off the road. Even the long, white trails that you
see behind jet aircraft are evidence of pollution in
our atmosphere. These trails are made up of water
droplets that form around unburned particles of jet
fuel.

How seriously the biosphere is being harmed   (12)
is not yet completely known. However, many
scientists have predicted that unless something is
done to correct these hazards, our air may become
so contaminated it can no longer support life as we
know it.

Something *can* be done if people are alerted to   (13)
the dangers and are willing to do something about
them. Already some new types of jet engines that
will leave less unburned fuel are being used. Also,
recent models of automobiles are all equipped with
devices that limit the amount of pollution
produced. Efforts have been made to reduce the
smoke given off by factories. This is difficult, partly
because the methods used are expensive and
partly because the development of more effective
methods costs additional money. Despite the
obstacles, if our environment is to be livable, we
must decide to spend the money, time, and effort
required. Pollution will not go away by itself; only
people can stop pollution.

Will your grandchildren feel that you have   (14)
helped ruin their natural environment? Or will
they live in a biosphere suitable for all living
things?

Norman Abraham, Richard G. Beidleman, John A. Moore,
Michael Moores, and J. Utley, "Pollution." Courtesy of Rand
McNally & Company, *Interaction of Man and the Biosphere,* Junior
High School Life Science. (New York: Rand McNally, 1979.) Pp.
226–230.

Finishing time: _____

To check your comprehension, answer the following questions without looking back at the selection.

1. In what ways has water become polluted? Give examples to explain your answer.
2. What causes the air pollution in our cities? What areas are most seriously affected by this kind of pollution?
3. What measures have been taken to control our pollution problem?
4. What other kinds of pollution have you observed?
5. What must people be willing to do to make their environment livable?

Now figure out your reading rate according to the formula on page 335. (There are 953 words in the selection.)

If you got more than one question wrong, go back and read the entire essay again. Then, answer the questions you missed.

Unit VI

The Writing Process

This unit outlines and explains the major steps of the writing process. Although writing is difficult for many people, it can be done most easily by taking the process step-by-step. Each chapter in this unit presents one major part of the writing process: prewriting, developing and organizing paragraphs, writing themes, and finishing. Checklists for various stages of the writing process are included at the end of each chapter.

Before you begin this unit, read the following student theme about high school, an experience most of us have shared, whether as recently as last year or as long as ten years ago. Look closely at the way the theme works as a whole to get the author's message across. Various exercises in this unit will ask you to return to this theme and show how certain parts of the theme actually work.

I have served my prison term, and I don't want (1)
to be locked up again. That is exactly how I felt
when I stepped forward at high school graduation
to receive my diploma. The days of cruel authority
with no room for exceptions were over for me. It
wasn't the actual process of education that made
high school like a prison for me. But high school,
governed like a prison by rules, routines, and
confinement, created an atmosphere that did not
encourage learning and self-improvement.

At the core, high schools and prisons are (2)

institutions based on rules with built-in punishments for any sort of disobedience. There are probably sound reasons for most of the rules the law enforcers have developed in both settings, such as safety, control, and efficiency. But it seems that the stress in both of these atmospheres is on punishment rather than on reward and encouragement for good behavior. Breaking the rules in both cases leads to punishment; following the rules leads to uninteresting routine in which the participant (student or prisoner) has little or no say.

(3)   As we all know, the authorities say that a routine is necessary to the operation of both establishments. Like prisons, high schools rely heavily on set routines and require people to get permission to break the routine. But such a practice certainly does not encourage an open, accepting atmosphere in high school. Even for a simple change like a day off of school, the system seems to fall apart if forms aren't filled out properly. Once, at the last minute, my father asked if I wanted to go on a day's business excursion with him to check some farms for insurance purposes. He thought the experience would be educational for me, and I was excited about it. My father and I left the city; my mother went to work as usual; and my high school went frantic trying to track me down. I cut school that day with the intention of broadening my education, but the next day I was sent to the dean by my first-period instructor, was humiliated by the dean's secretary, and was forced to call my mother to vouch for my story. Because of this disciplinary action, I missed all of English and part of chemistry. But most important, the dean made me feel like a criminal for doing nothing wrong.

(4)   Along with not filling out the proper forms, socializing in high school is practically treated like a minor offense. I for one would much rather see the teachers put their energy into the classroom

than have teachers waste their time seeking out the petty criminals. Students aren't even allowed room for growing, learning, and playing between classes. As soon as the bell rings, teachers take their posts in the halls and begin telling students to be quiet, keep their hands to themselves, and get to the next class. Most students find it easiest to get along in high school when they actually consider themselves prisoners, stop thinking, and simply do what they are told. Is this the type of person our secondary school system should be producing?

(5) A feeling of confinement is the focal point of my high school experience. I very seldom sensed encouragement to make free choices and deal with different learning situations. As with small children, all decisions were made for me and my peers. Even the classrooms were confining—maps and chalkboards on the front walls, windows on one side wall, a clock in the back of the room, a door and a bulletin board on the fourth wall, and in the center of each room the desks, nailed to the floor. Perhaps freedom was once given to high school students, who continually abused it. Or perhaps present students no longer care about the quality of their time in high school, so they let others make decisions for them. But there is a reason for the current state of affairs, and I think this sense of confinement is a major part of the problem. As in prison, a student must serve his or her time, or term of confinement, without exception—until age sixteen. The conditions under which students are kept in school are often not pleasant. Classrooms and prison cells hold groups of unhappy people, and, supposedly for the sake of improvement, confinement is enforced often against a person's will.

(6) It seems to me that in high schools rules and regulations must be set and carried out to a certain extent. A routine is also important to the success of any school system. My objection is the degree such rules fill our lives. High schools are not prisons.

They are institutions that should mold the minds of free-thinking citizens who can function successfully in a fairly complicated society. Encouraging students to stop thinking for themselves and punishing them for every slight change from the norm is bound to stifle rather than encourage students. So they are sent to college or into society with a feeling of helplessness as a result of being confined for years. A routine may be necessary but should not be carried out to the extent that it produces "prisoners" unable to take responsibility for the rest of their lives.

42   Prewriting

The first step of the composing process is called **prewriting** or inventing, which can be defined as the process of discovering subject matter. This stage can help you overcome any fear you may feel when you sit down with a pen and a blank piece of paper. An important part of the composing process, it is directly related to the practice of writing an essay and to the final product.

The prewriting stage takes place before you do any writing. In fact, prewriting occurs before an idea even takes shape. Because most prewriting is mental, explanations of this stage of the composing process vary somewhat. For our purposes, prewriting is divided here into six parts: exploring a subject, limiting the subject, discovering additional details, classifying the details, selecting the most appropriate details, and ordering the details.

42A   Exploring a Subject

In most cases, choosing and exploring a very general subject are the first prewriting activities. You can approach this step in one of two ways: brainstorming or asking routine questions.

42A(1) Brainstorming

Brainstorming essentially means stimulating the brain to get at ideas within. It involves making free associations with a general subject. The result of brainstorming can be a list of questions, statements, words, or any combination of these. Write down these questions, statements, or words as they occur to you. Do not worry about spelling, grammar, order, or sentence structure. Your only objectives at this stage are speed and quantity; you can concern yourself with correctness and organization later. Asking questions is the most efficient way to brainstorm.

If, for example, your general subject is high school (as in the sample theme on pages 341–344), you might begin to brainstorm your subject by asking the following questions:

Is high school fun?
What did I get out of high school?
What made me feel helpless in high school?
Why was I frustrated most of the time?
Why did I want to cut classes?
Why was a strict routine enforced?
Do the teachers like their jobs?
How do the rules work?
What did I like about high school?
What was being in high school like?

Even at this early stage, these questions resulting from brainstorming are focusing on rules and regulations in high school; this gives you a start on limiting your subject (the next step). Another person, however, might develop a completely different list of questions.

42A(2) Routine Questions

Asking a routine set of questions about a subject means taking the same approach to all subjects. It does not include random questioning based on association as brainstorming does, but rather it is concerned with developing questions from standard cues that suggest other ideas and questions. These cues can be of any type but should be general enough to be applied to all subjects. One of the most common sets of cues is sometimes used by journalists: Who? What? When? Where? How? (and sometimes Why?). Following cues of this sort helps you make sure you are looking at a subject from all possible angles.

Using these journalistic cues as a springboard, we might develop some of the following questions about the general subject of high school:

Who: Who enjoys high school?
Who makes life miserable in high school?
Who are the law enforcers in high school?

What: What did I learn in high school?
What did I like about high school?
What did I dislike about high school?
What courses did I take?
What rules did I have to follow?
What extracurricular activities did I participate in?

When: When was high school the most fun?
When was high school the least fun?
When was I in high school?
When did I cut classes?

Where: Where did I attend high school?
Where did I do most of my learning?
Where did I want to be—instead of in class?
Where did I feel like I was when I was in high school?

How: How did I graduate?
How did the teachers manage to teach?
How did the general atmosphere in high school affect me?

This approach to a subject is much more controlled than brainstorming.

42B Limiting the Subject

This step involves limiting the subject so that it is easy to handle in a theme. Specifically, you need to limit (or restrict) your subject so that you will be able to support all your main ideas with specific details (while remaining within the assigned length). Rarely do students limit their subjects too much; more often, they do not limit enough. Consider the following example:

Unlimited: How are men restricted?
Limited: How have men in my family been restricted by society's expectation that men be very competitive in everything they do?

You can limit your subject by focusing on one question or a few related questions that result from your exploration of the subject. From the brainstorming exercise, you might focus on the following related questions:

Why was a strict routine enforced?
How do the rules work?
What was being in high school like?

These three questions can be rewritten as one:

With various rules and strict routine, what was being in high school like?

From the questions generated by the routine questions, the following questions might be chosen:

Who are the law enforcers in high school?
Where did I feel I was when I was in high school?
How did the general atmosphere in high school affect me?

These three questions can be rewritten as one:

> Where did I feel I was when I was surrounded by law
> enforcers in high school?

According to one student, the answer to both questions is that she felt as though she were in prison when she attended high school. So a theme based on these questions could describe the similarities between high school and prison.

Limiting your subject must often take place throughout the writing process. You should limit your subject as much as you can at this initial stage and then continue to limit it whenever necessary as your paper develops. If, for example, you have written ten pages when you finish the first section of your outline and the assignment calls for only two pages, you must go back, limit your subject further, and adjust your outline.

42C Discovering Additional Details

At this point, you must think of details that might be used to support your specific subject, which you arrived at after exploring and limiting your general subject. The best plan for adding new ideas at this point is to think of as many answers to your main questions as you can. Let us take a look at the possible answers to one of the limited questions:

Question:
With various rules and strict routine, what was being in
    high school like?

Answers:
The halls are filled with teachers and administrators who
    observe students throughout the day in high school,

just as the corridors are lined with guards to watch the prisoners in jail.

Attendance is required till age sixteen in high school, just as confinement is enforced until the prisoner has served his or her time in jail.

Classrooms and prison cells hold groups of people who are there against their will.

Both high schools and jails are supposedly designed for a person's improvement.

In both high schools and jails, misbehaving is not allowed.

In both high schools and jails, the inmates may feel helpless.

Both high schools and jails are governed by rules and regulations.

The food in both high schools and jails is mass produced.

Breaking the rules in both high schools and jails leads to punishment.

If a person escapes and gets caught in either high school or jail, he or she gets punished.

In both high schools and jails, everyone lives by a set routine.

In both high schools and jails, a person has to get permission to break the established routine.

Different writers might have different answers to some questions. In any case, the answers should then be grouped so they can be developed into a theme.

42D   Classifying Details

General labels can help you group or classify these answers. This process is much like labeling the items on a grocery list—fruits, vegetables, meat, poultry, spices, and so on—except that you must develop your own labels. The labels should be broad but exact and not overlapping. Take a look at possible labels for the answers from 42C:

Answers	Classification
The halls are filled with teachers and administrators who observe students throughout the day in high school, just as the corridors are lined with guards to watch the prisoners in jail.	Law enforcers
Attendance is required till age sixteen in high school, just as confinement is enforced until the prisoner has served his or her time in jail.	Confinement
Classrooms and prison cells hold groups of people who are there against their will.	Confinement
Both high schools and jails are supposedly designed for a person's improvement.	Improvement
In both high schools and jails, misbehaving is not allowed.	Misbehavior
In both high schools and jails, the inmates may feel helpless.	Feeling
Both high schools and jails are governed by rules and regulations.	Rules
The food in both high schools and jails is mass produced.	Food
Breaking the rules in both high schools and jails leads to punishment.	Rules
If a person escapes and gets caught in either high school or jail, he or she gets punished.	Escape
In both high schools and jails, everyone lives by a set routine.	Routine
In both high schools and jails, a person has to get permission to break the established routine.	Routine

The main categories, which appear on the list more than once, are the following: confinement, rules, and routine. The minor topics, which are mentioned only once, include law enforcers, improvement, misbehavior, feeling, food, and escape.

The next step involves choosing which of these answers will be used in the final paper.

42E Selecting and Ordering Details

Including only major topics, or topics that are mentioned more than once in the classification stage, is an easy way to select your details. The minor topics can be dropped at this stage. Selecting your topics is actually another way to limit your subject further.

Now you must decide how you want to order your major topics. In this case, these topics include confinement, rules, and routine. The most logical order would be to discuss how rules and routine confine people and, therefore, create a negative atmosphere. So the order of the topics is now set by their logical relationship to one another.

rules
routine
confinement

Now only two prewriting steps remain: writing a thesis statement and outlining.

42F Writing a Thesis Statement

Writing a thesis statement is still another way of limiting your subject. It states the controlling idea of your theme and gives focus and direction to the thoughts in the rest of the theme. It gives an overview of the topics you will discuss (rules, routine, and confinement, in this case) and indicates what you are going to say about those topics. To write a thesis statement for the sample theme, you need only answer the questions posed in 42B. A possible thesis

351

statement for this theme follows; note the topics, printed in color.

> Thesis statement: High school, governed like a prison by rules, routine, and confinement, creates an atmosphere that does not encourage learning and self-improvement.

Every essay has only one thesis statement, which is part of the introduction of an essay. This general statement is usually the first or last sentence of the first paragraph of an essay and the first statement in an outline.

42G Outlining

At this point, you must recall the statements, or answers, from 42C that are related to your major topics.

Topics	Answers
Rules	Both high schools and jails are governed by rules and regulations. Breaking the rules in both high schools and jails leads to punishment.
Routine	In both high schools and jails, everyone lives by a set routine. In both high schools and jails, a person has to get permission to break the established routine.
Confinement	Attendance is required till age sixteen in high school, just as confinement is enforced until the prisoner has served his or her time in jail. Classrooms and prison cells hold groups of people who are there against their will.

This material can now be outlined in either phrase or sentence form. The phrase outline appears here. In either type of outline, the thesis statement should appear as a complete sentence at the top of the outline.

Thesis: High school, governed like a prison by rules, routines, and confinement, creates an atmosphere that does not encourage learning and self-improvement.

I. Introduction
   A. Rules
   B. Routine
   C. Confinement
II. Rules
   A. Both high schools and jails governed by rules and regulations
   B. Breaking the rules in both high schools and jails—punishment
III. Routine
   A. A set routine in both high schools and jails
   B. Permission to break the established routine in both high schools and jails
IV. Confinement
   A. Attendance required till age sixteen in high school; confinement enforced until the prisoner has served his or her time in jail
   B. Classrooms and prison cells holding people against their will
V. Conclusion
   A. Summary
   B. Concluding remarks

Following these prewriting activities, you are ready to develop your thoughts into paragraphs, which will make up the substance of your final paper. The answers to two more questions, however, will prepare you even more specifically for writing:

What will be the tone of your essay?
Who is your audience?

The first question asks how you will approach your subject (seriously, humorously, and so on). The answer to the first question is closely related to your answer to the second question. In other words, the tone you take depends to a great extent on whom you are addressing.

Checklist for Prewriting

1. What is the general subject of my paper? (42A)
2. Have I thoroughly explored my subject through brainstorming or routine questions? (42A)
3. Have I limited my subject adequately? (42B)
4. Have I thought of details to support my subject by answering the questions I developed? (42C)
5. Have I grouped my answers by labeling them? (42D)
6. What are my major topics? (42E)
7. Have I written my thesis statement? (42F)
8. Have I outlined my paper? (42G)
9. What will be the tone of my essay? (42G)
10. Who is my audience? (42G)

Review Practice 42–1 Go through the prewriting process by following the checklist for prewriting for all the following topics. Write notes detailing all your thinking.

1. My College
2. Sports
3. Hobbies
4. Activities After School
5. Activities Before School
6. Relaxing
7. Study Methods

43   Writing Paragraphs

Paragraphs provide a means for writers to expand upon each topic in an outline. The first line of each paragraph is indented to show that a change in topic or subtopic is taking place. Although paragraphs vary in length, typical paragraphs in student themes usually range from 50 to 250 words, averaging about 100 words.

A paragraph is a unit in itself, the result of logic and planning. Each paragraph usually includes a topic sentence, which is a general statement about the content of the paragraph, and details that support and/or explain the topic sentence. In writing and revising paragraphs, writers often follow specific guidelines like those explained in this chapter.

43A Topic Sentences

Most paragraphs have topic sentences. Each topic sentence contains the controlling idea for its paragraph. Although a topic sentence can appear anywhere in a paragraph, it functions best as the first or last sentence in a paragraph, serving as either an introduction to the details in the paragraph or as a conclusion. In either case, it gives shape and direction to a paragraph.

Topic sentences are developed from the main topics of a paper. In the comparison of high schools and prisons, the main headings were rules, routine, and confinement. From these topics, sentences containing these ideas can be formed.

Topic	Topic Sentence
Rules	Both high schools and prisons are institutions based on rules with built-in punishments for any sort of disobedience.
Routine	The authorities say that a routine is necessary to the operation of both establishments.
Confinement	In both cases, confinement is enforced—often against a person's will.

As you will see, these sentences will become an important part of the theme. They are logically related to each

355

other and to the main questions asked in Chapter 42: With various rules and strict routine, what was being in high school like? Where did I feel I was when I was surrounded by law enforcers in high school?

Practice 43–1 Write topic sentences for the following paragraphs.

If we never saw Babe Ruth hit a home run, we can still feel the thrill by reading about it. If we never saw a four-minute mile, or a hundred-yard run for a touchdown, or a yacht race, we can still read about them. And stories like those in the following pages help bring back our own memories of things we saw, or things we did—our own collection of great moments in sports.

Helen C. Derrick, Wilbur Schramm, and Charles G. Spiegler, *Adventures for Americans* (New York: Harcourt Brace Jovanovich, Inc., 1962), p. 335. Reprinted by permission of the publisher.

First, the automobile encouraged Americans to move farther and farther away from cities, out into the suburbs. From about the time of Lindbergh's trip to Paris, the "lure of the suburbs" attracted more and more middle-class Americans. Second, cars and buses transformed American education, especially in small towns and farm areas. The school bus made it possible to consolidate school districts into larger units. Gradually the simple one-room schoolhouse, with one or two teachers for all the grades, disappeared.

Allen Weinstein and R. Jackson Wilson, *An American History: Freedom and Crisis* (New York: Random House, 1974), p. 644. Reprinted by permission of the publisher.

Of course these are sensible ideals; few would claim that education ought to be undemocratic and useless. The difference between the British and the American approach lies in their respective definitions, or at least implicit definitions, of democracy and usefulness as applied to education. A democracy, in British eyes, has the duty of providing free education to every child according to his "age, ability, and aptitude" (in the words of the Education Act of 1944). The more democratic the educational system, the more the schools will strive to give to each pupil, whatever his class or economic background, that education which encourages and makes full use of whatever abilities he possesses.

David Daiches, "Education in a Democratic Society," in *Contexts for Composition*, ed. Stanley A. Clayes and David G. Spencer (New York: Prentice-Hall, 1969), p. 75. *Commentary*, April 1957. © 1957 by Commentary. Reprinted by permission of the American Jewish Committee.

43B Adequate Details

When expanding upon topic sentences, make sure that you furnish enough details to support an idea and make it interesting. In addition, these details should be developed in a manner that fits your purpose and subject matter.

First, a paragraph must contain enough details to explain or support an idea. Some paragraphs are not adequately developed.

Children who watch television are exposed daily to some of the highest-pressure advertising in mass media. They hear about toys, candy, and new kinds of gum until they essentially become salespeople to their parents for the children's market in America.

In this paragraph, information on specific products that are sold this way and examples of this type of advertising should be included to complete the paragraph.

Some paragraphs are too long and should be broken up, resulting in several paragraphs on one general topic. Long

357

paragraphs often become difficult to follow, especially for impatient readers; shorter paragraphs break the material into pieces and serve to remind the reader of the topic at hand:

> A shy, consumptive, thirty-nine-year-old spinster teacher, Dorothea Dix, entered the East Cambridge, Massachusetts, House of Correction to conduct a Sunday school class for the inmates. When Miss Dix emerged from the House of Correction, shocked and shaken by what she had witnessed, she was a changed woman. The harrowing experience started her on a crusade that would last four decades and reform the treatment of the mentally ill and insane in the U.S. and England. In that time, it was believed that the insane were born defective, were depraved, were hopeless, and therefore should be treated as animals. There were few insane asylums. Inmates were often kept in the worst parts of jails, prisons, almshouses. More often than not they were chained and whipped. Dorothea Dix set out to improve those conditions radically.

> "U.S.A.—Year by Year, 1770–1975." Excerpt from THE PEOPLE'S ALMANAC by David Wallechinsky and Irving Wallace. Copyright © 1975 by David Wallace and Irving Wallace. Reprinted by permission of Doubleday & Company, Inc. (Garden City, N.Y.: Doubleday, 1975.) P. 168.

This example could easily be divided into two unified pieces.

> A shy, consumptive, thirty-nine-year-old spinster teacher, Dorothea Dix, entered the East Cambridge, Massachusetts, House of Correction to conduct a Sunday school class for the inmates. When Miss Dix emerged from the House of Correction, shocked and shaken by what she had witnessed, she was a changed woman. The harrowing experience started her on a crusade that

would last four decades and reform the treatment of the mentally ill and insane in the U.S. and England.

In that time, it was believed that the insane were born defective, were depraved, were hopeless, and therefore should be treated as animals. There were few insane asylums. Inmates were often kept in the worst parts of jails, prisons, almshouses. More often than not they were chained and whipped. Dorothea Dix set out to improve those conditions radically.

Other paragraphs are too short and should be combined.

Aristotle, on the other hand, is rather of the opinion that there were originally eighteen letters, A B G D E Z I K C M N O P R S T U Ph, and that two, Th namely and Ch, were introduced by Epicharmus and not by Palamedes.

Aristides says that a certain person of the name of Menos, in Egypt, invented letters fifteen years before the reign of Phoroneus, the most ancient of all the kings of Greece, and this he attempts to prove by the monuments there.

On the other hand, Epigenes, a writer of very great authority, informs us that the Babylonians have a series of observations on the stars for a period of 720,000 years, inscribed on baked bricks. Berosus and Critodemus, who make the period the shortest, give it as 490,000 years.

From this statement it would appear that letters have been in use from all eternity. The Pelasgi were the first to introduce them into Latium.

Harry E. Neal, "World History—Eyewitness Reports." Excerpt from THE PEOPLE'S ALMANAC by David Wallechinsky and Irving Wallace. Copyright © 1975 by David Wallace and Irving Wallace. Reprinted by permission of Doubleday & Company, Inc. (Garden City, N.Y.: Doubleday, 1975). P. 484.

In this example, no single idea is developed adequately, but, when combined, the sentences complement and support one another.

> Aristotle, on the other hand, is rather of the opinion that there were originally eighteen letters, A B G D E Z I K C M N O P R S T U Ph, and that two, Th namely and Ch, were introduced by Epicharmus and not by Palamedes. Aristides says that a certain person of the name of Menos, in Egypt, invented letters fifteen years before the reign of Phoroneus, the most ancient of all the kings of Greece, and this he attempts to prove by the monuments there. On the other hand, Epigenes, a writer of very great authority, informs us that the Babylonians have a series of observations on the stars for a period of 720,000 years, inscribed on baked bricks. Berosus and Critodemus, who make the period the shortest, give it as 490,000 years. From this statement it would appear that letters have been in use from all eternity. The Pelasgi were the first to introduce them into Latium.

Practice 43–2 Expand the following ideas with appropriate details.

1. Mass media has a tremendous hold on the people of the United States. From cartoons and billboards to newspapers and television, we are all exposed to a great deal of advertising.
2. Wages control a firm's cost of doing business and affect the quality and amount of work that can be done.
3. Severe mood changes are a sign of depression. This mental state usually begins in early childhood.
4. Questions about who wrote a piece of literature should be solved. If they are not solved, they can create a number of problems.
5. Most people learn their sense of right and wrong. Then,

they use this sense to make major decisions in their lives.

Practice 43–3 Mark logical breaks for paragraphs in the following passage.

According to an Egyptian legend, men first learned how to write from the great god Thoth. Thoth had the head of a long-billed bird called the ibis. The story goes that by scratching his bill in the sand, Thoth showed people how to make the signs with which to record their thoughts. The Chinese, the Babylonians, the Greeks, and many other ancient peoples had different legends about how writing began. All of them considered it a precious gift from the gods, for they knew it was something of great importance. They saw that by learning to write man could pass on what he had learned and could constantly widen his knowledge. Exactly where and when writing originated is hidden in the past. But over the years historians have searched for clues as to how it began and how it developed. The earliest form of writing grew out of drawing pictures. It was a kind of shorthand. Instead of drawing a single picture of a man eating a fish, people drew a sign for a man, a sign for a fish, and a sign indicating eating. At first these signs looked like the things they represented, but as they were drawn more quickly and with different kinds of writing tools, each sign was reduced to just a few marks. These signs became a kind of code. This code, unlike pictures, had to be studied before anyone could understand it and write it. In this kind of writing, there had to be signs for ideas as well as for objects. So from the word "idea," it came to be called ideographic writing. Although most modern writing is not ideographic, we do use some signs that are. Traffic markers, for example, use a curved line to tell you that there is a bend in the road or an X to warn you of a railroad crossing. Chinese writing, mainly ideographic, contains some 40,000 characters. Of these, four thousand must be learned in order to write fairly well. In contrast, only twenty-six characters are needed to write English and most European languages. Written Hebrew calls for twenty-two characters, Arabic twenty-eight, and Russian thirty-two.

Joanna Foster, "Writing." From THE NEW BOOK OF KNOWLEDGE, Vol. 20, 1979 © Grolier Incorporated. (Danbury, Conn.: Grolier, 1979.) Pp. 317–318. Reprinted by permission of the publisher.

Practice 43–4 Combine paragraphs when appropriate in the following passage.

There were very few places in the world that Jules Verne, the *writer*, did not visit.

He went round the world a hundred times or more. Once he did it in eighty days, unheard of in the nineteenth century. He voyaged sixty thousand miles under the sea, whizzed around the moon, explored the center of the earth, and chatted with natives in Australia.

Jules Verne, the *man*, was a stay-at-home. He was more apt to be tired from writer's cramp than from traveling.

He did make a few visits to Europe and North Africa. And he made one six-week tour of New York State. But that was all. He spent less than one of his seventy-seven years really traveling.

Yet he was the world's most extraordinary tourist.

His books are crowded with hunting and fishing expeditions. Jules actually went hunting only once.

Then he raised his gun and shot off the game warden's hat!

He never held a test tube in his hand. But he was an inspiration to the scientist in the laboratory.

Long before radio was invented, he had TV working in his books. His name for it was phono-telephoto.

He had helicopters fifty years before the Wright brothers flew their first plane at Kitty Hawk.

In fact, there were few wonders of the twentieth century that this man of the nineteenth century did not foresee. In his stories you can read about neon lights, moving sidewalks, air conditioning, skyscrapers, guided missiles, tanks, electrically operated submarines, and airplanes.

Excerpt from "Around Today's World With Jules Verne" by George Kent, *Reader's Digest,* July 1954. Reprinted by permission of the publisher.

43C   Developing Paragraphs

The three levels of reading are literal, interpretive, and evaluative. These same levels, which are explained in detail on pages 402–404, exist to a certain extent in writing and can be explained through examples of various techniques that can be used in writing paragraphs.

Basically, details are building blocks that you combine to construct a paragraph. The techniques explained here can help you develop your topic sentence with details that will provide information on all three levels.

43C(1) Definition

Explaining the meaning of a term or phrase adds information to a paragraph on a literal level.

A species is a class or type with distinguishing characteristics.

Practice 43–5 List any uses of definition that you find in the student theme at the beginning of this unit.

43C(2) Description

A description draws a verbal picture of a situation on a literal level. This picture can appeal to any one or more of the five senses: sight, touch, taste, smell, and hearing.

Item	The nap of his brown suede jacket was
Description	flattened by the heavy bag he carried on his back. The flatness made the jacket look used
Item	and worn out. His shoes were the same color
Description	as his jacket but did not show their wear.

Practice 43–6 List any uses of description that you find in the student theme at the beginning of this unit.

43C(3) Example

Giving an example of what you are talking about is a way of making yourself clear on a literal level. Not only do examples give logical support to your ideas, but they can also make your ideas specific, interesting, and memorable. As a result, they can help the reader understand each part of your discussion.

Definition	A species is a class or type with distinguishing
Example	characteristics. A whale, for example, is one species of mammal.

Practice 43–7 List any uses of example that you find in the student theme at the beginning of this unit.

43C(4) Grouping

To explain an idea on a literal level, you might want to group similar items. For example, houses may be grouped by style of architecture, building material, size, cost of construction, and so on.

Grouping	On our block, the brick houses sell much faster
Grouping	than the stucco houses.

Practice 43–8 List any uses of grouping that you find in the student theme at the beginning of this unit.

43C(5) Analogy

To help your reader see the relationships between your ideas, you might use an **analogy,** which is a comparison of two seemingly unlike items. Items compared in this way usually have several characteristics in common. Making comparisons demonstrates an interpretive level of thinking.

> A library is like a gold mine in many ways.

Practice 43–9 List any analogies that you find in the student theme at the beginning of this unit.

43C(6) Cause-Effect

Explaining the causes that lead to a particular effect or the various effects of a particular cause requires you to draw relationships among the ideas and facts you have gathered. As a result, this technique also represents the interpretive level of thinking.

> Thanks to the studies conducted by ecologists and   Cause
> the new emission control regulations placed on   Cause
> factories, America's industries are becoming more   Effect
> aware of their effect on the air we breathe.

Practice 43–10 List any uses of cause-effect that you find in the student theme at the beginning of this unit.

43C(7) Comparison-Contrast

Comparing or contrasting requires you to point out similarities (comparing) or differences (contrasting) between elements in the same category—for example, similarities or differences between Republicans and Democrats. This technique calls for you to draw relationships on

365

an interpretive level. Some words and phrases that signal a comparison are *both, similarly, likewise,* and *in like manner;* some words and phrases that signal a contrast are *but, yet, however, still, nevertheless, on the other hand, on the contrary, in contrast to (this), at the same time,* and *otherwise.* In the example that follows, the signal words are italicized.

Comparison   Judo and karate are *both* oriental martial arts. Judo,
Contrast   *however,* is more defensive in nature than karate.

Practice 43–11 List any comparisons or contrasts that you find in the student theme at the beginning of this unit.

43C(8) Analysis

To analyze something, you must break it into its basic parts. Then, you should examine these parts, their relationship to each other, and their relationship to the whole. Analysis often includes your opinions or judgments and your reasons for those judgments. This level of writing demonstrates that you have mastered the evaluative, or most difficult, level of thinking and understanding.

Basic parts
Relation of parts
to each other

Relation of parts
to the whole

      Regardless of the source of stress, states Dr. Selye, your body has a three-stage reaction to it: (1) alarm; (2) resistance; and (3) exhaustion. In the alarm stage, your body recognizes the presence of stress and, through a release of hormones from the endocrine glands, prepares for fight or flight. In the resistance stage, your body repairs any damage caused by the stress. If the stress does not go away, however, the body cannot repair the damages and must remain alert. This plunges you into the third stage—exhaustion. If this state continues long enough, you may develop one of the diseases of stress. . . . Although Dr. Selye believes that the only complete freedom from stress is death, he also points out that humans thrive on stress because it makes life more interesting. Recognizing stress as an ongoing part of life can be the first step in turning it into a positive rather than a destructive force in your own life.

Paragraphs by Joan G. Roloff and Virginia Brosseit. Copyright © 1979 by Glencoe Publishing Co., Inc. (Encino, Calif.: Glencoe, 1979.) P. 106. Reprinted by permission of the publisher.

Practice 43–12 List any uses of analysis that you find in the student theme at the beginning of this unit.

3D   Organizing Paragraphs

The sentences in a paragraph should be placed in a logical order that reinforces the purpose of your essay. Most details in a paragraph are related in a variety of ways. Often, one example grows out of another; a second definition is needed to explain a previous definition; or an example is necessary to explain an idea.

Basically, there are five patterns for organizing details in a paragraph:

1. from general to particular
2. from particular to general
3. by time
4. by arrangement in space
5. by movement between extremes

If, for example, your intention in a paragraph is to explain how to put legs on a coffee table, most of the details should probably be arranged in spatial order, beginning at one end of the table and working to the other. On the other hand, if you are trying to convince a reader of the importance of working with one's hands, the details in the paragraph should probably be arranged from least important to most important (or from one extreme to the other).

367

The method you choose to organize your details in a paragraph depends on the argument in the paragraph and on the nature of the details themselves. Any combination of these methods of organizing details in a paragraph is also acceptable, as long as your reasoning is clear to your reader.

43D(1) General to Particular

This common method of organizing details in a paragraph begins with a topic sentence (general statement) and then offers particular details to prove or explain that topic sentence. Its structure can be diagrammed as follows (though the number of details can vary in each paragraph):

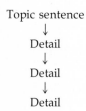

Here is an example:

Topic sentence	Today a new significance has been attached to
Detail	word games by educators and psychologists. Tests
	to determine both the aptitude and achievement of
	students place much emphasis on vocabulary. In
Detail	the 1930's Johnson O'Connor, who created the
	Human Engineering Laboratory, published an
	article in which he claimed that there is a direct
	relationship between the size of a person's
Detail	vocabulary and his success in business. The result
	has been an increased use of vocabulary tests in
Detail	schools. In multiple-choice tests the proper word
	to fit a given definition, or vice versa, is chosen
Detail	from a list. Another type of test lists several words
	as possible choices to fill a blank space in a
368 Detail	sentence. For still another test it is necessary to

match synonyms or antonyms from parallel rows
of words. All these tests now appear as word   Detail
games in magazines and newspapers for the
general public.

Mary Morris, "Word Games." From THE NEW BOOK OF
KNOWLEDGE, Vol. 20, 1979, © Grolier Incorporated. (Danbury, Conn.: Grolier, 1979.) P. 237. Reprinted by permission of
the publisher.

Practice 43–13 Label any uses of the general-to-particular
method of organization that you find in the student theme
at the beginning of this unit.

Practice 43–14 Write a paragraph organized from general
to particular that begins with this sentence: "Several
people I know have broken bad habits."

43D(2) Particular to General

In the particular-to-general method, examples lead up to
the topic sentence, which appears at the end of the paragraph. This type of organization is particularly effective if
you suspect that your reader might not agree with the final
point you are going to make. Its structure can be diagrammed as follows (though the number of details varies
here, too):

Detail
↓
Detail
↓
Detail
↓
Topic sentence

Here is an example:

The old house is located deep in the woods   Detail
about halfway up a hill. The smell of fall and a row   Detail
of poplar trees leads up to the front door. The   Detail
house itself holds my childhood toys and my

369

Topic sentence   memories of my grandmother. The entire scene
                  reminds me of the peace and warmth of my past.

Practice 43–15 Label any uses of the particular-to-general
method of organization that you find in the student theme
at the beginning of this unit.

Practice 43–16 Write a paragraph organized from particular to general that ends with this sentence: "Some people
put their free time to good use."

43D(3) Time Order

The third way of organizing details in a paragraph is by
time. This order is especially appropriate when describing
a series of experiences. In such a case, neither of the previously discussed methods of organization would be very
helpful, but time is important. With this method, words
that express time—such as *first, then, next,* and *finally*—are
signals that help the reader follow the writer's train of
thought. Look at the following example:

> Paper training is an easy way to housebreak a
> puppy. *First,* locate a box that is low enough for
> the puppy to climb in and out of easily. *Then* line
> the box with newspapers and place it in an area
> that is *always* available to the puppy. *Now* place the
> puppy in the box at regular intervals and
> commend him if he performs satisfactorily. *As soon
> as* the puppy begins to understand what is
> required of him, scold him when he makes a
> mistake. *Finally,* bestow lavish praise and affection
> when the puppy uses the box properly, and you
> will *soon* have a well-trained puppy.

Roloff and Brosseit, *Paragraphs,* p. 69.

Practice 43–17 Label any uses of organization by time that
you find in the student theme at the beginning of this unit.

Practice 43–18 Make up a topic sentence that introduces
the following sentences. Then, write a paragraph putting

the following sentences in time order. Add words, phrases, or sentences when necessary.

Directions for Making Candles
Add the color of your choice to the melted wax.
Drop a wick in the melted wax.
First, melt some paraffin in a saucepan.
Put the mold in the refrigerator overnight. (This way, the wax will contract and will be easy to get out of the mold the next day.)
Finally, take the candle out of the mold and admire your creation.
Pour the melted wax in a candle mold of any shape.

Practice 43–19 Make up a topic sentence that introduces these details. Then, write a paragraph putting the following details in time order.

wake up early   wash up
go to class   turn off the alarm
get out of bed   eat breakfast

43D(4) Space Order

Another method of organizing details is by their relationship to each other in space. You might describe someone's outfit, for example, from head to toe or from toe to head; or a discussion of your summer travels across the country in a camper might be organized from east to west or from west to east. Beginning at one end and moving detail by detail to the opposite end is the simplest way of organizing by space. With this method, words or phrases that express space or place—such as *here, there, beyond, nearby,* and *opposite*—are signals that help the reader follow your train of thought. Look at the following example:

It was in Burma, a sodden morning of the rains. A sickly light, like yellow tinfoil, was slanting over the high walls into the jail yard. We were waiting outside the condemned cells, a row of sheds fronted with double bars, like small animal cages. Each cell measured about ten feet by ten and was quite bare within except for a plank bed and a pot for drinking water. In some of them brown, silent men were squatting at the inner bars, with their blankets draped round them. These were the condemned men, due to be hanged within the next week or two.

"A Hanging." From SHOOTING AN ELEPHANT AND OTHER ESSAYS by George Orwell, copyright 1950 by Sonia Brownell Orwell; copyright 1978 by Sonia Pitt-Rivers. Reprinted by permission of Harcourt Brace Jovanovich, Inc., and A. M. Heath & Company, Ltd. (New York: Harcourt Brace Jovanovich, 1950).

Practice 43–20 Label any uses of organization by space that you find in the student theme at the beginning of this unit.

Practice 43–21 Make up a topic sentence that introduces the following sentences. Then, write a paragraph putting the following sentences in order by space. Add words, phrases, or sentences when necessary.

Arranging My Room
Actually, the plant should separate the bed from the door.
I'll begin by putting my bed against the west wall in the north corner of the room.
I would like my floor plant to be next to the head of my bed.
My bureau fits perfectly in the southeast corner of the room.
The desk will be best in the southwest corner of the room where the window is.
The entire east wall is covered with closets.
My bookcase will go between the bed and the desk (on the west wall).

Practice 43–22 Make up a topic sentence that introduces these details about the features of a car. Then, write a paragraph putting the following details in order by space.

Features of a Car

seat	radio
trunk	radiator
roof	bumper sticker
hood	carburetor
front fender	tail pipe

43D(5) Movement Between Extremes

The final method of organizing details in a paragraph can follow any line of reasoning that makes sense out of the details at hand: most important to least important; most troublesome to least troublesome; least serious to most serious; most humorous to least humorous; least appealing to most appealing; and so on. For example, you might explain the courses you are taking this term from most important to least important in terms of a career. On returning from a trip, you might talk about the places you have visited from least interesting to most interesting. These methods of organization have one distinct advantage over the other four: when no other method of organization works, you can always arrange the details from one extreme to the other.

Practice 43–23 Label any uses of organization by extremes that you find in the student theme at the beginning of this unit.

Practice 43–24 Make up a topic sentence that introduces the following sentences. Then, write a paragraph arranging the following sentences from one extreme to the other. Add words, phrases, and sentences when necessary. Label your system of classification (from _____ to _____).

Trials and Tribulations of College
I am failing math.
I still do not understand when to use semicolons in my
    writing.
My English instructor says my style of writing is loose.
I am barely passing music theory.
I have cut my philosophy class twice.
My tennis coach is mad at me.
I have not written home in two weeks.

Practice 43–25 Make up a topic sentence that introduces these details. Then, write a paragraph arranging the following details from one extreme to the other. Label your system of classification (from _____ to _____).

Dorm Activities
a pillow fight
a person studying in a yoga position
skating on a skateboard down the dorm hall
Vaseline on the dorm doorknobs
short-sheeting a bed
eating pizza in bed
talking until 3 a.m.
drinking behind closed doors
staying out all night

These methods of organizing details in paragraphs can be useful to you in your reading and in your writing. They can help you understand individual paragraphs, chapters, articles, and books by helping you see the structure of your reading assignments.

43E Unity: Interrelationship

Two guidelines can help you make your paragraphs unified: the first concerns the relationship of your sentences to one another and to your topic sentences; the second concerns the transitions between your sentences and your paragraphs. Guidelines such as these can help you write well-developed paragraphs and, therefore, good compositions.

A paragraph presents the development of only one idea, which is introduced in a topic sentence. All sentences in a paragraph expand upon this controlling idea and grow out of each other. Information that is not related to the main idea of a paragraph should be dropped.

> *Watering and fertilizing are both important to the growth of indoor plants.* I have many indoor plants and am learning how to care for them. Water gives plants the nourishment they need on a regular basis, and fertilizer stimulates their growth once or twice a month. The plants should be moist, but not drenched, at all times; putting your finger in the soil tells you if your plants are dry; dry plants are not happy. Leeching, which is a method of washing salt and other minerals from the soil by letting the plants sit in a sink of water, should be done every four to twelve months. Fertilizing in small doses is also important; over-fertilizing may kill plants. Plants are interesting to watch and care for, especially when you know their needs.

Topic sentence

In this case, the information about the writer's owning and learning how to care for many plants and about the un-happiness of dry plants is irrelevant to the topic sentence, which is the first sentence in the paragraph. The revised paragraph would read:

> *Watering and fertilizing are both important to the growth of indoor plants.* Water gives plants the nourishment they need on a regular basis, and fertilizer stimulates their growth once or twice a month. The plants should be moist, but not drenched, at all times; putting your finger in the soil tells you if your plants are dry. Leeching,

Topic sentence

375

which is a method of washing salt and other minerals from the soil by letting the plants sit in a sink of water, should be done every four to twelve months. Fertilizing in small doses is also important; over-fertilizing may kill plants. Plants are easy to care for when you know their needs.

Practice 43–26 Rewrite the following paragraph, deleting all irrelevant material.

Astronomy is the oldest of the sciences. It began several thousand years ago, when people first wondered about the stars at night. I sometimes enjoy using a telescope to look at the stars. Most of the people who used to wonder about the stars were hunters and shepherds, although I'll bet people from other professions also wondered about the stars. These people could not write, perhaps because they did not have a school system like we do today, and we do not know much about their thoughts. Yet they used the stars as guides on their journeys. Have you ever used the stars as guides at night when you were outdoors? In fact, it is likely that they learned to predict the seasons, such as spring, summer, fall, and winter, by looking at the sky.

43F   Unity: Transitions

Transitions show the relationships between parts of a sentence, between sentences themselves, and between paragraphs. The word *transition* is a form of the word *transit,* meaning "the act of passing across or through" (as in "Since I am moving, my belongings are *in transit.*"). In written work, then, transitions are words or phrases that help the reader pass from one idea to another. Transitions provide logical links between your ideas, which, in turn, make your sentences and paragraphs readable and clear.

In other words, transitions can make the movement from one idea to the next and from one sentence to the next natural and logical.

Various parts of speech and various techniques can serve as transitions in your writing. These include pronouns, specific transitional words and expressions, repetition, and parallel structure.

43F(1) Pronoun References

Sentences can be linked by pronouns that refer to nouns in previous sentences.

> Choppy: Even though *Beth* is slightly overweight, a condition that *Beth* is aware of, *Beth* ate some cheesecake. *The* lack of self-control might be with *Beth* forever.
>
> Smooth: Even though Beth is slightly overweight, a condition that *she* is aware of, *she* ate some cheesecake. *This* lack of self-control might be with *her* forever.

43F(2) Transitional Expressions

Transitional words and phrases can show relationships between ideas and sentences. Transitional words include coordinating and subordinating conjunctions; see 1G. Transitional phrases include *in fact, in other words, in addition,* and *for example.* Following is a list of some common transitional words and expressions:

> Addition: moreover, further, furthermore, besides, and, and then, likewise, also, nor, too, again, in addition, equally important, next, first, second, third, in the first place, in the second place, finally, last
>
> Comparison: similarly, likewise, in like manner
>
> Contrast: but, yet, and yet, however, still, nevertheless, on the other hand, on the contrary, after all, notwithstanding, for all

	that, in contrast to this, at the same time, although this may be true, otherwise
Time:	meanwhile, at length, immediately, soon, after a few days, in the meantime, afterward, later, then, still
Place:	here, beyond, nearby, opposite, adjacent to, on the opposite side
Purpose:	to this end, for this purpose, with this objective
Result:	hence, therefore, accordingly, consequently, thus, thereupon, as a result, then, so
Summary, Repetition, Example, or Emphasis:	to summarize, to sum up, to conclude, in brief, on the whole, in sum, in short, as I have said, in other words, that is, to be sure, as has been noted, for example, for instance, in fact, indeed, to tell the truth, in any event, after all

Each of the transitional expressions added to the following example shows the relationship between two ideas. And each expression has a specific meaning.

Choppy: You think the world has many good qualities and it could be better? You have a realistic attitude about government. You show some promise as a political scientist.

Smooth: *If* you think the world has many good qualities *but* it could be better, *then* you have a realistic attitude about government. *Furthermore,* you show some promise as a political scientist.

Since transitional phrases should connect ideas in a logical way, you should choose them carefully. Notice that poorly chosen transitional expressions can be distracting to a reader.

Incoherent: *When* you think the world has many good qualities *and if* it could be better, *as a result* you have a realistic attitude about government. *In other words*, you show promise as a political scientist.

43F(3) Repetition

Key words or phrases can be repeated for emphasis (stress) and coherence (the quality of sticking or holding together).

Choppy: I feel sure that the American people want a *forceful leader*—who will stick by his or her decisions and accept the consequences.

Smooth: I feel sure that the American people want a *forceful leader*—*a leader* who will stick to his or her decisions and accept the consequences.

43F(4) Parallelism

Key words and phrases can be written in parallel form to show their relationship to one other.

Choppy: *Because of* the price of food, *with* low wages, and *as a result of* poor benefits, I do not think I can afford a vacation.

Smooth: *Because of* the price of food, low wages, and poor benefits, I do not think I can afford a vacation.

Some of the transitional devices (pronouns, transitional expressions, repetition, and parallelism) are at work in the following paragraph, showing the relationship of one sentence to the next:

> If most of us were asked what we knew about Isaac Newton, we should probably reply that he discovered the laws of gravity through watching an apple fall from a tree in his garden. So far as it goes the answer would be true; for years after that charming story had gone into circulation, his niece, who was also his housekeeper, confirmed the truth of that incident in the garden of the old house at Woolsthorpe in Lincolnshire. But it tells us too little of this man whose mind was one of the most remarkable in the history of human thought; whose discoveries marked the end of one period of

379

mankind and the beginning of another; whose
genius in mathematics laid the foundation for the
scientific discoveries of the ages of mechanical
triumph which followed; and, strangest of all, who
lost interest in this—if, indeed, he ever had any.

Horace Shipp, "Magic in Mathematics," in *Ideas That Moved the
World* (London: Evans Brothers, Ltd.). Reprinted by permission
of the publisher.

Practice 43–27 List all the transitions that you can find in
the student theme at the beginning of this unit, and explain how each helps to make its paragraph coherent.

Practice 43–28 Rewrite the following paragraph, supplying logical transitions in the blanks. Use pronouns, transitional words or phrases, repetition, or parallel structure.

Modern scientists might think _____
Aristotle worked under great disadvantages.
_____ had no books to consult,
_____ no _____ on natural history
had been written. _____ had no scientific
training, no scientific instruments, _____
colleagues with _____ he could discuss
_____ findings. What _____ did
have was inexhaustible energy and enthusiasm
and a love of living things. Sometimes when
_____ wrote of _____ observations
_____ drew diagrams to make
_____ meaning clear—the first such
_____ in scientific writing. He refers to
_____ often in _____ writings; but
unfortunately these _____ have been lost.

"The First Biologist." From MEN, MICROSCOPES AND LIV-
ING THINGS by Katherine B. Shippen (New York: Viking
Press, Inc., 1955). Copyright © 1955 by Katherine B. Shippen.
Reprinted by permission of Viking Penguin Inc.

Practice 43–29 Revise the following paragraphs so that
they are unified and logical.

She found it difficult to park on the mysterious plot of land, lock the car door, and make her way over to the meeting place. Her back was turned on the car that drove up, but she whirled around to see her enemies. A puddle of oil stood between the gangsters and her. She walked toward them to deliver the money as she had been told to do. There was no change in their facial expressions. As she approached the kidnapers, she caught one off guard, grabbed his gun, and belted the other one in the stomach with the money bag. Both of them darted forward in surprise, trying to regain control of the situation. One tried to run, but she put a bullet through the front right tire of the kidnapers' car. As she tightly held the handle of her gun, she felt a sense of confidence for having untangled a very complicated case.

Every one of us has potential for improving his or her daily life. In most instances, a sick person does not function as well as usual, but this is only for a limited time. Often, as a result of having gotten well, the individual will learn to function at a higher level than he or she did before the illness. One goal of all professional health workers is to help their patients apply what they learn in one situation to another situation. If this goal is achieved, all patients will be able to cope better with sickness and being healthy. Ideally, we are all constantly learning to adjust to different levels of health—whether we like it or not. I personally don't like to be sick.

Checklist for Writing Paragraphs

1. What is the topic sentence of the paragraph? (43A)
2. Is each sentence in the paragraph related to the topic sentence? (43A)
3. Do I have enough details in the paragraph to support my idea and make it interesting? (43B)

4. Is the paragraph developed fully, using the following techniques when appropriate: definition, description, example, grouping, analogy, cause-effect, comparison-contrast, or analysis? (43C)

5. Are the details in the paragraph organized logically according to one of the standard methods: from general to particular, from particular to general, by time, by arrangement in space, or by movement between extremes? (43D)

6. Are all the details in the paragraph related to the topic sentence and to one another? (43E)

7. Are there logical transitions between sentences and between paragraphs? (43F)

Review Practice 43–1 Develop each of the following topics into topic sentences. Limit the topics as much as possible. Then, by following the guidelines in the checklist for writing paragraphs, develop each topic sentence into a paragraph. Use as many different methods of developing your ideas as possible; see 43C. Then, label your methods of organization. Use at least three different methods of organization; see 43D. And underline your transitional devices. Use at least three transitional devices in each paragraph; see 43F.

1. My English Class
2. My Favorite Sport
3. My Favorite Hobby
4. After School
5. On the Way to School
6. When I Relax
7. The Best Study Methods I Know

44 Writing Themes

For most people, writing at this stage involves two steps: making writing conditions suitable and writing the theme.

But the process does not end here. Although it is a relief to get the first draft on paper, the composing process is not complete until you revise and proofread your work.

44A Writing Conditions

No standard formula exists for getting ready to write the first draft of a theme, because different people do their best writing under different conditions. Though writing the first draft of a paper is often difficult, certain personal writing conditions can relieve some of the anxiety connected with this task.

To find the conditions that work best for you, you should experiment with time of day, place, and method of writing. First, you might want to determine both the time of day during which you do your best writing and the length of time you can spend at one sitting. Some people write best at night, some in the morning, others in the afternoon; some can write on and off all day, and others can write only a few hours a day. The place you write can also be important to you: at a small desk, at a large table, on the floor, in a chair, with the radio on, in complete silence, or with no one around. Tradition has it that Thomas Wolfe did his best writing on top of a particular refrigerator, which he shipped around the country with him when he traveled. Finally, different methods of writing are effective in producing the first draft. You could write the first draft out in longhand, use a typewriter, or talk your paper into a tape recorder and then write it out.

Those who regularly write more than one draft of a paper often prefer to turn out the first draft by the method that is fastest for them, since revising is generally easier than writing a first draft. Any writing conditions are acceptable as long as they produce good results.

44B   Theme Parts

An essay or theme has three parts: (1) the beginning or introduction, which includes your thesis statement; (2) the middle or body; and (3) the end or conclusion.

44B(1) Beginning or Introduction

The introduction of an essay captures the reader's interest, establishes the tone of the theme, is short, and gets to the point. To capture your reader's interest, you might cite some specific details with which your reader can identify, tell a story that is related to your general subject, or cite a revealing fact or statistic. Introductions often have a "funnel effect," beginning with general information and narrowing the reader's focus to a particular issue (your thesis). You should, however, avoid presenting a long string of boring or unrelated generalizations in your introduction. Introductions are important because they create the reader's first impression and may well determine whether the reader continues to read your paper.

In the example comparing high schools and jails, the introduction would include the thesis statement and a brief explanation of the controlling idea (that high schools create an atmosphere that does not encourage learning and self-improvement).

Catchy statement	I have served my prison term, and I don't ever
Story	want to be locked up again. That is exactly how I felt when I stepped forward at high school graduation to receive my diploma. The days of cruel authority with no room for exceptions were
Fact	over for me. It wasn't the actual process of education that made high school like a prison for
Thesis	me. But high school, governed like a prison by
Topics	rules, routines, and confinement, created an atmosphere that did not encourage learning and self-improvement.

Practice 44–1 Write an appropriate introduction to the following student theme.

It seems like ages since I first wanted to take a trip like this. It has always been my dream to go to some of the high-country fishing lakes, but I have not really had the time to do so. That has been the excuse I have been giving myself for the last year and a half. The truth is that I had two worries about a trip like this. The first is that I didn't have anyone to go with, and the second is that I wasn't sure if I wanted to go all the way up north just to go fishing. Well, I finally stopped kidding myself and arranged a trip to Union Lake up in the Stanislaus Forest above Sacramento.

My friend and I left Sacramento happy but unprepared on a Friday night. Threatening clouds hung above us through the entire trip up to the lake. It was a rather spooky experience for me because it was the first time that I have driven in the forest other than in the daytime. I had never seen the dancing of my headlights on the gigantic trees surrounding us. It seemed as if the whole forest had come alive with wild animals that would attack us at the first signs of hostility. Driving along, we at last came to the final thirteen miles of hard, rough dirt road that would take us to our fishing paradise. But so many sharp rocks at any time could end my long-awaited fishing trip. And if the tires weren't sheared to ribbons, the shocks would be sure to give out from the beating they took from the mile-high bumps. When it seemed that we were never going to get to the lake, the car rolled quietly up to the shoreline.

To our surprise and satisfaction, the clouds had floated over the horizon leaving a breathtaking view of the millions and millions of tiny lights in the sky. I spotted many falling stars, which streaked across the sky forming a maze of silver dots. Neither words nor pictures can describe the events and scenery I experienced in the mountains.

Rising out of a sleeping bag on a very cool morning can be quite different from getting out of a warm bed in a bedroom. The first thing I noticed was the extreme stillness of the lake. Like a sheet of glass, the calm surface made a double image of all its surroundings. Only when I tossed a small pebble onto the surface did the lake come to life, sending out small, speedy ripples.

All that day we fished, only to be disappointed with a few small trout. It didn't really make much difference what we used on the fish; we were still being defeated in the game of fishing. When it looked as if we were losers, my long-time fishing pal hooked onto that prize catch we had been waiting for. Along with that last rainbow and the peacefulness surrounding the setting sun, I would say it was well worth my time and effort to have taken this trip. I will always have cherished memories of the clear skies, pure air, still lake and—the best memory of them all—that lunker-sized trout.

44B(2) Middle or Body

The body of a theme fully develops the controlling idea (or thesis) and all the topics included in the outline that was written during the prewriting stage. Each topic is developed into at least one paragraph by using some of the following techniques you learned about in 43C: definition, description, example, grouping, analogy, cause-effect, comparison-contrast, and analysis.

Then, each group of details is organized in a paragraph according to the methods described in 43D: from general to particular, from particular to general, by time, by space, and by movement between extremes.

In the sample composition about high schools, the most effective method of organization will be comparison-contrast because of the nature of the topic. But some topics are best expanded by a combination of other patterns and techniques. If a combination of organizing techniques were applied, the body of the sample paper might look something like the following. It is printed here with the typical changes that might occur as you write. Topic sentences are italicized.

At the core, both *high schools and prisons are* ~~*social settings are rule-oriented*~~   Transition
institutions based on rules   Grouping
with built-in punishments for any sort of disobedience.

There are probably ~~many~~ sound reasons for most   Cause-effect

of the rules the law enforcers have developed in
settings,
both ~~high school and prison~~, such as safety,   Examples
even
control, and efficiency. But it seems that   Analysis

the stress in both of these ~~restrictive~~ atmospheres
reward and
is on punishment rather than on ~~positive~~
encouragement for
good behavior. Breaking the rules in both cases   Paragraph/summary

leads to punishment; following the rules leads to   Comparison
an
stifling, uninteresting routine in which the   Transition to next topic
(student or prisoner)
participant has little or no say.

the authorities say that
As we all know, ~~*a rigorous*~~ *routine is necessary*   Transitional phrase

to the operation of both establishments.

Comparison

Comparison

Description

Example

Like prisons,
ˌHigh schools ~~and prisons both~~ rely heavily on

set routines and require people to get permission

to break the routine. But such a practice ~~is~~
                    does   encourage
certainly ˌnot ~~conducive to~~ ˌan open, accepting

atmosphere in high school. Even for a simple

change like a day off of school, the system seems

to fall apart if all the forms aren't filled out
                    Once,
properly. ˌAt the last minute, my father asked
                              business
if I wanted to go on a day's ˌexcursion with him

to check some farms ~~and agricultural situations~~

for insurance purposes. He thought the

experience would be educational for me, and I

was excited about it. My father and I left the

city; my mother went to work as usual; and my

high school went frantic trying to track me

down. I cut school that day with the intention of

broadening my education, but the next day I was

sent to the dean by my first-period instructor,
      was   dean's secretary, was
ˌhumiliated by the ˌ~~dean~~ and ˌforced to call my

mother to vouch for ~~the truth of~~ my story.

Because of this disciplinary action, I missed all of my English and part of chemistry. But most important, the dean made me feel like a criminal for doing nothing wrong. Analogy

Along with not filling out the proper forms, socializing in high school is practically treated like a minor offense. I for one would much rather see the teachers put their energy into the classroom than ~~to~~ have teachers waste their time seeking out the petty criminals. Student's aren't even allowed room for growing, learning, and playing between classes. As soon as the bell rings, teachers take their posts in the halls and begin telling students to be quiet, keep their hands to themselves, and get to the next class. ₍Most students find₎ ~~I found~~ ₍it₎ easiest to get along in high school when they ~~thought~~ ₍consider₎ themselves prisoners, ~~I~~ ₍actually₎ ~~stopped₎ ₍do₎ thinking, and simply ₍did₎ what ~~I was₎ ₍they were₎ told. Is this the type of person our secondary school system should be producing?

A feeling ~~and reality~~ of confinement is the

Transition
Continuation of previous topic
Examples
Analogy
Summary: thought-provoking question
Description

Description focal point of my high school experience. I very

                                    free

seldom sensed encouragement to make ˄choices

                            learning

and deal with different ˄situations.

Comparison   As with small children,

˄All decisions were made for me and my peers.

Even the classrooms were confining—maps and

chalkboards on the front walls, windows on one

side wall, a clock in the back of the room, a door

and a bulletin board on the fourth wall, and in

the center of each room the desks, nailed to the

Cause-effect floor. Perhaps freedom was once given to high

Cause-effect school students, who continually abused it. Or

perhaps present students ~~in high school~~ no

longer care about the quality of their time in high

school, so they let others make decisions for

Analysis them. But there is a reason for the current state

of affairs, and I think this sense of ~~unconditional~~

Comparison confinement is a major part of the problem. As

in prison, a student must serve his or her time,

Definition or term of confinement, without exception—until

Summary age sixteen. The conditions under which

390 students are kept in school are often not

pleasant. *Classrooms and prison cells hold groups of*   Comparison

unhappy people and, supposedly for the sake of

improvement, confinement is enforced ͺagainst a
                                                    often

person's will.

Practice 44–2 Write an appropriate body for the following introduction and conclusion from a student theme.

Introduction

Who needs big business in America? All of us, in one way or another, need big business if we want to live as comfortably and as cheaply as we are living right now. Doesn't big business supply millions and millions of automobiles to consumers at moderately low prices? Do the American people really believe that the consumer would be better off if these corporations were broken down into smaller, privately owned businesses? I believe that this cannot be what this country needs.

Conclusion

Big business is necessary for the American society if we expect to live in the style we want. Big business shouldn't be insulated, but instead it should be praised as "Yankee know-how" in managing a huge economic system. It creates thousands of jobs for both skilled and unskilled workers. Big business has brought this country to the richest and highest standard of living in the world. So, when the subject of big business comes up, I cannot see how Americans can reject the basic reason for our success in the economic world.

44B(3) Ending or Conclusion

A conclusion summarizes and concludes. In many respects, it mirrors the introduction, summarizing the main ideas in a theme and highlighting the most important issues. It represents your final encounter with your readers and should leave them with a strong statement or impression of the theme's argument and conclusion(s). Under no circumstances should it introduce new information.

Our sample theme might conclude as follows:

Summary: topic 1

Summary: topic 2

It seems to me that in high schools rules and regulations must be set and carried out to a certain extent. A routine is also important to the success of any school system. My objection ~~and~~ fill our lives. ~~bitterness~~ is the degree such rules ∧ ~~are enforced~~.

Concluding analysis

Grouping/ definition

High schools are not prisons. They are institutions that should mold the minds of free-

function

thinking citizens who can ∧~~fare~~ successfully in a fairly complicated society. Encouraging students to stop thinking for themselves and punishing them for every slight change from the norm is bound to stifle rather than encourage students. So they are sent to college or into society with a feeling of helplessness as a result of being

Summary: topic 3

confined for years. A ~~prison-like~~ routine may be

Concluding remark

necessary but should not be carried out to the

"prisoners" unable

Analogy

392

extent that it produces ∧~~citizens untrained~~ to
take
∧~~face~~ responsibility for the rest of their lives.

The first draft of the sample theme on high school, then, is six paragraphs long. The paragraph structure can be broken into three parts as follows:

Introduction: 1 paragraph
Body: 4 paragraphs
Conclusion: 1 paragraph

In reference to the outline of the sample theme from 42G, some topics required more than one paragraph but none required fewer.

Outline	Number of Paragraphs
I. Introduction	1
II. Rules	1
III. Routine	2
IV. Confinement	1
V. Conclusion	1

This proportion of topics to paragraphs is fairly typical, but there is no set formula for this relationship. You should simply develop as many paragraphs as needed to explain your topic.

The final draft of this essay is the student theme at the beginning of this unit.

Practice 44–3 Write an appropriate conclusion to the following student theme.

Man is what he allows himself to become. Once he discovers the power within himself to be anything he sets his mind to, a human being invariably begins to venture out of the realm of self and lets his curiosity lead him on an external search for happiness. Perhaps the latter statement sounds paradoxical. Why wouldn't the discovery of such will power insure an eventual culmination of his search? The answer is that one of the vices of humankind prevents the utopia to which a virtue could lead. This evil to which I refer is greed. The more he acquires, the more man desires. If only people would take the biblical passage about Adam and Eve to heart. In their lust for power, their desire to be like God, to be all, the couple allowed themselves to become nothing. This is surely a lesson for all.

Despite their downfall, Adam and Eve survived, and as all great lessons teach, the only way to regain strength is to get back up and move onward. Nations crumble, empires die, but oh, the glory of a people rebuilt and a new land found! Man will go to great lengths to create or discover. He will sweat and bleed to analyze a problem, to prove a theory, or to write a novel. He is, by nature, always striving to do. And when an action is completed, the pride of accomplishment gleams in his eyes. The effort, the pain, the failure all somehow are worth it when man can step back and admire the mastery of his will.

Picture the delight in the eyes of a child when he puts the final touch on a bucket-shaped, popsicle-stick-and-sand castle. And what does the same child do when he sees daddy and mommy planting a garden? He immediately imitates. The parents' creations won't quench his thirst for success. Christmas cookies made by grandma were always neater than the ones the children made, but grandma praised the odd-shaped masses of dough highly, and mom and dad "oohed" and "ahed" between "mm's." That made the little ones squeal joyously and continue to create. The flowers the kids found were always more special than the perfect arrangements from the florist. Why? Because what we search for and what we make are reflections of our person.

Student theme by Barbara A. Nonnemaker.

Checklist for Writing Themes

A. Introduction, 44B(1)
   1. Does my introduction have a thesis statement that includes the topics and controlling idea of my theme?
   2. Does my introduction introduce my topics and make a statement about them?
   3. Will my introduction capture my reader's interest?
   4. Does my introduction establish the tone of the theme?
   5. Is my introduction short and to the point?

B. Body, 44B(2)
   1. Do I expand upon each of my topics in my theme?
   2. Is each paragraph in the body of my theme thoroughly developed?
   3. Are my sentences effective and grammatically correct?
   4. Have I used traditional patterns to develop my paragraphs: definition, description, example, grouping, analogy, cause-effect, comparison-contrast, or analysis?
   5. Have I used effective patterns to organize my paragraphs: general to particular, particular to general, time, space, or movement between extremes?

C. Conclusion, 44B(3)
   1. Does my conclusion summarize the highlights of my theme, including all my topics?
   2. Does my conclusion contain concluding remarks?

Review Practice 44–1 Following the guidelines in the checklist for writing themes, write a theme on any of the following topics that are assigned to you. (You have completed prewriting exercises for each of these topics in Review Practice 42–1 and written a body paragraph for each on a related topic in Review Practice 43–1.)

1. My College
2. Sports
3. Hobbies
4. Activities After School

5. Activities Before School   7. Study Methods
6. Relaxing

45   Finishing

This chapter is designed to lead you through the final steps of a written assignment. The following guidelines are considered standard and are generally accepted in college courses, but an instructor may give other directions to suit the specific purpose of a course. The suggestions here assume that you want your work not simply to look polished but also to be polished—from the content to the form of the final draft.

45A   Plagiarism

Plagiarism is the offense of representing someone else's words or ideas as your own. Some students plagiarize, or steal, other people's material intentionally; this is the worst offense connected with college papers. Others plagiarize accidentally, because they have taken notes poorly, have been careless in keeping track of sources and direct quotations, or have misunderstood a research assignment. Whether planned or accidental, plagiarism is a serious legal and moral offense, punished in different ways at different schools.

As you are completing your paper, you should make certain that all your writing is original and that it represents your own writing style and sentence structure unless it is material you have quoted from another source. If you are working with quotations or someone else's ideas, they should be introduced and footnoted carefully. You must give credit to the people whose words and ideas you are using in your paper.

Footnoting means inserting a number in your paper after a quotation or an original idea that you have borrowed and giving the source (author, book or article, and publishing information) of that material at the foot of the page or at the end of your paper. All quotations and someone else's original ideas (for example, a unique interpretation of a certain movie) must be footnoted. But you do not need to footnote general knowledge (such as the fact that the movie was made in 1975).

Plagiarism can usually be avoided by careful note taking. Plagiarism often begins when you copy a word or two or even a paragraph from a source onto a note card and do not put it in quotation marks. The same material might later slip into your paper with no reference to its real author. That is stealing, and it will gain you no recognition for the original work you have done—reading a variety of material and working it into your paper, activities that your instructor is looking for.

45B General Information

Following is some general information that might be helpful to you in turning in an assignment to an instructor in any department.

Every paper should have a title, for the title stimulates a reader's interest and helps give a paper focus. You can put your title 1½ inches from the top of the first page and begin your theme 1 or 2 inches below that, or you can add a title page to the paper.

Whether your title is on a separate page or on the first page of your paper, only the first letters of major words are capitalized. In no case is the entire title capitalized. Conjunctions, articles, and short prepositions are not capitalized except when they begin a title. In addition, titles are not underlined or put inside quotation marks; these two forms of punctuation show that a title is borrowed and not original.

Practice 45–1 Write out three different titles for the student theme on high schools at the beginning of this unit.

The introduction and the conclusion should generally not be separated from the body of a paper.

Next, in preparing your material, you should know how many carbons you will want. The type of carbon paper you choose makes no difference, since the carbon is the copy that you will keep. You may prefer to photocopy your paper. But it is always a good idea to keep one copy of each paper you write, just in case the original is lost.

45C Proofreading and Revising

To complete the composing process, you should proofread and revise the first draft. Some students prefer to write out a second and possibly a third draft; others simply make all of their corrections on the first draft. The changes in the student theme comparing high schools to prisons are written right on the first draft on pages 387–391 and 392. If you expect to turn in a final product that is polished, proofreading and revising are absolutely necessary. They can be done in three steps.

45C(1) Content and Purpose

First, you should read the theme thoroughly for content and purpose, asking yourself these questions:

1. What is my purpose?
2. Is my thesis clear?
3. Do I stick to my thesis throughout the theme?
4. Are my arguments clear?
5. Are my arguments effective?
6. Do I accomplish my purpose?

You should revise your paper until your purpose is clear and you can answer yes to each of the other questions.

Practice 45–2 Explain how four of the changes made in the student theme on high schools improved the content and purpose of the theme.

45C(2) Sentence Structure and Diction

Second, you should read your paper again with a close look at sentence structure and diction. See Chapters 28 through 41 for an explanation of sentence structure and diction.

1. Does my language usage (informal or formal) fit my subject and my purpose? (28)
2. Is my word choice exact? (29)
3. Have I used words correctly? (30)
4. Have I used idioms correctly? (31)
5. Have I avoided clichés? (32)
6. Have I avoided wordiness? (33)
7. Have I included all words that are needed in my sentences? (34)
8. Are my pronoun references clear? (35)
9. Have I avoided misplaced and dangling modifiers? (36)
10. Is my sentence structure parallel when necessary? (37)
11. Have I avoided shifts in tense, voice, mood, person, and number? (38)
12. Have I used subordination effectively? (39)
13. Are my sentences varied in length and structure (40)
14. Are my sentences unified and logical? (41)

The numbers in parentheses following these questions are the chapters where explanations of these guidelines can be found. Again, you should revise your paper so that you can answer yes to each of these questions.

Practice 45–3 Explain how four of the changes made in the student theme on high schools improved the sentence structure and diction of the theme.

45C(3) Punctuation and Mechanics

Finally, you should read the theme to find and correct punctuation, mechanical, and spelling errors.

1. Have I used end punctuation properly, making sure a complete sentence comes before a period, question mark, and exclamation point? (12)
2. Have I avoided run-on sentences (6) and fragments (5)?
3. Have I used commas (13), semicolons (14), apostrophes (15), colons (16), quotation marks (17), dashes (18A) parentheses (18B), and brackets (18C) properly?
4. Have I used capitalization (19), underlining or italics (20), abbreviations (21), and numbers (22) properly?
5. Are all the words in my theme spelled correctly? (23–27)

The numbers in parentheses following these questions are the chapters where explanations of these guidelines can be found. Again, you should revise your paper so that you can answer yes to each of these questions.

When properly used, punctuation, mechanics, and correct spelling can help you explain your ideas, aid your readers in understanding each sentence and each paragraph, and lead your readers smoothly to your conclusion.

Practice 45–4 Explain how four of the changes made in the student theme on high schools improved the punctuation and mechanics of the theme.

Checklist for Finishing Themes

1. Have I been careful not to plagiarize someone else's words or ideas, misrepresenting them as my own? (45A)

2. Does my paper have a title to stimulate the reader's interest and give the paper focus? (45B)
3. Are the introduction and the conclusion of my paper connected to the body of my paper? (45B)
4. Do I have a copy of my theme to keep after I hand in the original to my instructor? (45B)
5. Have I proofread and revised my paper at least three times:
   a. for general content and purpose (45C[1])
   b. for sentence structure and diction (45C[2])
   c. for punctuation, mechanics, and spelling (45C[3])

Review Practice 45–1 Finish and proofread the theme or themes you wrote in Review Practice 44–1 by following the guidelines in this chapter. Show all the changes and corrections that you make on the theme itself.

Reading Tasks

No matter what you are reading, there are three levels on which you should understand the material: literal, interpretive, and evaluative.

Literal Level

The first level of understanding, known as the **literal level,** involves knowing what the words on a page mean—as individual words and together in phrases and sentences. This level of comprehension requires an understanding of both general and specific references. To learn the meanings of unfamiliar words, you will find a dictionary can be particularly helpful.

You should usually approach an assignment on the literal level, because you will need a literal understanding of the words and their meanings before you can move to any higher level of understanding. You must know the meanings of all the words in a reading assignment and should understand how they work by themselves and in their sentences. In particular, the key words in your assignments require your special attention.

Answer the following literal questions about the student theme at the beginning of this unit. Refer to the selection when necessary.

1. Define the following words with the help of a dictionary: *process, confinement, self-improvement, disobedience, efficiency, encouragement, humiliated, atmosphere,* and *objection.*
2. What does the writer compare high schools to?
3. What are the three main topics in this theme?

4. Write two literal-level questions of your own based on the student theme at the beginning of this unit.

Interpretive Level

The second level of understanding involves **interpreting** the words on a page. To reach this level of understanding, you must identify the writer's suggestions and then draw relationships between them. This stage is more advanced than literal understanding, and its mastery is also more valuable to you in your other school work. The best way to become skillful at interpreting is to practice. Read what is on a page and try to draw your own conclusions from the facts that are given to you.

Answer the following interpretive questions about the student theme at the beginning of this unit. Refer to the selection when necessary.

5. How do high school rules create a negative atmosphere?
6. How can a high school routine be made more flexible than it was for the student who wrote this theme?
7. Why don't confinement and encouragement go together?
8. Write two interpretive-level questions of your own based on this theme.

Evaluative Level

The third level of comprehension requires you to react critically to what you are reading. In other words, you must **evaluate** your reading material: Are the writer's points realistic? Why or why not? Do they persuade you? Do you want to act on what you have read? Do you find what you have read interesting?

This level of understanding involves skills that you must practice every time you read. However, when you

403

judge your reading material, you should remember to support your opinion with reasons: Why do you think a certain suggestion is good or bad? What reasons do you have for disagreeing with an author's point of view? This is a very demanding part of reading; it is easier to avoid this task and to let your classmates or your instructor do it for you. But if you arrive at this level of understanding for yourself, you will increase your ability to remember and will be able to respond more thoroughly to what you read.

Answer the following evaluative-level questions about the student theme at the beginning of this unit. Refer to the selection when necessary.

9. Do you agree that high schools are like prisons? Explain your answer.
10. Do you think that rules and regulations are necessary in high school? Why or why not?
11. What do you think the main purpose of high schools is? What do you think the main purpose of high schools should be?
12. Write two evaluative-level questions of your own based on this theme.

For further practice with these levels of reading, turn to the Unit VI Appendix Selection.

Discussion/Writing Assignments

The following questions are based on the reading selection at the beginning of this unit and the Unit VI Appendix Selection. To complete these writing assignments, go through the steps you learned in this unit, including prewriting, developing and organizing paragraphs, writing themes, and finishing. Follow your instructor's directions for discussing and/or writing on the topics here. All discussion and written work should be in complete sentences.

13. Describe your impression of high school by completing this comparison: For me, high school was like _____
_____.

14. "Many observers of our society claim that modern man, immersed in materialism, is 'owned by his objects.' Yet many of us have objects that we treasure not just for their material value but for a variety of other reasons. Assignment: Describe one or more objects which are important to you. Explain what values they represent and comment on those values."* (See appendix selection.)

*The 1973 California State University & Colleges Freshman English Equivalency Examination, Edward M. White, Project Director. © The California State University and Colleges. Printed by permission of Edward M. White and the Division of New Program Development and Evaluation. P. 34.

Unit VI Appendix Selection

We have in our living room a music box, (1) which for three generations has given pleasure to the eyes and ears of my family. It stands about a foot high and measures about two feet in length and width. Except for a spray of flowers carved on its face, the outside is unadorned. Inside, pasted to the lid, is a turn-of-the-century lithograph of a pair of plump cherubs. There is a set of tin records, perforated here and there, that goes with the music box. It is run by winding it up and releasing the spring. Its tunes are dated; "My Gal Is A High-Born Lady" and "I Guess I'll Telegraph My Baby" haven't been among the top ten for quite a while, but this does nothing to lessen the enjoyment they give.

My grandfather was the first to own the music (2) box. He traded a horse for it and presented the music box to my grandmother as a gift. They had been married for only six months. At first it was a very big deal. A music box in a Nebraskan farming town can cause quite a commotion, but as time went by and the popularity of "victrolas" grew, the music box passed into oblivion.

(3) Ignored and dusty was the way my father discovered it in the cellar. He cleaned it up and got it running and showed it off patronizingly to his friends as a relic from his parents' youth. It was played at parties as a novelty, but again it lost out against the incoming rage: the radio. So back into the cellar went the music box to await rediscovery one more time.

(4) This time it was my sister and I who resurrected it. We hauled it out into the light, dusted off its rosewood sides, and listened to the songs first heard what seemed to us to be eons ago.

(5) My grandparents grew old and, being practical people, decided to divide their possessions with their children before their death to avoid a tragic scramble afterwards. To my father went the music box, and he carefully brought it to our home and revived it one more time.

(6) Now, despite its years, it keeps on playing its old familiar songs. I love the old music box. It can never be associated with a price tag. My grandfather acquired it with an honest trade, and it has been handed down through the years. The music box symbolizes my grandfather's love for my grandmother, my father's years at home, my sister and I exploring in the dark cellar, and countless fine memories. I love it for its beauty, the rich, soft red of the rosewood, and the way it gleams in the sun. I love hearing the whir of the motor and vigorously cranking the handle. I love the corny song titles and the feel of the rough surface of the records. And although its value is largely sentimental, its worth stems from the fact

that it has survived many years with grace and beauty, something very few *people* can claim.

"Comparison and Contrast," in *The 1973 California State University & Colleges Freshman English Equivalency Examination,* p. 34. First draft student writing has been edited for consistency with this text.

Answer the following literal questions about the appendix selection. Refer to the selection when necessary.

1. What object was special to the writer of the selection?
2. Who was the first to own the object?
3. What does the object symbolize for the writer?
4. Write two literal-level questions of your own based on the selection.

Answer the following interpretive questions about the selection. Refer to the selection when necessary.

5. Why was this object special to the writer of the essay?
6. About how old is the object?
7. Why is the writer unable to put a monetary value on the object?
8. Write two interpretive-level questions of your own based on the selection.

Answer the following evaluative questions about the selection. Refer to the selection when necessary.

9. Why do you think the object was resurrected over and over?
10. What do you have that you value as much as the writer of this essay loved the music box?
11. Do you agree with the writer that very few people survive many years with grace and beauty?
12. Write two evaluative-level questions of your own based on the selection.

Glossary

accent–See **stress.**

active voice–The voice of a verb indicating that the subject performs the action of the verb: "Meg *hit* Martha." See also **passive.**

adjective–A part of speech that explains or modifies nouns and pronouns by giving information about their quality or quantity.

adverb–A part of speech that explains or modifies verbs, adjectives, and adverbs.

analogy–A comparison of two seemingly unlike items.

antecedent–A word or group of words that a pronoun refers to. It must appear before the pronoun.

antonyms–Words that have opposite meanings.

appositive–A noun or noun substitute that is next to another noun or noun substitute that it renames or explains: "Have you met Fred, *our neighbor?*"

association–Relationships you can draw mentally between items, especially to aid your memory.

auxiliary–A helping word in a verb phrase: "I *have* known her for three years."

body–The middle of a selection; the portion of a selection that contains several topics.

case–The name of the function of a noun or pronoun in a sentence. It explains how a word relates to other words: subjective, objective, and possessive.

chronological order–A method of organizing details that is based on the time sequence of those details: for example, from morning to night.

clause–A group of words that contains a subject and a predicate. The two types of clauses are independent (or main) and dependent (or subordinate).

collective noun–A noun that is singular in form but plural in meaning: *family* or *senate.*

comma splice–A run-together sentence made up of two independent clauses with a comma and no coordinating or subordinating conjunction between them.

comparative form–The form of adjectives and adverbs that expresses a degree of difference between two persons or things: *happier* or *more happily.*

complement -A word or group of words that completes a verb, a subject, or an object.

complex sentence–A sentence containing an independent clause and at least one dependent clause. See also **clause.**

compound sentence–A sentence containing at least two independent clauses. See also **clause.**

compound-complex sentence–A sentence containing at least two independent clauses and at least one dependent clause; a combination of a compound sentence and a complex sentence. See also **clause.**

comprehension–Understanding of the material you read.

conclusion–The end of a selection; the portion of a selection that contains a summary of its main points.

conjunction–A structure or function part of speech that joins words, phrases, or clauses. There are two kinds of conjunctions: coordinating conjunctions and subordinating conjunctions.

conjunctive adverbs–A part of speech used to connect independent clauses.

connotation–The meanings that a word suggests or implies beyond the dictionary definition. See also **denotation.**

consonants–All the letters in the alphabet except the vowels *(a, e, i, o, u).*

content words–Vocabulary words or words that convey the most meaning in our language: verbs, nouns, adjectives, and adverbs.

context clues–Signals in your reading that can help you figure out the meaning of unfamiliar words and phrases. There are four types of context clues: definition, comparison, contrast, and example clues.

coordinate adjectives–Adjectives that modify the same noun but are not connected by a coordinating conjunction. They can be identified because they sound natural when you put *and* between them.

coordinating conjunction–A part of speech used to connect words, phrases, or clauses of equal weight.

correlative conjunction -Coordinating conjunctions used in pairs:

either . . . or, neither . . . nor, not only . . . but also, whether . . . or, not . . . but.

deduction–A logical pattern of organizing details that moves from general to particular.

definition–A standard, accepted meaning of a word.

denotation–The standard meaning of a word as explained in the dictionary. See also **connotation.**

dependent (or subordinate) clause–A group of words that contains a subject and predicate but cannot stand alone as a sentence. It is usually introduced by a relative pronoun or subordinating conjunction and can function as a noun, an adjective, or an adverb in its own sentence.

derivations–The history of a word that notes the language or languages a word comes from and its meaning in the original language.

detail–A piece of information that expands upon, explains, clarifies, or illustrates a main idea.

direct object–A person or thing that receives the action of a transitive verb in a sentence.

evaluative understanding–Understanding that involves reacting critically to reading material.

expletive–The word *it* or *there* when used as a filler in a sentence.

finite verb–A verb that can serve as the main verb in a sentence.

fragment–A part of a sentence (usually a phrase or a dependent clause) capitalized and punctuated as if it were a complete sentence.

function word–Also called structure word; a word that indicates the function and relationship of words in a sentence: prepositions, conjunctions, pronouns, and interjections.

fused sentence–A run-together sentence made up of two independent clauses with no punctuation and no subordinating or coordinating conjunction between them.

gerund–A verb form that ends in *-ing* and functions in a sentence as a noun.

gerund phrase–A group of words beginning with the *-ing* form of a verb and functioning in a sentence as a noun.

imperative mood–The mood of a verb used to give a command, make a request, or give directions.

independent clause (or main clause)–A group of words that contains a subject and predicate and can stand alone as a sentence.

indicative mood–The mood of a verb used to make a statement or ask a question.

indirect object–A person or thing to (or for) whom or what an action is done.

induction–A logical pattern of organizing details that moves from particular to general.

inferences–Implications that can be drawn from reading material.

infinitive–A verb form that is made up of the word *to* plus the present stem of a verb: *to go, to make,* or *to explain.*

infinitive phrase–A type of verbal phrase that consists of a group of words beginning with an infinitive. This phrase can function in a sentence as a noun, an adjective, or an adverb.

inform–To present information in an objective, factual manner.

interjection–A word or phrase of exclamation that expresses emotion.

interpretive understanding–Understanding that involves drawing relationships, coming to conclusions, discovering the author's intended purpose, and drawing implications.

intransitive verb–A verb that describes action that is not done to someone or something.

introduction–The beginning or opening of a selection; the part of a selection that contains the thesis statement.

key words–Important words in a selection that capture the highlights of that material.

linking verb–A verb that describes a state of being.

literal understanding–Basic understanding of the words on the page and their meanings.

main ideas–The highlights or major points of the material.

mnemonic device–From a Greek word meaning "memory"; a calculated way of remembering something, such as the technique of making associations.

mood–The manner in which an action or state of being is expressed: indicative (for statements and questions), imperative (for commands, requests, and directions), and subjunctive (for motions, resolutions, recommendations, commands, demands, or conditions).

movement between extremes–A method of organizing details that is based on any system of classification that is related to the material: for example, from least serious to most serious.

narrate–To tell a story.

nonfinite verb–A verbal or a verb that cannot serve as a main verb in a sentence: participles, gerunds, and infinitives.

nonrestrictive modifier–A clause or phrase in a sentence that is not needed to identify the noun before it. This type of modifier is set off by commas.

noun–A part of speech that names persons, places, things, animals, actions, qualities, and ideas.

noun phrase–A group of words beginning with a noun that can replace a single noun in a sentence.

number–The form of a noun, pronoun, or verb that indicates singular (one) or plural (two or more).

objective case–The case of a noun or pronoun that is an object in a sentence.

outline–A format that highlights the main ideas of a selection and demonstrates their relation to one another. There are two types of outlines: sentence outlines and phrase outlines.

parts of speech–A label that identifies a word by its form, position, and function in a sentence.

participial phrase–A type of verbal phrase that begins with either a present participle or a past participle.

participle–A verb form that can function as an adjective. There are two types of participles: past and present.

passive voice–The voice of a verb indicating that the subject receives the action of the verb: "Martha *was hit* by Meg." See also **active.**

past participle–A verb form that usually ends in *-ed, -t,* or *-en;* one of the principal parts of a verb.

persuade–To convince.

phonetics–The sound system of the language.

phonics–The sound system of the language as related to the spelling system.

phonograms–The various combinations of letters that represent the sounds of our language.

phrase–A group of words that does not have either a subject or a predicate and, therefore, cannot stand alone as a sentence.

plural–The form of nouns, pronouns, and verbs that refers to two or more items.

possessive–The case of a noun or pronoun that indicates ownership.

predicate–The part of a sentence that says something about the subject. The simple predicate is the main verb and its auxiliaries. The complete predicate consists of the simple predicate and its modifiers.

predicate adjective–A word that follows a linking or state-of-being verb and describes the subject.

predicate noun–A word that follows a linking or state-of-being verb and renames the subject.

prefix–Letters or syllables that can be added to the front of a root and that have meanings of their own.

preposition–A structure or function part of speech that relates a noun or pronoun to another word in a sentence.

prepositional phrase–A group of words that begins with a preposition and ends with an object of the preposition. This phrase can function in a sentence as either an adjective or an adverb.

present participle–A verb form that ends in -*ing*.

present stem–One of the three principal parts of a verb. It is also the stem of the infinitive.

principal parts–The three forms of every verb from which the verb's six tenses are formed: present stem, past tense, and past participle.

progressive verb–A verb form that ends in -*ing* and is preceded by a form of the verb *to be.* It shows an action or state of being in progress: "I *am taking* that class."

pronoun–A structure or function part of speech that can take the place of a noun in a sentence and must refer to an antecedent. There are eight types of pronouns in English: personal, reflexive, intensive, interrogative, reciprocal, indefinite, demonstrative, and relative.

restrictive modifier–A clause or phrase in a sentence that is needed to identify the noun before it. This type of modifier is not set off by commas.

retention–The act of remembering or retaining in memory.

root–The basic element of a word.

scanning–A very fast reading procedure that should be used when looking for specific information.

sentence–A group of words that contains a subject and predicate and can stand as a unit. There are four types of sentences: simple, compound, complex, and compound-complex.

simple sentence–A sentence containing one main clause. See also **clause.**

singular–The form of nouns, pronouns, and verbs that refers to one item only.

skimming–An exceptionally fast reading technique intended to help the reader get a general sense of the main ideas of a selection.

space order–A method of organizing details that is based on the space relationship of the details: for example, from head to toe.

stress–The place in every word where the main accent falls in the pronunciation of that word.

structure word–Also called function word; a word that indicates the function and relationship of words in a sentence: prepositions, conjunctions, pronouns, and interjections.

subheading–A heading that is a subdivision of a major heading.

subject–A word or phrase in a sentence that tells who or what is doing the action expressed by an action verb or who or what is in a state of being expressed by a linking verb.

subjective case–The case of a noun or pronoun that is a subject in a sentence.

subjunctive mood–The mood of a verb used to make motions, resolutions, recommendations, and commands or to express conditions.

subordinating conjunction–A part of speech that connects words, phrases, or clauses of unequal weight.

suffix–Letters or syllables that can be added to the end of a root to form other words.

summary–A coherent version of the main ideas of a selection presented in your own words; a very brief review of the contents of the material.

superlative form–The form of adjectives and adverbs that expresses a degree of difference among three or more persons or things: *happiest* or *most happily.*

syllabication–The division of a word into syllables.

syllable–A unit of a word or a word that contains one vowel sound.

synonyms–Words that have similar meanings.

thesaurus–A book of synonyms.

thesis statement–The most general statement in an essay or article. It is usually only one sentence long and can be found at the beginning or end of the first paragraph. The thesis statement is the main point the writer will prove in the body of the essay.

topic sentence–The one sentence in each paragraph that explains the topic of that paragraph.

transitions–Devices that show relationships between parts of a sentence, between sentences themselves, and between paragraphs. They include pronouns, transitional expressions, repetition, and parallel structure.

transitive verb–A verb that describes action done to someone or something.

verb–A word that describes an action (transitive or intransitive verb) or a state of being (linking verb) and indicates the time of that action or state of being.

verb phrase–A main verb consisting of more than one word.

verbal–A verb form that cannot serve as a main verb in a sentence: participles, gerunds, and infinitives.

verbal phrase–A group of words consisting of a participle, gerund, or infinitive and various other words that go with those verb forms to make a unit.

voice–A feature of a verb indicating whether the subject performs (active voice) or receives (passive voice) the action of a verb.

vowels–Sounds represented by five letters in the English alphabet: *a, e, i, o, u.*

Reading Progress Chart

Record your reading rate for the number of comprehension questions you answered correctly. See the reading tasks in Unit V to find out how to figure your reading speed.

	Selections					
---	Unit I	Unit II	Unit III	Unit IV	Unit V	Unit VI
750						
700						
650						
600						
550						
500						
450						
400						
350						
300						
250						
200						
150						
100						
Total Number of Questions						
Number of Questions Correct						

Index

419